THE FUTURE OF TRUTH

(AND HOW TO GET THERE)

SECOND EDITION

LINDLEY GOODEN

The 1st Edition of The Future of Truth (and How to Get There) was published in April, 2024.

Typeset in Adobe Garamond Pro 12.5pt / Gibson 13pt

The Future of Truth (and How to Get There) | 2nd Edition

ISBN (Paperback): 978-1-7636194-5-6
ISBN (Hardback): 978-0-9925231-8-3
ISBN: (eBook): 978-0-6450371-1-1

This book is dedicated to everyone trying to build a happier, healthier future of truth in a time when nothing really feels true.

Whether we want to help our loved ones, friends or just our online network to be safe from mis- and dis-information, there is hope.

But we'll need to do this together.

CONTENTS

We start with the building blocks of mis- and dis-information, why they are so powerful, and how they make us look to the wrong people for 'the truth'.

Stories are our warm embrace and our worst nightmare. They're the foundation of our world views, and when they're weaponised effectively, they can make us believe almost anything.

We've come a long way since our time in the trees, but our brains are still based on those of our great ape ancestors. Chapter 2 shows how to use our 'chimp brains' differently to spot lies in real time.

CHAPTER 3 – THE TRUTH IS OUT THERE   **89**

Conspiracy beliefs are everywhere, so how can we handle the harm they do? Chapter 3 looks deep into the rabbit hole and comes back with simple techniques to manage our addiction to fiction.

CHAPTER 4 – THE BEARERS OF BAD NEWS   139

Now we understand how mis- and dis-information work, we can see them in the world around us. Chapter 4 starts with news – on social media, in the conventional news business and our own conversations with loved ones.

CHAPTER 5 – THE GOOD, THE BAD AND THE UGLY   176

When disinformation changes our beliefs, things can get ugly, fast. This is the chapter where we start to name names. Who does information well? Who uses it to exploit our biases? And how hot does the water need to be for us to jump out?

CHAPTER 6 – LAW MAKERS AND LAW BREAKERS — 208

This chapter is one for the legal eagles. We cast a sharp eye on the laws that some – but not enough – countries have brought in to defend us against mis- and dis-information. And we ask, 'what do we need right now, for mis- and dis-information to stop?'

CHAPTER 7 – RESOLVING OUR DIFFERENCES — 230

If we can't have grown up conversations about difficult things, we'll never know the truth when we see it. This chapter is all about opening a dialogue with people who think differently, especially when we think they're completely wrong.

CHAPTER 8 – AI THINK, THEREFORE AI AM   246

The future of truth will look very different to today. We are in the early years of an age of artificial information, but is truth about to die? Not if we know how deepfakes and AI-generated disinformation work.

CHAPTER 9 – REALITY HAS LEFT THE BUILDING   279

It's always darkest before the dawn. And before we can build a healthier, happier future of truth, we need to face facts. The fact is that we're reaching peak polarisation. This chapter (new for the 2nd Edition) looks at the alt-reality we're in, and how to face the real world again.

CHAPTER 10 – CREATING THE FUTURE OF TRUTH   316

In Chapter 10, we showcase and summarise the best efforts worldwide to help us to fight mis- and dis-information wherever our timelines take us. What can we do in our own lives to fight false information? This chapter is about our next steps together.

Finally, let's bring together the crucial steps forward for information guardians everywhere.

FOREWORD

Thanks to Aarti for her unwavering belief and support throughout my time buried in the world of mis- and dis-information. It's been challenging and fun, and her belief has driven me every day as I pushed through the hurdles to release this book.

The Future of Truth (and How to Get There) is based on hundreds of conversations with people with a wide range of beliefs. They provided important fuel, ideas and perspectives on how we interpret the information we're fed. And it's a genuine tribute to the varied, sometimes opposing, beliefs of the tens of thousands of people I've interviewed during my news career and beyond that this book has been possible.

I'm honoured to have been able to listen to every story.

Special thanks to David Gooden, Pete Cohen, Ranj Begley, Edosa Odaro, Wendy and Bob Levingbird, Bob Sinfield, Frederick Archer, Simon Hotchkin, John Cottiss, the late, great Martin Woodward and others along the way who've shared their own thoughts, experiences and expertise with me. They've challenged my beliefs, offered their own, and that's helped me to continue the conversation into this 2nd Edition.

And thanks to you for being here. This is the true story of mis- and dis-information and it won't always be easy to listen to. You'll disagree with me in places, and that's just as it should be. We'll never come back together to have grown-up conversations about difficult things if we don't listen to people with another point of view.

i

BEFORE WE START

i

'Truth that's told with bad intent beats all the lies that you can invent.'

WILLIAM BLAKE

1. THE LIES THAT TORE US APART

I think we can all agree on one thing in life. Whatever our views, however we feel about the big issues, we really, really don't like being lied to.

That, above all, separates our friends from our foes.

Friends don't lie.

Well then, how did we end up here? How did we end up so bitterly divided in our beliefs, standpoints and world views? The facts are often simple, clear and hard to argue with, but our opinions still drag us apart. And they're destroying the social bonds that used to hold us together. It's a puzzle that sometimes seems too complicated to piece together.

But that's why we're here. To work out why we've fallen so hard for mis- and dis-information and how to fight them both. It's time to make our information 'great again', and it is possible.

We're going to arm ourselves with strong defences against extreme views. We'll understand why 'the truth' is so important to us all – particularly in tough times, and how to instantly spot lies in the stories we see, hear and read. Together, we'll take an honest, practical view of our own beliefs and calm our reactions to stories that are designed to tear us apart. The tools we bring together will help us to instinctively spot mis- and dis-information well into the era of AI and beyond.

Hey, the truth is that you're a nice person, most of us are really good at heart. But we can be convinced that pizza-eating Satan-worshipping Democrats were trafficking kids through a non-existent restaurant basement in Washington DC. We might believe that Japan created Finland as a secret place to fish – for free. Or that Bill Gates really did stuff a tracking chip into every drop of COVID vaccine like some sort of evil Willy Wonka.

In fact, while the pandemic devastated lives worldwide in the early 2020s, another disease swept societies globally, infecting our beliefs and attitudes and turning us against each other.

That disease was the rise of mis- and dis-information. It's so serious that the shared values and beliefs that normally unite us are being dismantled faster than they can be repaired.

The good news is that our nasty break-up doesn't need to be permanent.

We just need to do some work to fix it.

2. WE'RE GETTING DIVORCED (FROM REALITY)

A great relationship mediator will start their work with a request for honesty and a real, two-way conversation when a couple tumbles into their office with a break-up brewing.

It's a very similar situation when our relationship with the truth breaks down.

During our time together we'll cover a lot of crisscrossing reasons why it's happening, how each of us can stop it and find our way back. But the mediator would tell us that honesty, empathy, listening to others, and knowing the very human causes of the breakdown will help us to cross the divide.

So, let's do that.

The World Economic Forum (which some among us might believe is at the heart of a conspiracy to control what we own and eat – but let's shelve that for a moment) laid out the threats it believed the world is facing in its Global Risks Report, 2025.

Whatever you believe about the WEF, the headlines made a lot of sense – and they were following a pattern:

> Misinformation and disinformation would be the biggest short-term risk to social cohesion – for the second year in a row.
> The previous year, they'd come in at number 5.
> The next biggest risk we face would be extreme weather events – and that'll be the top risk of the future.
> Third and fourth place went to state-based armed conflict, followed by societal polarisation.
> And in general, societal fractures – through false information and inequality - are at the heart of the overall risks facing us all in the coming years.

No politics, no conspiracies, just a warning.

Let's bring in thoughts from other global organisations who have their own share of critics, but despite their differences, are also working on it.

In late 2023, UNESCO (the UN's educational, scientific and cultural arm) commissioned a survey of 2.5 billion people in 16 countries with national elections on the way. It found that a staggering 85% said yes, false information and hate speech online are major risks to social cohesion, peace and stability.

What do you think? That sounds very reasonable to me.

Let's complete the hat-trick with The World Health

Organization. The WHO – which featured in multiple conspiracies during the COVID-19 pandemic and was ditched by the US government in early 2025 – has also declared that misinformation genuinely damages people's mental and physical health.

Whatever our beliefs, our politics, our hopes, this issue affects us all. From an independent point of view, whether you feel that these organisations are hiding a set of secret agendas or not, it's hard to deny. They all believe that our societies – and our health – are at serious risk unless we put a stop to misinformation and disinformation.

And I have no doubt that that's correct. We're now living in a time when the truth - reality itself - is difficult to distinguish from made-up, inverted, harmful ideas spewed out by people from the bottom to the top. But it's more than that. When a young man can walk into a place of worship with an assault rifle driven by medieval beliefs that had nothing to do with their life, upbringing or beliefs a few years earlier, we need to agree that mis- and dis-information are incredibly bad for our health.

So, here's what we'll do to change the game.

We'll learn how to spot, step back from and sidestep false information wherever we find it, even when it's almost flawless. We'll combine lessons from history, psychology, neuroscience and journalism to build a healthier relationship with our information. And here's the key: once we know why we're so susceptible to false information and fake news, we can instinctively feel manipulation in real time and do something about it.

It's going to be challenging, and it'll sometimes push back on some of our most heartfelt beliefs.

But our brains were built for simpler times. So, let's scan our vaccine chips, hit okay on our 5G mobiles and get to understanding what on flat Earth has brought us here, and how to get out of it.

3. DISARMING THE WEAPONS OF FALSE INFORMATION

There are lots of things driving us apart, but the facts aren't one of them. Our interpretation of them most certainly is.

The sad fact is that … facts are boring.

They're just simple reality without the feelings attached.

But you can't get anywhere near 'the truth' without the original facts. They are everything.

Sure, they don't contain the spice and intrigue of gossip, secret plots, scare stories or scandals. They don't fit some people's core beliefs. But they're nothing to do with our opinions or experiences and don't require our input to be 'true'. They just are. They're what happened, when, where and with whom. We'll get to the more delicate question of the 'why' later.

The facts are our first defence against people who want to weaponise information. Those types of opinion-makers want us to fight so that they can take a heartfelt, moderate, humane view and twist it until it hurts, triggering doubt and division, and making themselves seem more important.

But ultimately, we have the power to control the supply. And it starts with a few key words that can immediately point us in the right direction, toward a future where truth is available, and recognisable, to us all.

They are: and at the heart of them all:

a TRUTH

b TRUST   SOURCES

c BALANCE

d BIAS

e CONVERSATION

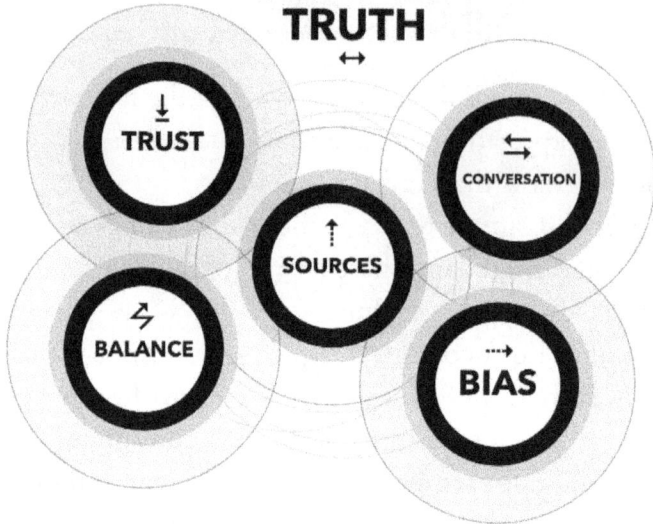

TRUTH
↔

TRUST
↓

CONVERSATION
⇆

SOURCES
↑

BALANCE
⚡

BIAS
⋯→

a TRUTH

If we want to uncover the truth, we need to deal with all of those things: trust, balance, bias, conversation and sources.

Our brains haven't evolved much in the last few thousand years, never mind in the last few decades since the internet drew its first breath.

But the tools that we use to access, absorb and share information have gone through a total revolution, and the information we receive and share every day is a universe away from what we're ready to cope with.

For people who remember the bad old days of shared landlines where you'd call your friend, only to have mum or dad telling you to get off the line, there have been vast improvements.

Privacy from mum and dad, for one.

But our younger people, the next generations, have had no choice but to grow up in a digitally exposed, physically separated, more divided world. Connected by device, separated by distance, and isolated from people that they could genuinely trust.

That digital divide is a big part of our problem. Physical distance has been shown to drive conspiracy thinking (for example, research in the British Journal of Developmental Psychology: www.bpspsychub.onlinelibrary.wiley.com/doi/full/10.1111/bjdp.12368

From a distance, 'the truth' is almost impossible to find without building up our nose for – excuse my language – bullsh*t.

There are so many potential answers at the end of a Google search, for one thing. And it's not just young people hitting the wall. The landline generation have also spent their years reading newspapers and watching conventional coverage that wouldn't know 'the truth' if it kicked them in the pension pot.

But yes, social media is the vehicle for most of it. It was a technical miracle that united the globe. It spread brilliant ideas, brought classmates together and overthrew corrupt regimes. It made communication possible in a way that humans have never seen. But shortly after the banking crisis made our world a lot less affordable, the tone of voice turned, stories got darker, conspiracies and arguments opened up, and opinions became the new cryptocurrency of our online world.

And for younger people, that's effectively the way it's always been. It's bred anxiety in the young, and anger in the old.

The state of play is that we live in such an opinion economy that we've forgotten how to spot original, definitive facts. In some ways, our opinions are more valuable. But that was always going to leave us feeling rootless. We need to know what's going on in our lives, or we lose our power.

The good news is that once we know how to extract the facts, and separate them from fiction and opinion, we'll finally be able to trust what we're seeing, hearing and reading – or throw it out. Then, we'll be in a position to make choices that help us, rather than harm us.

And it's really exciting when you know how to extract the facts. It gives us real power.

So, let's talk about the other key words I've just mentioned. Starting with trust, and why it's not always a force for good.

b TRUST

We all want to trust the people around us to have our backs, don't we?

But when the truth is hard – or impossible – to find, we quickly lose trust in the systems and the people around us. We get suspicious. Less trust leads to weaker relationships, greater conspiracies, more doubt and more division.

It's a process that fuels our online friendships, our likes and shares, our politics and much more.

When we're driven away from each other, we normally place our trust somewhere else. It can happen online when someone claims to believe the same thing as we do, or to be like us. Or to have the keys to a world-shattering secret. In the real world, we'd spend much more time with them, carefully weighing up their ideas, before we placed that kind of trust in them.

But of course, there are millions of people out there saying whatever it takes to be heard. So, when it comes to trust, here's a bit of information from the get-go that we all need to know, whatever our age, gender, background or beliefs.

The only truly trustworthy places to get our information are:

1. The person at the heart of the story.
2. Or a person qualified to accurately report what they say without political, commercial or ideological bias.

I count myself very lucky.

I'm proud to have investigated thousands of news stories – sometimes clashing with the orders of my superiors who'd just read a juicy headline in the papers but hadn't looked into the story detail. That was my job for many years, and the job of people like me, to check the facts and pass them on to our viewers and listeners.

And that's what we'll do together.

But more than that, we'll step back to understand the blinding human reasons why we believe the stuff we do, and how to fight back against false information wherever we see it.

It's a tightrope, and it's all too easy to fall off.

Let's take the next step.

c BALANCE

The next key word.

It's a sad fact that balance isn't really offered to us in most of the information we see, hear or read. It's all over the place. And every ideological nudge, left and right, can force us to fall.

Normally, we'll only ever see a narrow set of quotes and opinions from our chosen platform, friends, family or news channel – possibly only one opinion if we're getting our news on social media.

What we really need is the source of the story – the original voices, even if they're biased, balanced by commonly held opposing views, in the right proportions.

That is balance.

Sadly, it's so, so easy to misunderstand balance. Balance is absolutely not a case of giving different voices equal coverage.

That's dangerous, because it raises up views that might only represent a tiny, niche idea - often a very extreme one. We've seen that many times over the last few years, particularly in some of the elections, votes and referenda that we're all too aware of.

In fact, balance only comes from reporting the main angles and witness or expert accounts, weighted exactly as they appear in the real world. Not 50-50!

And why is balance so important?

Well, real balance keeps us on the right track. It's our guide through a story. If we don't have it, we lurch quickly into the number one cause of mis- and dis-information: bias.

d | BIAS

Looking back at this book (and I don't want to spoil the ending), I've written the word bias more than one hundred times.

It's so crucial to mis- and dis-information. It's almost the most important word.

That's because it's really important – whoever we are, whatever our backgrounds and experiences – to check ourselves for bias. It's like taking a quick audit of our core beliefs.

If we don't do that, we won't be able to see our own prejudices, and won't be able to accept the full facts of any story. Even the best of us have bias. And it's much more likely to spiral out of control in a world where a million loud opinions back up our existing core beliefs. The over-used term 'echo chamber'.

One of the best antidotes to bias is simply to listen to other people.

Particularly when we listen to people who don't share our outlook on the world. We learn a lot just by looking through another person's eyes.

Once you've listened, perhaps you can open up a dialogue.

But it can be really challenging – especially with so much mis-
and dis-information out there to confuse us. But we'll tackle that
very carefully later in the book.

Onto the next word …

e CONVERSATION

No conversation, all opinion. All opinion, no perspective.

You might not always agree with the other side of an
argument, and they might even be wrong based on the facts that
you've seen. But it's absolutely crucial that we listen properly and
respond reasonably.

The point here – as we'll talk about a lot – is that we never
have a full view of the facts until we hear all of them. And the
facts always contain pro- and anti-elements, whatever the side of
the argument that you're on.

I've had a lot of professional conversations with people who
held controversial, sometimes aggressive and threatening views.
It's a slow process to open the door to conversation, and you need
to do it very gently, by listening first, especially when the person
across from you is suspicious of you.

Breaking down bias starts by looking seriously at the other
sides of the argument – and sometimes that's your (and my) job –
especially with everyone taking sides today.

Nobody's perfect, but unless we really listen to all sides,
we're not listening at all.

That means that you need to be genuinely interested in
what the other person has to say. You also have to earn your
place in the conversation. We'll work hard to generate healthy
conversations around conspiracy beliefs, politics and more, a little
later on.

It's a skill that we could all improve, especially face-to-face.

But – and I've brushed past this already in the key words – there's one thing, above all, that we need to get right if we're going to head toward a happier, healthier future of truth.

4. SOURCES

Whenever I hear a story that surprises me, the first question I ask is: 'Where did it come from?' That's followed swiftly by: 'Where did they get their information?'

Checking where our information's coming from is just about the most important thing that we can do, whether or not we think we're being lied to.

It's right up there with bias.

Sources come first, whether you're a hard-nosed journalist or someone looking for a holiday recommendation.

I mean, it's fun to listen to people's opinions, especially when they jump into a conspiracy and come back with a satisfying nugget of tasty gossip. But they're not sources that we can stake our reputation on. They don't know the truth, they're probably a long way from the facts, perhaps heavily biased and at very least see the truth from their own perspective.

So, information is all about good sources.

And here's how we find them.

We certainly need to ignore any account whose name is a series of symbols and letters followed by a few numbers. That can only be a human hiding their name, or a bot trying to look like a human who's hiding their name!

Putting that to one side, good information starts with good, known sources.

Here's the crucial recipe of where to go for our information:

Primary sources - the best.

First and foremost, we want to hear from the people who were at the scene of a story, or experts who know the subject better than anyone else. They might be biased, or only have one side of a story but they are the nearest thing we have to the original facts.

The next best - secondary sources.

We can probably rely on trained reporters if they're not from a newsroom with a well-known political, ideological or commercial agenda, or lots of pre-proven bias.

Third-hand or tertiary sources.

We sadly can't rely on anyone who's telling us what they heard or think – including our best friend, their workmate or their husband's dad. We might trust those people, but it doesn't mean they know what's going on. Also in this group are many newspapers, professional influencers and some TV and radio channels, because of bias in their storytelling. You probably know who yours are, even if you still like to get your news from them. As long as you know, you can dodge the bias.

Fourth-hand or quaternary sources.

Sadly, there's one more layer. And it's where a lot of us get all of our news. Social media relies on our opinions of what someone else has said about a genuine report of the original facts. It's chit-chat, opinion and core beliefs exposed. Sometimes the source of a big story will talk about it, but most of the conversation is a big reaction that fits someone's world view. And the more contentious the issue, the more biased it gets by the time it's filtered through a couple of hundred opinions.

News on social media is hardly ever accurate. It's opinions of opinions of reporting of the facts.

If we could step away from news on social - or 'anti-social' media - we'd be a lot better informed, and a lot less angry. And let's not forget balance. If we genuinely want to claim we know the truth, we'll need those primary and secondary sources plus accounts from the other sides, in the right balance.

Remember, when we don't listen to all sides of an argument – in the correct proportions – we never have access to the full story. It's that simple. And what about motives? You and I know when someone isn't 'on the level'. There's something driving them that they haven't told us. A secret motive.

Well, it's exactly the same with sources of information. Perhaps our source is a friend or family member who's swallowed something nasty on social media. Perhaps they're an expert or a politician or a member of an organisation that backs one side of an argument.

The lie is in the why.

Bias isn't always obvious, but if you're given a view that's completely one-sided, it's a clear sign of bias in action.

And whenever we share news and information – even when we know it's false, we're spreading the bias.

By using our account we're essentially washing it clean – or laundering – the biases of people who we're trusting too much.

Okay, what if I've 'done the research'?

If anyone tells you to 'do the research' on a niche belief or theory, you might find that something very tantalising happens. The writing or videos on that subject might agree with the theory. Normally, that would mean that they're right, right? Sadly not.

On this very specific point, made famous by early QAnon followers in the US, the only people talking about some of their far-out theories were their own members. The 'research' was actually written by people with exactly the same views as them. So, if there are no opposing views in all but the most clear-cut, fact checked and balanced cases, it's another reason to watch the sources.

And one thing is always obvious with any of those.

The opposing side is accused of being part of the conspiracy because they don't agree with us.

That them-and-us issue is a big part of the disinformation problem so I'll get onto very simple, intuitive ways that we can re-balance the information that we're given. It starts with emotion, understanding our core beliefs, and learning how to slow down our reaction even when we're called to arms by people we support.

And look, it probably sounds like too much work to investigate every piece of information you see, and that's true. But during our time together we'll develop simple checks, tips and tricks that will make the process feel natural, quick and reliable. It's a toolkit we'll turn into a set of ultimate questions about the information we're fed.

There is hope.

When we stop for a moment, we really can build up immunity to the bad diet of information that we're forced to digest every day of the week.

5. YOU SAY TOMATO, I SAY TOMATO

Okay, so let's get ready for Chapter 1.

We're about to investigate the causes, the feelings, the practical steps and safeguards we need to beat mis- and dis-information. And with that in mind, this book is absolutely, fundamentally and categorically not going to convince you to believe in any specific theory or to take any one stance.

Every belief is yours. As long as they're not hurting anyone, they're completely up to you.

And I don't care how you say tomato. Or, for that matter, tomato.

I also won't ask you to stop caring deeply about the things that drive you, or the people who annoy you.

Here, in plain language, without jargon, mystery or conspiratorial psychobabble, is what we'll work out together:

1. The issues that we're facing right now because of the spread of false information.
2. The very human reasons why we've fallen for it so far, and how we can kick the habit when strong emotions and beliefs are triggered.
3. The key pillars of storytelling and why mis- and dis-information are so perfectly attuned to exploit them.
4. The 'tells' that separate facts from fiction.
5. Why the views of others are so important to the whole.
6. Techniques to – thanks to careful conversations with each other – create a happier, healthier future of truth in the era of deepfakes and beyond.

And full disclosure: I am someone who's been on both sides of the divide as a creator and a consumer. A fact checker and a storyteller.

But I was fanatical about fact checking in my time on TV and radio.

So, let me be really honest. This won't be easy.

We're going to talk about some painful and challenging things during our time together. We might have to look into the eyes of some dark beliefs and learn from them.

Also, you won't always agree with my thoughts. And I hope

that you're someone who disagrees with me in places because that's the whole point of establishing the facts of a story from all sides – especially yours. Occasionally, I will come out from my magnanimous hidey-hole to knock a few heads together, but that's one for later.

There are simple ways we can improve our information diet, so I'll pass the baton to you after we're done. Listen or don't, choose to believe or disbelieve. But you'll have the facts. Although 'the truth' can be much, much harder to find.

6. RIGHT, WRONG AND THE GREY BIT IN THE MIDDLE

As we head into the false information maze, I'd like to add one final thing.

Mis- and dis-information may be the externalised ramblings of people who don't fully realise that they're wrong. But we're all susceptible. So, the last thing any of us should do is to blame other people for their beliefs.

There's a huge grey area in the middle, and somewhere in there – if we can get the facts straight – is 'the truth'. Our decisions about who to listen to, who to fight with, who to vote for and what to stand for can often skew our view of right and wrong. We might try to avoid facing the facts by throwing in a 'what about that person - they did far worse than my person' what about-ism. We might say terrible things just to hold onto the truth we want to believe in.

Ultimately, none of us like being lied to, but some lies make it through despite our best efforts. For now, let's just agree on one thing ...

If you set out to harm someone, to misinform them or make them feel bad, you're in the wrong.

We'll investigate what that means later.

Okay, so let's start by following that white rabbit down its hole, travelling a few hundred years into history to one of the most enduring conspiracy theories that humans have ever created.

Welcome to The Future of Truth (and How to Get There).

1

WE ALL LOVE TO TELL TALL TALES

1

'Stories are a communal currency of humanity.'

TAHIR SHAH

1. LET'S START WITH WHY

It's so very human to tell stories.

They've been the warm embrace holding small groups of people together for tens of thousands of years. They're our creative spark, our place in the world. They've passed down important knowledge and given our brains a place to go. They're new, they're exciting, and they're really, really scary.

A good story is a reason to come together. It's probably been added-to, sexed up and embellished around campfires and smartphones since time began. It's an absolutely fabulous way to spread knowledge and come together around shared beliefs, and an incredibly effective way to scare us into action.

The problem is that our brains haven't evolved much over the last few thousand years.

They're still built to get our weak, fleshy bodies out of the jaws of lions and to propagate the species. Once we escape the physical danger, the other stuff: the complexity of thought, creation of tools, culture, society and art are there to pull us closer together, to entertain each other, to solve problems and grow.

For ancient humans, brains and brawn became the best combination on the block, and storytelling was the cultural currency.

So, what's changed?

2. STORYTELLING 2.0

Unfortunately, our naturally grown addiction to good stories is being overfed.

We want more. We like to make them bigger and more gripping. And it's all too tempting to update the original story with an extra detail or two that makes us part of it.

There's been a lot of research into the history of storytelling in small groups. One was carried out in 2017 by anthropologists from University College London.

Let's look at the study that showed how powerful storytelling is today, and how it can build morality, community and egalitarian values without the need for religious belief.

Stage 1

The team carried out a search of 89 different stories told by seven different forager societies in countries including Thailand, Malaysia and across Africa.

The stories contained lessons about social cooperation, empathy and justice, and some even included discussions about sexual equality. The researchers narrowed down their study to a group called the Agta – a small society of around 1,200 people, spread across dozens of villages on the island of Luzon in the Philippines.

Stage 2

They asked one community 'who are your best storytellers?'. The scores were collected, and the better storytellers were identified within the community.

Stage 3

They then asked another group within the same community to vote separately – using tokens – for the person who should receive a special share of rice. The researchers gave them 12 possible recipients of the token. Each voter could also keep the token for themselves. Importantly, a few of the potential recipients were on the list of the best storytellers.

The results

Almost two-thirds of the group decided to keep the token for themselves. And who can blame them? But there was a small and significant trend in the remaining third. Essentially, for every one 'good storyteller', the token holders would be twice as generous to the group they were in.

Among the Agta, having good storytellers made the community more generous.

As if that result wasn't interesting enough, the research also showed that good storytellers would also be more likely to have a partner and on average have 0.52x more surviving babies than others. One extra baby for every two good storytellers.

So, telling good stories made people popular, more attractive, and more likely to have healthy children.

I've slightly simplified the summary of this part of the research, but those are the headlines, and those trends are backed up by other studies of different communities.

The incredible result is that stories really do bring us together and – through our increased generosity and positive values – make communities of people more successful. I should add, and there's a lot of research on this too, that the storytellers' success can be counteracted when they tell stories that are later found to be untrue.

You can have a look at the research yourself at https://www.

nature.com/articles/s41467-017-02036-8

ADDICTION TO FICTION

That piece of research – and the others like it – go at least part of the way to explaining why stories are so important. And you can see that anything that makes us more united will also make us more successful as a group.

Teamwork really does make the dream work.

But after more than 30,000 years of storytelling, our compulsion to tell – and listen to – them is not a conscious choice. It's not something that we need to think about. Stories, fiction, tall tales are something that naturally shape us, our innermost beliefs and values from birth.

So, let's go back to childhood for a moment and think about the magic and horror of fairytales. What lessons did we all learn from the jeopardy of *Hansel and Gretel* (Germany), *Mamad, The Man Who Never Lied* (Africa), or *The Kingdom of the Ogres* (China)?

Do you have a favourite fairytale? Did one story make you clutch your parent tightly when you were young?

I think mine might be *Jack and the Beanstalk*. My dad would chase us around the kitchen booming '*Fee-fi-fo-fum, I smell the blood of an Englishman!*' You'd think that he'd have got tired of that by my and my brother's 51st birthdays. Apparently not.

But whatever your favourite, fairytales made us feel a tantalising moment of fear, childish excitement and then relief. And this is a clue to the process that makes stories so gripping whatever age we are.

Threat, emotion, relief, repeat.

Folklore acted in a similar way on our ancestors. That word of mouth taught them to think about the dangers they faced, to understand the world around them, the acceptable codes of conduct and what happened if they didn't follow them. It's the same today, and the second part of it is that we enjoy telling those harmless little horror stories because it gives us popularity and status.

If you've ever shared or listened to a ghost story with the lights low, you'll know that there's nothing like it for quickening the heartbeat.

It was claimed by cognitive psychologist Jerome Bruner that stories are 22 times more memorable than plain facts, statistics or other factual interactions. This may or may not be mathematically correct, but live medical scans have shown that stories fire up better recall by activating visual centres of the brain, emotions and imagination – as well as the language comprehension areas that help us to understand things.

I won't take you too far into this area for now, but if you'd like to get creative, there's a nice article about 'Our Fiction Addition' on the BBC website here: www.bbc.com/culture/article/20180503-our-fiction-addiction-why-humans-need-stories.

Ultimately, great stories help us to process information. Our brains are perfectly evolved to respond to – and pass on – information through storytelling.

In the next chapter, we'll talk about the chemicals that keep us safe, make us fight, fly and tell scary stories around the social media campfire. But for now, let's think about this: what happens when a good storyteller tries to get their own way by making us scared, excited, attached and then relieved?

You can see where we're going with this.

That's right, the way we feel is an integral part of mis- and dis-information.

If they can create a plausible threat that taps into our core beliefs or the values we've been taught, they can weaponise a story.

It's how false information-mongers design stories that

intentionally tap into our fear, our natural need to listen, to share and act on information that seems, at first look, to make sense.

THE ANTHROPOLOGY OF IT ALL

Here's a story that you might know and love.

There was a tortoise and a hare. The hare was very fast and boasted to the other animals about how fast he could run. One day, the tortoise said 'Okay, I'll race you'. The hare scoffed and laughed and taunted the tortoise but agreed to the race.

Later, it was race day … the hare ran off at speed, knowing that there was no way the slow tortoise could beat him. So much so, that he took a nap along the way, under a tree. But in his arrogance, he lost track of time and when he woke up, he realised that the tortoise had overtaken him. No matter how fast he ran, he couldn't catch up, and the tortoise won the race – against all of the odds.

The lesson? Slow, steady – and humble – wins the day.

It's Aesop's famous fable of the tortoise and the hare (with a few additions from me – like I say, we can't resist putting our own spin on a good story). It's about 2,500 years old but still teaches us valuable lessons about arrogance, complacency, about there being multiple ways to win in life.

It's a great example of how storytelling can communicate valuable lessons in a colourful, three-dimensional way, without a single real-world fact or instruction.

Widen this story out to other well-worn tales, and you'll find powerful hidden messages about the power of cooperation, that good behaviour is better, and bad behaviour – often arrogance – will land you in trouble, eventually.

On the flip side, you'll hear scary, fictional stories that encourage us to cooperate and defend ourselves against an evil threat from outside our group. Speaking of which, let's group together stories on social media. How does the fairytale storytelling approach show itself today?

> *Popularity*. It's great to be a princess or a prince. When we look great online, have followers and appear to be living our best lives, we're projecting the sexy and successful image that storytellers in centuries gone by flaunted to become the centre of attention – and successful as a result.

> '*Curiouser and curiouser*'. Telling stories online – not least in conspiracies – means that we can share our knowledge and curious insights with our people, our tribe, our social group, and grow it. Many minds add new information and take the group in a new direction. That's how conspiracy beliefs can quickly diverge from the original facts.

> *Sharing* and responding to stories gives you more social credibility and means that you go from outsider to a central part of the story. Almost from rags to riches, socially speaking.

> And let's face it, many of us dream of instant success without the hard work. Just like being granted *three wishes*.

This is just a glimpse of how our brains respond to stories. But already, we can see the very strong, ancient foundations of storytelling and success.

Let's talk emotion.

I GET SO EMOTIONAL, BABY

Our modern brains haven't quite managed to replace the natural fear they have of imminent attack, with a more helpful, relaxed, grown-up perspective. They're still a bit, well, chimp.

Whenever our emotions flare, it's a sign that our primal brains are getting a workout. The content that causes the reaction will be eye-catching and hard to ignore. And if there's one thing our brains do well, it's to turn threats and excitement into chemistry, followed by an emotional response, followed by an action.

The good news is that emotions are temporary, so we can move past the beliefs that they bury inside us in the heat of the moment. But why do we react like that in the first place?

Because a great story is like a rehearsal of a real danger.

It's a safe version of the original threat to test our responses, putting us into the frame of mind we'd be in if the danger was real. It's a practice run.

And this is the next piece in the puzzle. Just like balance, bias, conversation and sources. Emotion is the next big marker that we'll come back to, because it's at the heart of why we react so quickly to, and also share, mis- and dis-information.

THE RESEARCH THAT LINKED EMOTION TO FAKE NEWS

There's a great piece of research called '*Reliance on emotion promotes belief in fake news*', by Cameron Martel, Gordon Pennycock and David G. Rand: www.cognitiveresearchjournal.springeropen.com/articles/10.1186/s41235-020-00252-3

They looked at the relationship between emotions and our belief in a story. They asked: 'What happens if we feel heightened, a little emotional before we see, hear or read a fake story, compared to a genuine story?'

Probably not very different, right?

Wrong.

When we approach a fake story – already feeling emotional – we're more likely to believe that false information.

Conversely, if we're emotional when we look at a genuine

story, we're no more likely to believe it than if we read it with a cool head.

There's a direct link between our emotional state and the growth of fake news.

And I can tell you, from my years in the news business, that one phrase embodies a newsroom's story choice more than any other (although we rarely actually said it because it's pretty unpalatable). It's all about emotion:

If it bleeds, it leads.

The more emotionally testing a story, the more impact it has. So, let's build a good – potentially false – story. To make genuine information more gripping, it needs a strong emotional element.

So, we'd spend our time covering:

> Stories that are new and surprising. That's the nature of news, so no problem there.
> News that has a high emotional impact on the audience – i.e., makes them feel something which might be shock, fear or excitement. Stories that stoke a feeling of injustice, or are framed in a way that give us a feeling of control over our lack of power in the world. Tabloid and opinion-based news does this particularly well.

What next?

> You'll add in some emotive, big, bold and controversial language or adjectives to make things seem more outrageous.
> If possible, you'll reveal something important that your audience didn't already know – or perhaps give it a new spin.
> Or you'll go for the franchise approach – could you resurrect a subject that people already react strongly to?

But it's the emotional impact, the tabloid approach that has the biggest effect on us. Bad news delivered in salacious ways.

So, when is bad news bad for our health?

WHY WE LOVE BAD NEWS

Bad, biased, big, bold news is addictive.

But why?

Well firstly, humanity is really tuned in to self-preservation. It makes us prone to feel fear and anxiety – our 'negativity bias'. It's a well-known psychological effect based on our need for self-defence against threats.

Bad news threatens us, so we sit up and listen.

We also get ready to defend ourselves. So, we'll get angry, verbal, take sides. It's similar when we feel an injustice, especially when we're the ones losing out. And when we feel powerless in the real world, bad news can give us a target for our anger. It's all so very human.

Think about the reaction of friends, family and colleagues during the COVID-19 pandemic. An existential threat that initially brought us together, and then split many of us apart.

We now know from the research I just mentioned, that when we're already emotional, fake news fans the flames even more. At the opposite end, we don't react as strongly to happiness and contentment because positive emotions are exactly what we want, so we don't need to activate our bodies to fight them or run away.

That's why we love bad news.

We believe it, it makes us emotional, activates our brains and our bodies, and give us something to fight. The chemistry is strong, and we'll look at it inside our brains, in Chapter 2. But already, can you see why negative, high-impact stories get us so hot under the collar? Why the mass media are so tuned in to our emotions, and why bad news sells more?

Our response to fear, perceived injustice and the bad news that feeds it are key reasons why we're so angry, divided and opinionated.

So, anyone who's looking to manipulate our views can tap into that.

They can create a realistic-sounding threat based on our existing fears and core beliefs and prime us to fight. And the people who spread disinformation this way become just as addicted to the positive returns as we are to the negative effects.

But don't take the scientists' – or my – word for it. Let's wind back the clock to an age of squalor, fear and damnation.

Few conspiracy beliefs have lasted as long as the one coming up. It's been responsible for persecution, for murder, for genocide and holocaust. It's hard to believe that it still hits the headlines today, and how little we've learned over the last 900 years.

3. 900 YEARS OF CONSPIRACY

Before you read this section, I have a few important words to say. At the time of writing this 2nd Edition, the Middle East has been at war for over a year, costing the lives of tens of thousands of civilians in Gaza, Lebanon, Syria, Yemen – and Israel. It's impossible to ignore the terrible price paid by so many, and so I want to offer a small warning about the contents of this section. It explains a disturbing Middle Age conspiracy belief about Jewish people that might upset you. Please jump to the next section if you find the subject difficult to read or be reminded of, and please don't share this story with children. This is not intended to relate to any of today's events in the Middle East.

So, you've probably heard this story in some form. And I'm

including it here because it's as relevant today as it was when it began.

You may not know its name. Perhaps you've heard references to it in a news story, or in an online conversation. You might have thought that it's new, something quoted only by people with extreme views. But it's one of the most enduring and disturbing conspiracy theories of all time.

It's called the 'blood libel'.

We're going to race through 900 years of history over the next few minutes, and land right back here in the 21st century.

Here are the main milestones.

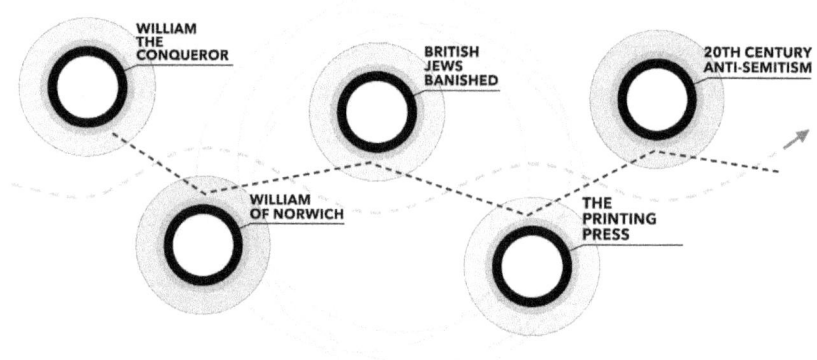

a 1100: THE STORY BEGINS

In around the year 1100, most of the population of early medieval England couldn't read, and they had no access to any information outside the edicts and orders of the Catholic church and the King.

Jewish people had been living in England for only 30 years or so, brought to the country for one specific purpose. Historians believe that William the Conqueror selected wealthy Jewish people in France and brought them to Britain to lend money, to put coins into circulation, to set up loans for business people, for families, so that he could charge them taxes. Previously, most people lived hand-to-mouth, trading what they could for food.

Simply, the new King wanted his slice, and the Jewish money lenders would be doing the dirty work for him.

In Biblical times – and throughout history – tax collectors were some of the most hated people in society and were seen as innately sinful. The Romans also used rich Jewish people to collect their taxes – but importantly, they weren't paid anything. They would need to charge a commission. They had no choice but to do the job that they'd been given, but equally, you can imagine some of the margins they charged, and the penalties for people who didn't repay the loan in full.

But in such an age of poverty, superstition and religious zealotry, it was a very bad look to have Jewish people collecting money from good Christian folk living in squalor.

And it didn't take long for the hatred to metastasise.

Within a few years, a rumour spread that every Easter – the time of the crucifixion of Jesus Christ – Jewish people were going around capturing Christian children, killing them, and using their blood in a recipe for bread (matzos). This was a time when everyone would be reminded of how the Romans in Jerusalem killed Jesus – supported by the Jewish authorities. So, when a child died, the fingers pointed at local Jews.

I can only paraphrase this early conspiracy theory. But of course, you can find a lot of background information on this from good sources including The National Archives: https://www.nationalarchives.gov.uk/education/resources/jews-in-england-1066/

So, what happened? The resentment, lack of money and a deep feeling of injustice exploded into the minds of the poor. They were powerless in the real world, but now they could claim some power back. And they quickly bit the hand that fed them.

Let's fast forward 40 years.

b 1144: WILLIAM OF NORWICH

By now, Jewish people had been living in the UK for just over 70 years.

In 1144, the body of a boy called William was found in Norwich. He'd been stabbed to death, his body left in woods near a Jewish house. Sure, there were non-Jewish houses nearby too but immediately, the finger pointed to the Jewish community.

Here's the charge against them. Can you pick up any subtle religious overtones?

'*The Jews of Norwich bought a Christian child (the 'boy martyr' William) before Easter and tortured him with all the tortures wherewith our Lord was tortured, and on Long Friday hanged him on a rood (road) in hatred of our Lord.*'

William went from boy to 'boy martyr' to miraculous healer within the blink of an eye. He was soon said to have had holy powers. The killer was never found, and the matter was laid to rest.

A few years later, a Benedictine monk – Thomas of Monmouth – came to town. He heard William's story and soon petitioned for two things: to make William a saint, and to blame William's death on local Jews.

He published a series of book volumes a few years later, the first edition in 1150, called *The Life and Miracles of St William of Norwich.*

This is where things changed.

In that first volume, Thomas of Monmouth wrote down the blood libel for the first time. How William had not just been stabbed but ritually murdered, crucified. The story soon included how William's body had been found with a crown of thorns placed on his head. Now, officially, the Church was accusing Jewish people of crucifying kids at Easter.

Where was the evidence? Well of course, there wasn't any. No-one saw anything. We're talking about a monk from the Middle Ages, not a scientific investigator. And of course, there are crisscrossing records, accusations and counterclaims.

But the word spread far and wide.

Thomas of Monmouth's claims about the Jews were read by fellow clergy, and the rumours spread hand-in-hand with claims that Jewish people were bribing local authorities to keep their crimes quiet.

They were essentially 'crossing their palms with silver' to gain power, so the story went.

The iron grip of the medieval Catholic church, fear of eternal damnation, a sense of injustice, and sheer, blinding white anger about the murder of a local child was a motivator like no other.

c THE 1200s-1300s

The persecution followed.

Violence against Jewish communities exploded. Perhaps one in 400 people in England were Jewish by then.

The rumours and violence spread far and wide, and Jewish people soon faced heavy financial penalties, culminating in their banishment from Britain on 18th July 1290. They weren't allowed back until the mid-1600s.

With Jewish people scattered, the Scottish leader William Wallace dead, a Welsh uprising quelled, and France and England united by royal marriage, who could people blame next? Who'd be the next dreadful threat to the Christian way of life?

Witches.

It began almost immediately. Just 11 years after Jewish people were thrown out of England, accusations began of sorcery.

One of the first was between Sir John Lovetot and Walter Langton (one of King Edward I's most important administrators). Lovetot accused Langton of using sorcery to gain influence over the King. Lovetot's dad owed Langton a lot of money (£1,000 in old money). At some point, it would have to be repaid, and some people will do anything to get out of a debt.

Lovetot went straight to the Pope, who put Langton on trial. But it didn't stick. Two years later, the charges were dropped because all of the supporting evidence came from Langton's rivals.

The point here is that there was now a double threat to good Christian folk in Europe: Jewish people and now witchcraft.

Slowly and surely, the mania continued by word of mouth until a new piece of tech would change the game completely.

d | 1400s: THE PRINTING PRESS

Let's jump forward.

A new piece of tech landed in Europe in 1436: the printing press. It was a communication revolution that would bring the written word to the masses, like social media, like AI.

Books could suddenly be printed more cheaply than ever before. Knowledge was power, and not just Biblical knowledge. All sorts of books could be sent to far flung corners of Europe.

One of them was *The Life and Miracles of St William of Norwich*.

Another was a book about witches. We'll talk about the *Malleus Maleficarum* shortly.

By 1473, the Jews had moved east to other parts of Europe.

When a toddler called Simon Unferdoben from Trent in Italy was found dead in 1473 near a Jewish home, you can guess who copped the blame.

Like William of Norwich, little Simon was labelled a saintly martyr, renamed Simon of Trent, and because he'd died at Passover eight Jewish people were blamed, tortured, and beheaded or burned.

Who needs evidence when there's fear, fury and an easy target living nearby?

But remember the name Simon of Trent if you can.

By this time, the witch panic was now in full effect, but luckily another book was landing on clerical bookshelves everywhere.

Again, it contained the writings (and indeed, rantings) of two Dominican friars Johann Sprenger and Heinrich Kraemer. They claimed that the devil was at work all around us, and women, not men, were the main targets – inherently weaker and more sinful.

So, hey – they might be witches.

That's right, this book was the *Malleus Maleficarum* – or Hammer of Witches, published in 1486.

And when this book hit the shelves, information would never be the same again.

This incredibly strange text said that witches lurked among us, that they hid in trees, that they ate babies (aka the blood libel) and could be tortured to secure confessions. But it didn't matter that these were the ravings of incredibly suspect sources. It created fear. It created a new threat and someone to blame the fear and horror on, just like populist politicians do today.

Soon, women across Europe who'd previously been valued – sometimes as healers – were accused of sorcery. This thing was reprinted 28 times and became the standard handbook on witchcraft and demonology until well into the 18th century.

The witch-hunting frenzy killed over 40,000 people – the majority women – over the next 200 years. All propelled by fear, religious zeal and gossip. Exactly the same process by which stories had moved people to fight or fly for millennia.

e 1600-1900

We're jumping very close to modern times.

And while some people were hunting witches, others were pushing Jewish people even further east, from Germany to eastern Europe, then into Russia, and as far east as Iran.

By the time people had stopped believing in the need to kill witches, tens of thousands of Jews had already been murdered.
But that was nothing compared to what happened next.

f 1900s

The blood libel was now held high in a new breed of anti-Jewish hatred.

A May 1934 edition of the antisemitic German newspaper *Der Stürmer* (The Attacker) ran the same story as Thomas of Monmouth had in his volumes 800 years earlier. The blood libel was back in print, and it became a populist cornerstone of Adolf Hitler's antisemitic propaganda, leading directly to the holocaust. Even after World War II, blood libel stories circulated in Poland and other countries, despite the recent horrors of the holocaust that so many people had seen firsthand.

Intense suspicion, a time of absolute horror and a sense of them versus us had blinded many to the evidence of their own eyes.

But surely, those days are over? We know what happened to our God-fearing ancestors, and we're over it, aren't we?

g 2016

Hillary Clinton – who'd already been accused of being a witch who'd ritualistically murdered a child – was then accused by Republican supporters of trafficking children through restaurants, specifically the basement of Comet Ping Pong pizza in Washington DC.

The QAnon conspiracy cabal – remember them? – simultaneously claimed that a Satan-worshipping Democrat, celebrity and Jewish group had been trafficking kids and harvesting life-extending chemicals from their blood.

Witchcraft, devil worship, ritual murder of a child, Jewish people taking children's blood …

It's all so very 1100.

And of course, the basement didn't even exist.

h 2019

A young man walked into a San Diego synagogue during Passover with an AR-15 rifle.

Nineteen-year-old John Earnest opened fire, killing Lori Gilbert Kaye who was there to pray for her late mother. Police quickly found that he's uploaded a manifesto to the site Pastebin, and also onto the message board 8chan saying, 'You are not forgotten, Simon of Trent'.

You remember Simon of Trent, don't you? The boy who died in Italy during the Middle Ages?

One murderous conspiracy theory, written by a medieval English monk after the death of one boy years earlier, spread by fear, fury and a means to spread the word.

This is exactly what can happen when doors are opened to conspiracy beliefs, alt-truths and disinformation.

When stories spread dark rumours freely, with no controls or fact checking, reality dies.

Let's be really clear. There was never any evidence of a Jewish conspiracy in 1100. No witnesses, no informants, just accusations from the medieval church, monks, and a frightened, impoverished population who had no choice but to believe what they were told.

Perhaps it's finally time to put down the parchment. This was clearly never true, but when we allow our primal chimp brain to run riot and dictate our feelings, it's no surprise that disinformation works as well now as it did 900 years ago.

4. ONE SCARY WORD LIES IN WAIT

And that word is fear.

We'll do almost anything to fight it, especially when there's a feeling of injustice or powerlessness mixed in. The worse the crisis, the more prone we are to feel fear, and anger to overcome it.

We've all been there. It's a huge relief when we find a simple explanation to take all the worry away.

The next chapter explains the human nature behind it, but here's a really good introduction to the way fear works on us by Arash Javanbakht and Linda Saab in the Smithsonian magazine – www.smithsonianmag.com/science-nature/what-happens-brain-feel-fear-180966992/

When it comes to our tendency to explain away fear, here's a great line from the article:

'*When we are able to recognize what is and isn't a real threat, re-label an experience and enjoy the thrill of that moment, we are ultimately at a place where we feel in control.*'

The big question is how to separate a real threat from a made-up one when social and mass media feed us a world of extreme (at very least fabricated) opinion, quickly, wherever we want, without fact checking or safety checks.

And we'll find some answers to those problems together. We have lots of solutions to follow, once we can see how easy it's been to be manipulated on social media, in the news, by politics and more. Once we know that, we can move on.

5. THE DEFINITIONS OF MIS- AND DIS-INFORMATION

Before we go any further, this book is all about mis- and dis-information and how to fight them, so we'd better define them! At their core, they are this:

> **Misinformation** is basically false information spread by us, by mistake. Perhaps the person sharing the article didn't check the facts of the story for themselves. They may have trusted the person that the information came from just a bit too much. Enough to spread it further without checking that they were correct (or being honest about it). Either way, the information is false, but the infection wasn't necessarily spread on purpose.

> **Disinformation** is intentional. Whatever the motivation, whatever the detail, anyone who spreads information that they know – or strongly suspect – is false, IS the problem. They're also more likely to create it, add their own spin on it, with a malicious or moneymaking ulterior motive in mind. You're also likely to find governments, businesses, trolls and groups with biased views and a big agenda in this category.

Looking back, the creators of the world wide web were so trusting. Geniuses, but a bit naïve. They thought we'd use their invention as a power for good.

For all their tech prowess, you've got to admire their positivity. Innocence, even.

But what would Plato say?

Whenever I'm facing an existential crisis of trust in the

societal structures that hold us together, I like to ask, 'What would Plato say?' He never fails us, although some of his gender references might need a bit of updating these days.

In Book Two of his *Republic* – one of the world's most influential journals – he talks seriously about how stories need to be made safe for the young:

'*...our first business is to supervise the production of stories, and choose only those we think suitable, and reject the rest. We shall persuade mothers and nurses to tell our chosen stories to their children, and by means of them to mould their minds and characters which are more important than their bodies. The greater part of the stories current today we shall have to reject.*'

Seriously, that's some relevant, up-to-the-minute, ancient Greek philosophy, right there.

When we reach Chapter 6, we'll talk about exactly what's gone wrong with safeguards and moderation on social media – where young and old alike get so much of their information from.

One of the biggest issues is actually the freedom that we'd normally welcome. There aren't enough people on social media's payroll to reject the stories that Plato warned us about - especially after the Meta announcement in early 2025.

You could say that democracy made misinformation.

Democracy should be a good thing. A place for ideas to grow freely and creativity to flourish.

But the village gossip and word-of-mouth in Middle Age Europe was a cautionary tale. The stories, tall tales and gossip about Jewish people got worse and more widespread after the invention of the printing press. Word spreads fast, allowing frightening ideas to mutate and grow.

Sadly, there might be a problem with democracy.

Really, it's about how safe it is to listen to every single person's inner monologue, without penalties for information that leads to real-world harm.

In terms of information, the age-old problem is that, when the technology of storytelling overtakes the ability to keep people safe – whether that's the printing press, the internet, social media or generative AI – something very specific happens:

> Conversations quickly move from firsthand accounts, to opinions, to new media channels with an agenda to misinform.
> The newly misinformed community becomes more extreme and splintered.
> Malicious or opportunistic actors begin to intentionally mislead them – introducing disinformation into the mix.
> Mis- and dis-information coexist, become self-sustaining, more extreme and conspiratorial, and play off each other.
> And the process loops round and continues to create diverging views that now have enough support to be perceived as 'the truth'.

But why?
Surely that spiral into misinformation isn't inevitable, is it?

6. BAD NEWS TRAVELS FAST

The story of the last 900 years is a clue.

You might be surprised to hear that the old phrase 'bad news travels fast' is absolutely true. There's another phrase that says it in style: 'A lie is halfway around the world before the truth has put its boots on.'

Let's look at a fantastic bit of research that showed how addicted to fiction we are. Social media has moved on a lot since then, and we now know that fake accounts and bots are often created to start the original lie, particularly if a regime like the Russian government chooses to try to sway an election. But this study gives us a lot of insight into the role we humans play in the true story of misinformation.

In 2017, scientists at MIT (Massachusetts Institute of Technology) studied the way in which fake news spreads on X (or Twitter as it was then), and how that compares to genuine news. They looked at how far, wide, fast and deep 'bad news' travels among a huge sample of 3 million users.

And they found that:

> People spread false news much more quickly than real news – 70% faster in fact.
> Re-sharing people's posts is the main cause.
> It takes six times as long for a genuine story to reach you than the fake version.
> And bots aren't responsible for most of it. People are.

So, false stories that trigger surprise, outrage and gossip are up to twice as likely to spread as real stories because we're much more likely to share them.

Now, in the almost total secrecy around algorithms – and the much greater input of other countries' bots into political decisions since 2016 – we know that some of the big social media tycoons (you know the names) have a lot of questions to answer about how our news feeds are manipulated. But what's clear is that we're to blame for spreading most false, fake and bad news. These days, bots are much more involved. But we are the key spreaders. We are the target and the amplifiers of it.

And technology aside, it's exactly the same process as telling scary stories around the ancestral campfire. Outrageous, scary, exciting stories are more gripping and we're much more likely to spread them because they make us part of the conversation. Social media gives us that opportunity.

And that brings us to something that, after many moons

investigating mis- and dis-information, I believe is at the heart of every conspiracy theory under the sun.

7. CORE BELIEFS

Whenever we talk about mis- and dis-information, conspiracies or 'the truth', we need to take a step back.

One of the key drivers of every single judgement we make are our core beliefs about the world we live in.

Core beliefs dominate our reactions to the stories that we see, hear and read. We all have them, and they show themselves every time we express an opinion.

They might include:

> But the government is plotting to control us.
> My life is tough, so it's unfair that other people should get a bigger slice of the pie.
> I know right from wrong, and people on the other side of the argument are wrong.
> Those immigrants are taking housing and benefits from people like me.
> I am a left-winger/right-winger and will never vote the other way.

Can you identify any of yours?

They can be almost invisible. They can be darker than we'd admit to. And they can make us support really nasty ideas, even though we're otherwise nice people. And mis- and dis-information are great at twisting them. So, it's really important to hold up a mirror to our core beliefs, because they dictate how susceptible we are to certain extreme beliefs when a difficult subject comes up.

After more than 30 years asking questions of important people, one of mine is that I believe that we shouldn't trust everything we're told – especially when the motives are hidden. I'm very sceptical of big claims that don't ring true.

Of course, we still engage our brains to control what we really think. But let's face it, the way we really feel about an issue, story or argument influences us at our core. And our core beliefs move up and down in intensity depending on the information we're seeing.

It's a thick, conflicting blancmange of our:

> Underlying values – taught and trained when we're young.
> Childhood experiences
> Family.
> Work.
> Education and training.
> The political views that we were brought up on.
> Bad experiences and good.
> Our recent conversations.
> News and social media exposure.

Let's look at some core beliefs in action.

And I want to say that this example isn't chosen to take one side or another. It's simply a way to see core beliefs in action. It happened in the UK in 2023.

Question Time is the BBC's late-night, flagship political programme, touring Britain with a live audience plucked from the local area. On the stage is a panel of political people, mainly MPs, with someone from outside politics – perhaps an actor, musician or in this case a professor.

The audience gets to ask the panel questions and make their own comments about what's happening in public life.

In June 2023, the BBC decided to film an episode of Question Time on the 7th anniversary of the Brexit vote, with an audience made up exclusively of people who'd voted to leave the EU. They'd held it in Clacton-on-Sea in Essex, the town with the second biggest pro-leave vote per head.

How would the pro-leavers feel now?

Well, just one tiny detail before we find out. Someone important was missing.

Despite it being a home run for the Conservative government in an audience of Brexit believers, they didn't turn up. Not a peep from the Cabinet. But of course, the UK was in the middle of an explosive mortgage crisis, an interest rate and inflation crisis, a cost-of-living crisis, an import-export crisis, so they probably had more important things to do. None of it, of course, made worse by Brexit. But it's the audience – not the panel – that really made this show tick.

And the belief was definitely still strong. When former Prime Minister Tony Blair's Director of Communications Alastair Campbell (who was and still is strongly against Brexit) talked about how voters had been misinformed and lied to by the pro-leave camp, an audience member threw it back at him.

She said, '*It just makes my blood boil when I keep hearing that same thing about the fact that we were lied to… I wanted out, to be sovereign.*'

Shortly afterwards, an older woman spoke: '*The reason I wanted to come out of Brexit is because we seemed to keep to all of the rules, and many foreign countries didn't. I'm talking about people who go up on roofs for one thing. When they brought in the rules about the safety guards, we took that on board. But when you went to France, or Germany or something, they were all up on their roofs with nothing. And we were having to pay the cost of doing it the right way, and they weren't. And that's one of the biggest reasons why I voted to come out.*'

Now, apart from mixing up her words a couple of times, it's hard to know whether the second audience member was angry about safety measures on roofs specifically, or how unfair it was for the UK to follow rules that '*other countries don't*'.

It's unlikely that she's a roofer. It's more likely that she'd read stories about it or had a friend who'd complained about safety on roofs.

The bigger core beliefs were probably:

> Them and us – we follow rules, they don't.
> Injustice – we're paying for Europe's rules. It's unfair that they don't (so I've been told).
> Emotion – just like the audience member whose blood was boiling about 'being lied to', she was just angry about Europe telling us what to do. That was, after all, the narrative that the right-leaning press had run all day, every day during the Brexit vote.

What was surprising was seeing the small proportion of people telling the show that they'd changed their minds.

That's brave in an audience that still appeared strongly in favour of Brexit. They'd really stuck their necks out and challenged their core beliefs. And the emotion in some was clearly visible.

They'd opened themselves up to heavy criticism from their community, and risked losing a lot of social standing.

That's why it's perfectly acceptable to blame the storyteller and the story when it's full of false claims, but we should never blame the person exposed to it.

One way to break the chain of our core beliefs – if we want to get closer to 'the truth' – is to look at credibility.

The simple question we can ask is this:

Is our source of information credible, honest and free from bias?

When bias shows up, we're simply listening to opinion, potentially lies, but certainly not the whole truth.

8. HOW TO KICK THE HABIT AND MOVE TO THE MIDDLE

Disinformation is designed to split us up. In some ways, that's what it's all about – to separate people from the pack so that our social norms fail and we're more open to influence.

Remember the World Economic Forum Global Risks Report that said, '*Misinformation and disinformation would be the biggest short-term risk to social cohesion*'?

For the sake of our future relationships, that's why it's so important to find the centre of an argument. The core, unbiased middle that takes all sides into account.

When we lose sight of the middle ground, we lose our way back to the truth. And – as we know – we fight amongst ourselves. So, from now on, we're going to build up a set of tools to extract the facts from fiction in the information we see. Then, we can agree on the centre ground – even if we still disagree with it.

So, let's start to build our toolkit to fight false information.

We'll do it chapter-by-chapter to help us to build really good 'news sense' and intuition. It'll protect us from extreme views and conspiracy rabbit holes. And if there's a chance that one of us is in one right now, it might help us to see a safe way out. Look out for those toolkit summaries at the end of every chapter to keep us close to the centre ground.

9. 5Ws AND AN H

It starts by extracting the facts.

The question is: what really happened in the story we're looking at or listening to? And how do we find out?

The facts of any story are contained within the well-known 5 Ws: What, When, Where, Who, and Why. I also like to add an H to the mix – How. You might have used them before in your own life, but here's how a journalist uses them to uncover the facts.

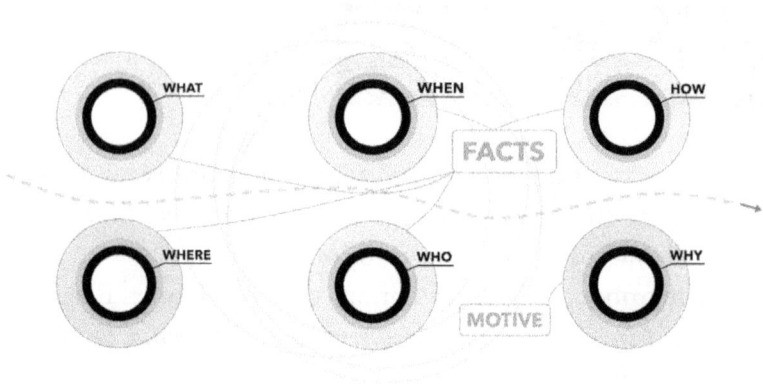

We ask something like this:

> What has happened? i.e. the basic details of the story. We also ask – do they make sense?
> Where did it happen? Does that tally with other accounts?
> When did it happen? i.e. any relevant dates or timeline
> Who was directly involved? e.g. do you know the sources, and are you hearing about or from people who know what happened? Or are you hearing it from people with third- or fourth-party opinions?
> How did it happen? Be careful here. Those details are only known by people very close to the story.
> Why did it happen? e.g. what were the motives? This is often the biggest question of all. Here above all, accuracy is crucial. If anyone claims to know the 'why', you have to ask, 'How do they know?'.

If you're trying to work out the facts of any story or piece of information, ask those questions, with a couple of variations of each, and you'll have everything that's available.

You can also go to a range of fact checking sites worldwide. They're definitely worth a look when you need to crosscheck specific pieces of questionable information. Just make sure you know who's doing the checking. Having a website with the words 'fact' and 'check' don't mean that they're on the level.

And if anything doesn't make sense, or there's missing detail, you can crosscheck it from another side, or another primary or secondary source within a few seconds.

Basically, assume that you don't know until you've checked with reliable primary or secondary sources, and assume you're wrong until the facts show that you're right. What else can we do to improve the way we soak up information?

LISTENING

It's so simple, but we're so bad at it.

By listening, we either confirm our view or fine-tune it based on other facts.

As we know, listening to the facts on all sides is the only way to uncover 'the truth'.

I'll mention this a few times, particularly when we talk about how to open a conversation with a loved one or friend who's built up strong conspiracy beliefs. For now, let's just say that it's absolutely essential to listen before we speak. What else helps us to move to the middle?

RESPECT

There's a lot of compromise involved in all of this.

And if you're anything like me, it's not always easy to stretch out a hand when someone's being really aggressive or demanding that you listen to their views.

But respecting their point of view is a very simple step. There are limits, obviously. But respect for the other side is at the heart of all kinds of mediation.

It helps us to step toward the middle and mean it. And once

you've paid a little respect to the other side – even if you dislike it – you're more likely to keep the conversation going.

CORE BELIEFS – WHAT ABOUT THEIRS?

It's not just our own core beliefs that we have to deal with when we're trying to spot lies and edge closer to 'the truth'.

The person giving us the information is also expressing their own. And sure, none of us are mind readers (unless you've evolved to that level), but we can still tell when someone's biases and prejudices are making their decisions for them.

Core beliefs – theirs and ours – make mis- and dis-information work.

But how can we spot them in someone else? When you're listening to them, can you guess:

> Their previously held ideas and values?
> Can you pick up signs of bias in what they're saying now?
> Are they saying something that you've never heard before, or repeating someone else on one side of the argument?
> Does their version of events differ strongly from others'?

Sometimes the bias will come from an agenda that their group, organisation or news channel has, or makes money from. You can relax if they're a reliable, unbiased source of news that's recognised as such on all sides, not just one.

The good news is that whatever we believe, we can naturally spot bias. The bad news is that we often make the choice to ignore it.

10. THE BIG ISSUE: HARM

So, we've made a start.

Already you can see how a little change of mindset – out of our natural tendency to apply our existing beliefs to the information we're fed – can help us to judge stories in real time.

But one thing that we haven't mentioned yet is harm. And in many ways, it's the biggest issue of all.

As soon as someone is aggressive, intimidating, willing for others to be harmed, it's very simple – they are in the wrong.

When you see that in the language they use, or in the way they express their beliefs, it's generally better to walk away than try to force them to change. In the case of far-out politicians, conspiracy community leaders or influencers making money out of our outrage, it's easy to be swept away by their carefully crafted manifestos.

But when they do harm, we need to raise a red flag.
I'll look at something new in Chapter 3 called 'The Harm Test'. As soon as false information becomes unsafe, there are ways to cut it out of our information diet immediately.

But we'll get into that.

COMING UP IN CHAPTER 2

In the next chapter, we'll get to know what's happening in our hearts and minds when mis- and dis-information hook us in.

Why are we so open to conspiracy beliefs, niche views and online bust-ups? Why do we always jump to the negative, not the positive? If we can answer these questions, we can understand what it feels like to be conned by mis- or dis-information.

Once we know it, we can fight it.

For now, what have we learned from the stories we've been telling each other?

11. CHAPTER 1 – THE TOOLKIT

Let's wrap together key bits of information from Chapter 1 into the first quick-reference toolkit:

- We are hardwired to tell, love and share stories. They're as powerful today as they were 30,000 years ago.
- Any story that carries a frightening message has the power change our views and behaviour, whether it's true or not.
- In fact, fake stories spread much more quickly than genuine ones. We are addicted to fiction.
- At the heart of it all is emotion. If a story makes us feel something strongly, we can quickly leave the facts behind.
- Bad news travels fast, and don't blame the bots for everything. Humans are doing most of it.
- At the heart of it all is our core beliefs. They guide us, show us what's right and wrong, and are easy to manipulate.
- The 5 Ws and an H are absolutely critical to unpack 'the truth'.
- The credibility of any source is at risk if they show bias.
- If anyone looks to harm you or others, they are in the wrong. Walk away.

12. WHAT DO YOU THINK?

We need to talk. So, what would you add to the toolkit? Is there anything in your experience that could add a useful insight to the list? Write it down, add it and perhaps you'll be able to improve on this toolkit and the others to come.

LINDLEY GOODEN

2

GREAT BIG APES

LINDLEY GOODEN

2

*'The worst cruelty that can be inflicted on
a human being is isolation.'*

SUKARNO

Why do we fall so hard for mis- and dis-information?

The process that feeds our addiction to false information is hard wired, perfect for modern media but made for much simpler times. There's a whole lot of psychology and neuroscience going on, but once we understand the process and how it feels, it's much easier to fight our information addiction and see clearly again.

The reasons go back a very long way, but we can see the signs every day.

1. OUR UNQUENCHABLE THIRST FOR MEANING

Let's start with this: why do we work so hard to give our lives meaning? What really IS meaning? And what's it got to do with the information we take in and share out?

Psychologists define meaning like this:

> Values drive and motivate us – justice, fairness, success, kindness, honour and many more ... psychologists often use these measures to evaluate our personalities.
> Meaning gives us personal priorities. Something feels

meaningful because it matters deeply to us, and we'll act on that. Purpose is the momentum that drives us forward – based on our values and the feeling that we're doing something meaningful.

There's something else, isn't there?

If we focus on the information world, meaning is what we take from a great story. It drives us, appals us, makes us happy, makes us do something.

Of course, it all depends whether we've really understood the story, or given it our own spin based on the experiences and views that have shaped us.

Meaning is incredibly deep and personal. It would have been a critical motivator for early humans who needed a good reason to fight the odds and survive. Meaning would have driven them to protect their family and friends, to hunt, fight and defend.

Lots of research has been done on this – including in the influential book Acts of Meaning: Four Lectures on Mind and Culture by Jerome Bruner in 1990. He argued that our minds are much more than calculation machines. They're 'creators of meanings' that gave rise to culture, storytelling and human community.

It's a bit like that in our work on mis– and dis-information: The information that we absorb isn't a simple set of facts and figures, but a set of value judgements that we apply to ourselves to give us identity, meaning and purpose.

Okay, let's get practical. How does meaning show itself? Meaning is fundamental to the way that we see ourselves (our identity), what we believe is true and false (our core values and beliefs) and what we choose to fight for (our purpose).

When we go online to shout about an issue we believe in, or read a certain website or newspaper because they agree with our views, we're satisfying our unquenchable thirst for meaning. We surround ourselves with information that fits our basic core beliefs and values, and we start to dismiss the other side because it shakes our world view.

But there's another layer that can seriously damage our health. If we give up on having conversations about controversial things altogether, the research shows that it can be bad for our health. Losing your social standing is directly linked to health problems, and there's even research showing that many of us would sacrifice our physical health above our social status. You can read an article about this fascinating area of psychology through the American Psychological Association's website: www.apa.org/monitor/2019/05/ce-corner-isolation

So, the lesson from this is not to go completely quiet, but that – for our health – we may need to choose healthier conversations. How is that possible? Well, how about sharing genuine information and reducing our intake of gossip – just a bit? A little more checking and a little less false claim-spreading would keep us connected, without doing us any harm.

Simple, practical and very constructive to the conversation.

2. FIGHT, FRIGHT AND FLIGHT

You're bound to have heard of 'fight or flight'. You might have heard of 'freeze, fight or flight'. Simply, it's the primal defence mechanism that flicks on when we're in sudden danger. It drives us to defend ourselves or run away as quickly as possible.

When we're looking at mis- and dis-information, the word 'fright' is absolutely central to the two, which is why I call it 'fight, fright and flight'.

So, let's go back to the time of our ancestors.

What's happening in our brains is ancient and it can get very creative in the way in which we fight or fly. It's not just a physical effect. It's emotional.

That's why I like to put the word 'fright' at the centre.

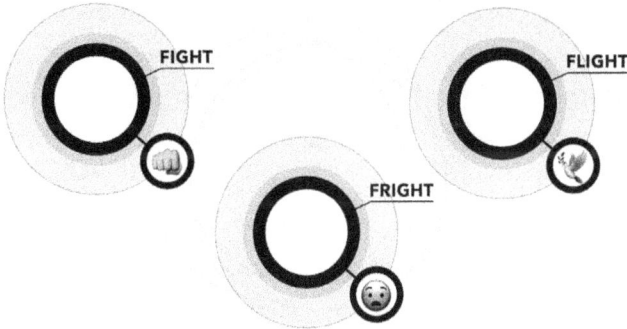

Here are the simple facts:

> 'Fight, fright and flight' is the brain and body's survival mechanism.

> It isn't consciously activated by us; we have no choice over it, although we can regulate our 'fright' in a couple of important ways that I'll mention in a moment.

> It happens in the amygdala – at the base of the brain. The ancient part that deals with primal functions.

> The amygdala activates and pumps stress hormones into our system – heightening our emotions, alertness and response speeds.

> The 'fight, fright and flight' response can be triggered by lots of things – anything we perceive as a threat, including physical danger or – importantly – information.

> So, it can be triggered by a work deadline, worrying about a life challenge, a news story or a threat to our wider world. That could be the cost of living, a political row, climate change or immigration.

Here is a good article from Harvard Medical School explaining – in plain English – how it works: www.health.harvard.

edu/staying-healthy/understanding-the-stress-response

Of course, I consciously chose the last example on that list: immigration. Why? Because we're here to understand how to heal the divisions and open grown-up conversations again. And immigration has been a big issue that's been used to drag us apart.

Ultimately, we're triggered all the time by words like … 'invasion'.

The word 'invasion' is used by the far-right to describe immigration, primarily because it makes people feel personally threatened by an attack from outsiders. There's also a huge amount of research showing that people further out to the right wing of politics and nationalism have a bigger amygdala – the primal area of the brain that fires up when we're scared. Having people around us who were more prone to fear would have been essential for our ancestors, but that superpower is easily manipulated by disinformation creators. It's a really interesting missing link as to why some of us lean naturally to the right, and you can dip into it here: https://neurosciencenews.com/brain-structure-political-ideology-27703/

So, fight, fright and flight was perfectly evolved to warn our chimp brains that we needed to get ready for impending physical danger. But when you add injustice to the story, it lifts untrue stories to feel more plausible – particularly in tough times - which hook us in and are hard to wipe from our minds. Quickly, our darkest core beliefs are confirmed – like 'how can those immigrants get free accommodation, when life is so hard for us?' – and we go from fear to anger to embedding a new core belief.

It's so simple, and so unbelievably effective at creating a 'them and us' division. That's why nationalists and other right-wingers lately (and left-wingers in history) get so hot under the collar about issues like immigration and tell stories about invasions to generate a strong following.

So, let's do something different – a short exercise. It's a good one to uncover our core beliefs with a current story in mind, just between ourselves obviously.

How do you feel about immigration?

3. QUICK EXERCISE

STEP 1

I'd like you to grade each of these questions. Which ones are most important, and least important to you? Grade them 1-5, with 1 being the most important and 5 being least important.

Q.　Are you angry about the number of immigrants coming into the country?

Q.　Are you angry that people are anti-immigration and even dehumanising of those people?

Q.　Do you feel that there should be harder controls over immigration?

Q.　Do you feel that it should be taken off the agenda completely?

Q.　What about the underlying causes – war, famine, drought, poverty, overpopulation? Are they an important reason for immigration to be high?

STEP 2

Now, look at the list. Which of those questions do you think – or feel – are the most important?

STEP 3

Next, try to look at the other side – even if you really dislike it – and consider for a moment the beliefs that might understandably drive a person who's pro- or anti-immigration. Why could their views be valid? There will be something, even if you've never shared those views.

STEP 4

Now, do you understand the other side of the argument a little more, or will you continue with your existing views unchanged?

Why?

The point of that exercise is to understand how it informs your view of the story of immigration. How does it change when you include the other side's view? Can you admit – just for a second – that their view adds valuable facts to the mix?

If you felt outraged, or angry, or intense sympathy during those questions, that's exactly the point to step back and sidestep the information or news that's tipped you over the edge.

When we feel strong emotion or fear flood our system, it's a warning that our core beliefs are being rattled. If we can spot that as it happens, we can start to pause and bring a useful perspective to stories that make us furious.

This can be extremely difficult, of course. The horrific Israel-Hamas war, for example, has left such utter devastation that you'd have to be inhuman to resist your emotions altogether. But the war of words across social media has done little for the tens of thousands of people who've lost their lives or the millions of people across the divide who've been living in fear. When polarisation and fury take over, the conversation is immediately closed down.

Even when there is so much understandable emotion, is there something that we can do to see the facts more clearly?

4. STOP, STEP BACK AND SIDESTEP

Let's talk about a simple idea, which is going to be with us from now on.

Whenever we're triggered or outraged by the information in front of us, what would we normally do? Perhaps we'd focus deeply on the content and say to ourselves 'I knew it – it confirms everything'. Or we might slam the laptop lid in disgust. We might copy the link and share it. Those reactions are exactly what our unfiltered emotion gives to us.

There is another way.
We can choose to stop, step back and sidestep.

Healthcare workers, police officers, fire officers and even journalists know that putting distance between themselves and a traumatic event is essential to cope with what they've seen or heard. It allows all of us to get important perspective, to process what we feel. And that helps us to widen our view, not narrow it.

Often, it's just a case of putting physical distance between us and the situation, or distracting ourselves from it. We all know that – even though it's sometimes slightly inappropriate – humour is also an important diffuser of tension, anxiety and anger, and it'll come up later in this book too.

Having a giggle could be one of the best, most natural ways to flush away fear.

Ultimately, when we slow down the emotions, take a breath and think, we are far less likely to fall for mis- and dis-information. That means turning away from some types of information – particularly the false information on social media and fake news which has been made to make us furious. It also includes taking time away from social and mass media, news feeds and news programmes – especially when we feel that flood of emotion take over. And let's always remember that this comes back to one, simple thing.

If we don't want to be lied to, the easiest defence is to stop, step back and sidestep one-sided views that enrage us and distract us from the facts.

5. SLAVES TO OUR RHYTHMS

What are the ancient rhythms that we simply have to dance to?

Well, we really are slaves to the physiology and chemistry that's evolved over millions of years to make us a successful species. Let's talk brain chemistry.

Our brains have incredible, chemical ways to make us act, react and behave. Our behaviours, choices, moods and values are all governed by the chemical signals that we transmit and receive. It's the Yin and Yang of physiology. We need a regular fix of happy chemistry or we can quickly feel lonely, isolated, low and depressed. That's why finding friends, telling and receiving stories, doing valuable things and having purpose makes us feel so good.

We receive:

> *Dopamine* – the motivational, positive-feedback chemical. When we feel successful, for example when we say something that people react well to, we receive a hit of dopamine. It's often been cited as the main cause of social media 'addiction'.
> *Oxytocin* – the 'relationship' chemical. Some people call oxytocin 'the hugging drug'. Basically, a positive community makes you feel safe, included, productive and happy, and that's as true online as it is in the physical world.
> *Serotonin* – also a social chemical, but not as huggy. When this fires off, it triggers a sense of status, pride and loyalty, particularly when you're an active part of a group. It's also

linked with having fun.

> *Endorphins* – these make us feel good when we're in pain. You'll often hear runners talking about endorphins. Online, our brains give us endorphins when we laugh.

When the chemistry flows it's a potent mix, and it's as old as the hills.

Unfortunately, when our brains 'come down' again our bodies tend to crave another hit of the happy chemistry, so we go back for more. That's why things like social media use and fighting for a cause can be so addictive.

Our less happy chemicals – released into our system when we're scared or feeling negative – are:

> *Cortisol* – regulates our stress response, blood pressure and metabolism – it's often called 'the stress hormone'.
> *Adrenaline* – this one is familiar to most of us. It gets our bodies ready to fight or fly when we feel fear, anxiety or stress.

Okay, a combination of those governs all sorts of actions and reactions. And there's another layer.

Have you ever heard of 'neuropeptides? These are amino acids (or chemical signals from our brain's neurons) that some scientists call 'the molecules of emotions'.

Biology wasn't my strong suit, so I'll boil it down to this: neuropeptides are released by the brain when we're stimulated in certain ways. They lead directly to emotions and then actions, which is how mis- and dis-information lead to behavioural changes in the real world.

Ultimately, this human chemistry set shows that our emotions are very tangible, physical things. So how do these chemicals flow when we see, hear or read stories?

Our social media channels and news give us threats, human

interactions, emotional support, stress, affirmation, a place to argue our points, laughter and social standing. Everything we need to kick start the chemistry.

And we can all feel it.

You and I have both felt the rush of adrenaline when we see something scary, or the warm glow when another couple of hundred people have liked our post. Our phones have driven the addiction in a way that humans have never experienced before, simply because they're with us all the time.

So, how does this bit of biology help us to fight false information and fake news?

The chemistry is a big clue.

If we're looking for useful signs of mis- and dis-information, the emotions that kept our ancestors safe from harm are a great warning system.

The more we feel, the more we need to stop, step back from and sidestep the information in front of us.

Walk away and crosscheck it, if you want 'the truth'.

6. BE MORE BONOBO

We've come a long way since our time in the trees. But you could definitely call our 'penchant for punch-ups' the undying obsession of great big apes.

We love a good fight, especially when we're presented with a story that makes us angry, or proves us right. Where does our need for conflict come from? We'll come back to information via a moment of pre-history.

The latest thinking is that the common ancestor of human beings and chimpanzees lived between 6 and 8 million years ago. I still find that amazing, and of course you might hold religious faith that tells you this can't be true.

But let's give science a chance.

The great apes diverged. And some of the characteristics diverged with them. For example, modern chimpanzees are well-known for their savage attacks on neighbours, devastating neighbouring populations to seize territory. Humans obviously exhibit similar traits combined with logical reasoning.

Gorillas are much calmer. So are orangutans. And bonobos – our closest evolutionary cousins – are positively Zen. They actually regulate their emotions to maintain peace. You can find out much more from The Proceedings of the National Academy of Sciences of the United States here: www.pnas.org/doi/10.1073/pnas.1522060113

It all gives their way of life the best chance of success.

So how can we be more bonobo, and a little less chimp? Well, it might help to think about how fast our natural traits kick in.

Steve Peters, author of 'The Chimp Paradox' said that people have three brains:

1 - THE CHIMP BRAIN

Our 'chimp brain' lives in our ancient limbic system, the amygdala – at the base of our brains – and reacts almost immediately to threats, well before our 'human brain' can.

Our inner chimp is emotional, impetuous and irresponsible.

And sometimes that's fine – and quite fun. But it's also where the negative 'othering' attitude runs riot through something called the 'us and them dichotomy'.

Basically, when someone enters a room, or a conversation, or a story, our split-second reaction is to get ready for trouble, and that thought can be very persistent if we're always primed to think of other groups that way.

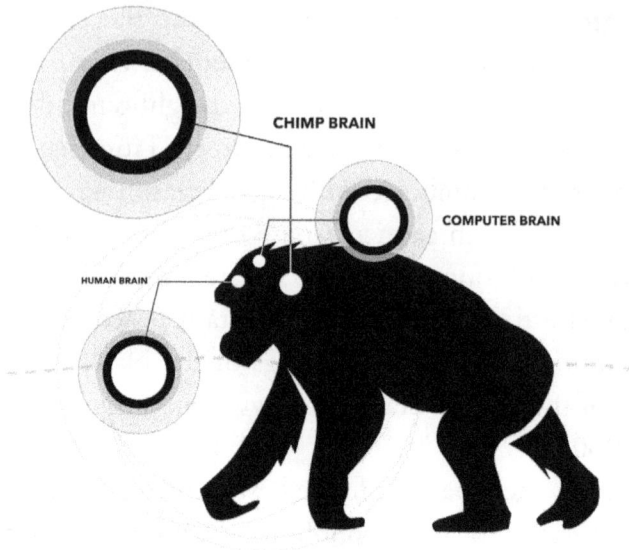

It's there for a reason, but sometimes we just need to give our inner chimp a 'hug', pat it on the back and move away. It's our friend – but only to a point.

2 - THE HUMAN BRAIN

Our 'human brain' is the grown-up, thinking part of our brain. It's controlled by our pre-frontal cortex at the front of our brains, and it's more rational, calm, in charge of our conscious mind.

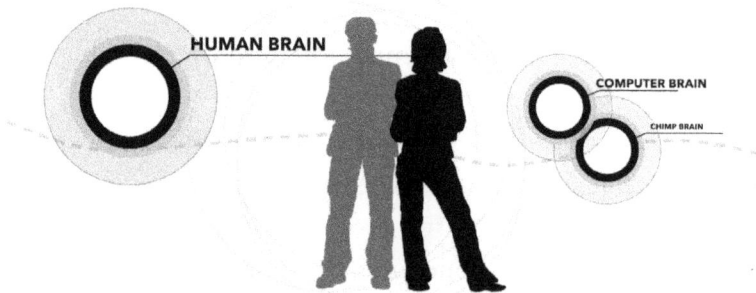

It helps us to cool a situation down, process it and gain perspective. But it's in direct competition with the emotional chimp, so we often need to calm down our feelings to see and think straight through the human brain.

3 - THE COMPUTER BRAIN

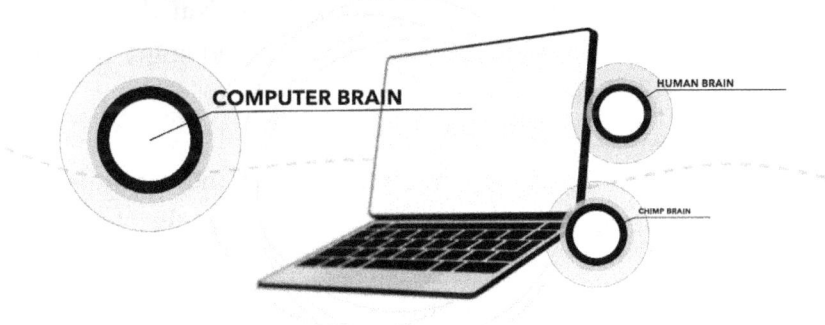

Finally, our 'computer brain' ticks away in the parietal lobe, and runs the background tasks, our unthinking habits and some of our quick, automated processes. It's always there, dealing with the subconscious stuff and assumed knowledge that we don't need to think too hard about.

As ever, evolution runs its long fingers through the pages of our story. And here's the crux of breaking our thought process down like this.

Neuroscientists have shown that our brains find it difficult to be human and chimp at the same time.

When we're kicking off emotionally, we're scared or angry, blood flows into our primal limbic system at the back of the brain. When we're calm, thoughtful and relaxed, blood flows around our frontal lobe just behind our foreheads. So, if we can control our chimp brain, we can engage the human brain and reduce the emotion that leads us to be fearful, angry, to believe in threats that aren't there.

A cool head is a clear head.

Another author Daniel Kahneman talked about it in his best-selling book *Thinking Fast and Slow*. He called the chimp brain

'System 1', and the human brain 'System 2'. Psychologists tend to use these labels rather than my more colourful chimp talk.

Either way, we can use the chimp-human-computer model to realise what's happening to us when we're activated by a story that makes us frightened (immediate reaction) and angry (our way of controlling the fear).

We all have it, it's perfectly human.

But we can also see much more clearly, and recognise the facts of a story if we give ourselves a moment to think.

Just for a second, try this little thought experiment:

> Think about what it feels like when your own furious inner chimp takes over, perhaps when a headline or friend's post rattles your cage. It could be anything – injustice, politics, something personal.
> Are you feeling angry, blind rage, irritation, maybe a dash of hatred? Or are you feeling intense sympathy and blaming someone for what's happening?
> Ask 'could the source of that story be biased?', 'could the information have been made up?'
> Pause, physically step away and give yourself a couple of seconds to process those thoughts.
> The classic 'count to 10' trick is more than enough time for most of us to engage the human brain, but a few quick questions also works.

Now, this might all feel like a frustrating process of quashing your natural feelings, but as ever, we have a choice. Believe something that could easily be a lie, or hug your inner chimp, stop for a moment and move past it.

The inner chimp is there for a good reason, but it really is very hard to reason with when we're bombarded with a hundred 'info-threats' every day.

Mis- and dis-information are perfectly attuned to activate our inner chimps. They work just like an ancient warning about an outside threat told around a communal fire. Even a little effort to bring up a controversial subject can trigger a big response.

It's very effective, and very devious.

But we can make a choice as soon as we see the signs – and be more bonobo if we so choose.

7. ENGAGING OUR HUMAN BRAINS

So how about this?

Let's engage our human brains again and think about what it takes to keep our inner chimp at bay. All our primal brain needs to kick off is a 'great story' filled with wedge issues or triggers. One little tall tale, and we're off again.

Here's the normal order – if we're not on our guard:

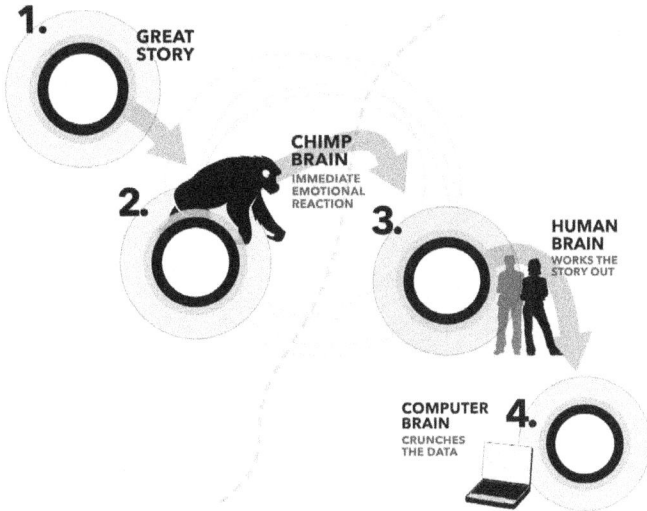

1. GREAT STORY

2. CHIMP BRAIN
IMMEDIATE EMOTIONAL REACTION

3. HUMAN BRAIN
WORKS THE STORY OUT

4. COMPUTER BRAIN
CRUNCHES THE DATA

The story goes first to the back of our brain where the chimp lives, and to our human brain second - if we're not already ranting about the story. The computer brain has background tasks to take care of.

If we fall for the emotion, our human brain will simply support it by working out the many ways that the story must be true. That won't happen if we close down the big, instant emotional reaction. Of course, a great story is layered, so it can also hook us in at the beginning, middle or end. The headline, or the quote from someone who sits firmly on one side of the argument, can set us off.

Also, a great piece of mis- or dis-information doesn't need to be logical. In fact, it would probably fall down if it was.

So, our job is to stand back and try not to 'live' the experience fully. We need to keep a little logic in the mix, to accept the emotion - to hug our inner chimp - but to think about the story more quickly. Where's it from? Is it biased? Is it designed to make me think something extreme?

We're bringing in our human reaction earlier:

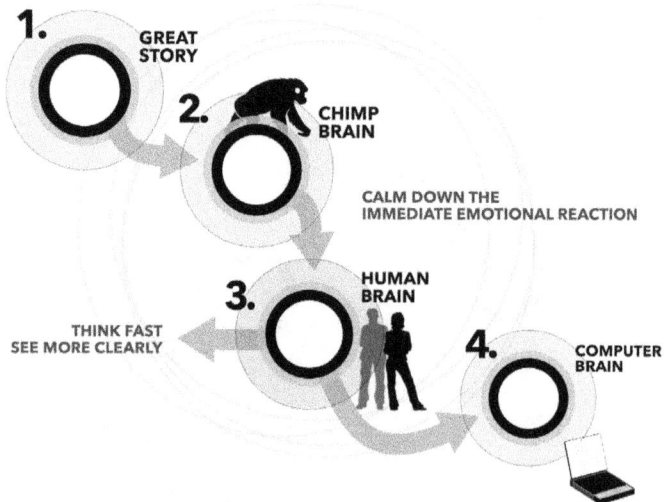

So, if this great story gives you a hit of emotion, stop, process it and observe how you feel. Sure, it's less exciting than letting your chimp run riot, but mis- and dis-information depend on us letting our chimps out to fight. That's how they get us.

Let's give our human brains a chance!

8. THE FOUNDATIONS OF DISINFORMATION

What else can we do?

Well, we haven't actually looked at the things that make that great story gripping. Let's open the hood and look at the missing links between what we say and what our ancient brains need to hear.

Here are some of the greatest emotional hooks, and the reasons why false information peddlers can smuggle mis- and dis-information into our conversations so effectively.

A GRAIN OF TRUTH

In all of the most gripping stories designed to spread false information, you'll find a common feature: a grain of truth.

It makes the rest of the story plausible. In fact, the starting point of any good lie is the truth.

The grains of truth might be basic facts that aren't in question. Perhaps there's a real problem underneath the story. Or the storyteller might use scientific language that sounds really plausible.

Let's just remember that we tend to support ideas that back up our core beliefs – confirmation bias. On the other side of the coin, we tend to disbelieve ideas that we don't already agree with, which is known as selective attention.

Honestly, I spit out my breakfast on a regular basis shouting, "that's definitely f***** not true!" We all shut down ideas that we don't like. It takes a moment to calm down and carry on.

So, a grain of truth is a very powerful tool in mis- and disinformation.

What other foundations are great stories built on?

ANGER, FURY, OUTRAGE

Outrage is so important, and I've mentioned it a few times.

Feeling outrage is probably the clearest sign that someone is trying to convince us to take a side. It's one of those telltale signs that manipulation leaves behind. Also – as you'll have seen many times – a really effective way to distract us from the facts.

When people try to stoke up your outrage, it's really important to ask 'why?'

What's making us feel under attack? And once we've stopped and stepped back can we put the video or article to one side and crosscheck the facts before our inner chimp kicks off?

Of course, sometimes, a bit of anger is justified, particularly in stories about genuine injustice. And luckily, we can always extract the facts using the 5Ws and an H:

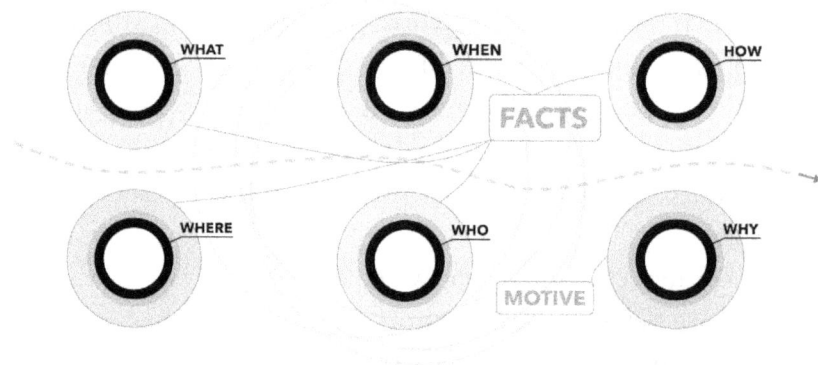

It's worth treating anger, fury and outrage as easy-to-spot signs of misinformation, disinformation and fake news.

Once you've crosschecked the facts from another reputable source (perhaps a reliable fact checking website), you'll know within seconds.

There are also really human needs in the mix. We all have them, and they can show up whenever we experience that great story - true or false.

SAFETY

We're safer in numbers. And disinformation-dealers love to make us feel isolated and exposed.

Consider how you feel when you're sitting alone on the sofa watching a horror movie.

The teenager is alone. She walks into the dark room behind her; the lights aren't working. Her friends have disappeared, and she has no idea that just behind her is a shape. Maybe it's another door. There's a small knocking sound, she turns slowly and sees nothing there. Two seconds, three seconds. She turns back around, and the shape is directly in front of her, crawling forward quickly on all fours.

Eww.

Of course, none of us feel as scared in the dark when we're surrounded by friends ready to fight with us.

Safety brings down the fear, whether it's created by threatening stories or a genuine dark shape in the corner.
And we've all reduced fear by:

> Sharing the news with friends to spread the weight.
> Feeling better when they say that they'll be with us all the way.

The more people explain the worry away, the more we feel a safety net form around us.

Whether it's a fishy bait ball in the Pacific, or a murmuration of starlings in the skies overhead. Cooperation and the safety it brings helps us to survive whether we have tails, wings or arms and legs. That's what friends, communities and gangs of all types are all about.

STATUS

I briefly mentioned in the last chapter how damaging it can be to lose our social status.

Social safety theory has shown that the prospect of 'social death' can be even more frightening than physical death.

One study called 'Social Relationships and Mortality Risk: A Meta-analytic View' by Julianne Holt-Lunstad, Timothy B Smith and J Bradley Layton found something really staggering. Almost unbelievably, they found that being isolated carries similar health risks to smoking and alcohol consumption. Social isolation carries far higher risks than physical inactivity and obesity: https://journals. plos.org/plosmedicine/article?id=10.1371/journal.pmed.1000316

Unfortunately, that makes status one of the greatest forces in our real – and online – lives. Most of us really want a voice, a place in the world. We'll sacrifice 'the truth' just to be an important part of something, which can lead us quickly into forming new groups that believe and spread views that leave the facts behind.

Picking out status as a foundation of mis- and dis-information explains a lot, which will come up again. And it brings us directly to a deeper issue.

BELONGING

A sense of true belonging is a magical thing.

It can be just the medicine that a person who feels outcast in the real-world needs. Let's face it, we all want to belong. Deeper than safety, deeper than status, lies the warmth of belonging.

Belonging satisfies our desperate need for relationships,

for social inclusion, and as we know from the research there are extremely good health reasons for that.

This is where we need to have a grown-up, give-and-take conversation with people who've found that sense of belonging in harmful beliefs. We just need to make sure that the people we love can still dip a toe in the real world so that they can return to it safely. Even if that's a long process.

We'll talk about this a lot more in the next chapter, but it's important to mark this as one of the key reasons why false information soaks into online communities and threads. Being part of something is a basic need of social animals like us.

CONTROL

There are probably hundreds of thousands of active disinformation creators who are attracting millions of followers and steering their beliefs, just to be in control. To have the upper hand.

And this is where reality and conspiracy meet.

Clearly, many governments, companies and influential people actively try to control our views with the information that they provide us with. Conspiracies, plots and private plans are hatched all the time.

But in the age of opinion, we need to keep our eyes open for 'gaslighting'. There's a reason I've chosen this form of control.
A gaslighter will manipulate and undermine someone, perhaps a partner or friend over a long period of time, causing them to question their own thoughts, choices or memories. You're basically putting the other person's views under so much pressure that they look to the gaslighter for guidance.

Convincing someone that their reasonable, tolerant views and beliefs are wrong is an insidious form of control.

And – as we'll see – conspiracy creators online and populist troublemakers often use this approach to separate believers from the other side of an argument. Cast doubt, distract and divide.

It helps those creators to stay in charge of the belief. Often, they'll do that by making a disbeliever feel stupid. It then becomes very difficult to question the leaders' views without being forced out of the group. It's exactly the same as being in a cult.

So, beware controlling people. The shouters, the bullies, the trolls and critics. Imposing views and banning people from asking questions is at the absolute heart of disinformation on social media, in politics, news and on the new channels who'll say anything to grab your attention tomorrow.

There are a couple more annoying, human traits that none of us like to admit to. But they can drive us straight into the comforting embrace of mis- and dis-information.

UNCONSCIOUS BIAS

Let's return to that important four-letter word.

Bias.

Starting with unconscious bias. We all have it, no matter who we are, our gender, sexuality, racial heritage or physical abilities. We'll jump to the wrong conclusions about someone because of their level of education, their hometown or football team. Anything is fair game for unconscious bias, because we don't realise that we have it.

In the fight against mis- and dis-information, it's this:

Unconscious bias leads us to believe theories that fit our core beliefs, without checking that they're untrue. It can also influence us to like, share or speak about issues – including social and political issues – that we're not qualified to comment on.

Look, we need to keep this stuff in check. Having unconscious bias doesn't make any of us bad people per se. But if we act on it, offend or harm someone, it needs to be tackled.

I know that there'll be someone reading this who's spitting

out their coffee right now, claiming that I – a middle-aged white man – can't possibly comment on unconscious bias because of who I am.

But that's the whole point … looking like this doesn't guide my views or actions, but I admit that I can't possibly understand things outside my frames of reference. I check that all the time. And if we're going to be more conscious of our biases, and make better decisions about who to believe we need to have an open conversation, whoever we are.

So, a regular audit of our biases, our core beliefs, is a really good idea if we're going to learn to come back together around 'the truth'.

SUNK COST FALLACY
AND CONFIRMATION BIAS

The pillars of an effective story are many. I hope that some of these have made sense to you.

We're almost there for Chapter 2, with just two pillars left:

> The sunk cost fallacy is our tendency to continue in a course of action, or belief, because we've already invested so much into it. It doesn't matter if it's harming us or others, we just can't let go.
> Confirmation bias is what drives us to support a standpoint that supports our core beliefs. It's similar to selective attention that I mentioned earlier.

Most of us – you, me, friends and families – have a habit of falling into both of those. They're really human, and go a long way to explaining why a small nudge into false information can push intelligent, tolerant people to extreme politics and conspiracy beliefs.

We'll hear more about these sorts of effects in the next chapter, and think about ways to talk ourselves out of the echo chamber. Before we talk conspiracies in Chapter 3, let's mention one more thing; something that we need to do a lot less of.

SHARING

A story dies at the first telling if no-one wants to share it.

During the pandemic, as we were cut off from our friends, colleagues and family, we began to share more. We shared more information, more theories and more controversial opinions.

And if you believe the results of the MIT study into the spread of mis- and dis-information online, you'll know that our sharing habits are the biggest driver of fake news online.

When was the last time you shared something without having a proper look at it? We've all done it, but were you right to do that? Did you check that it was above board and factual? Did you just like it, or re-post it with a message?

I ask these questions because the MIT research showed that we need to disengage from poisonous conversations, arguments, and share a lot less content if we also want to receive more reliable information. It's certainly not the global social media trend, but could each of us play our part tomorrow?

The problem is that it's easy to do. And when we hit share, we become the new source of every single element of the story.

It's now completely down to us.

We need to disengage a bit, and to choose the stories we spread with a bit more care. It's a sliding scale, something like this:

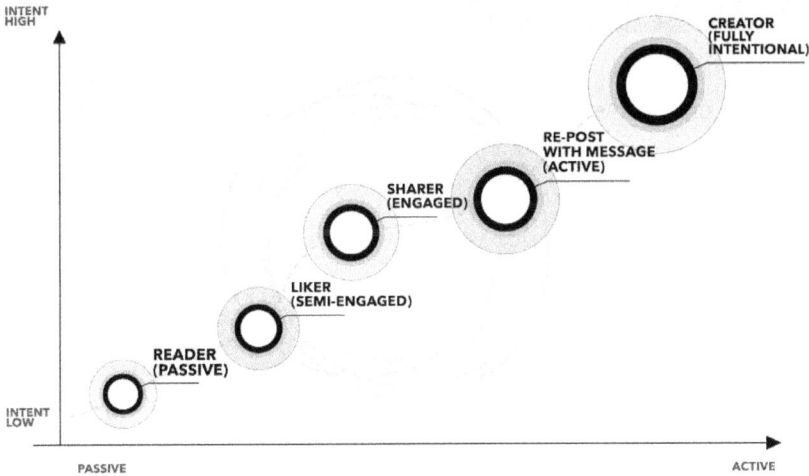

Where would you place yourself as a social media player?

Actively sharing without checking, or just liking stuff?

In Matthew Syed's book *Rebel Ideas*, he talked about how the sharing of ideas throughout history has been fundamental to our technological progress. Perhaps a neighbouring or far-removed society came up with a nice idea, they share it and spread the word to you though travelling messengers. When you hear about this great idea, your own innovation is boosted and takes your neighbours' idea to the next level. It might explain how large pyramids sprang up across the world at almost exactly the same time.

Therefore, the simple act of sharing can spread good news, or it can spread an equal amount of nonsense. Unfortunately, social media has made us very good at the second, and it becomes believable because we're the new fourth-hand source passing it on.

The positive point about sharing is that we can choose.

Are we okay to spread bias, misinformation or lies? I think most of us would say a categorical 'no'.

So, perhaps it's time to share less.

9. SO CLOSE, YET SO FAR

Beneath everything that we do online is something inherently physical.

As our online life has grown, we have physically grown far apart. It makes the stories we see, hear and read in near isolation much more powerful.

There's lots of research that shows that we're more likely to fall for niche beliefs and conspiracies when we're physically separated. When we're starved of normal interactions, we look online for social affirmation.

The National Library of Medicine in the US studied the effects of social separation during the COVID-19 pandemic and found that all of us were more susceptible to conspiracies because of the switch to social media. You can have a look at that here: www.ncbi.nlm.nih.gov/pmc/articles/PMC8420120/

In the next chapter, we'll talk a lot about what happened during the world's biggest moment of isolation: COVID-19.

Understandably, you might have felt the injustice of having to keep going into work wearing a mask when others could 'relax' at home. It might well have forced your business to close, which is terrible. Or perhaps you're just suspicious of big pharma and big tech, and COVID proved your suspicions.

Whatever you believe, the pandemic drove us apart physically but triggered an explosion in social media use. And for reasons that we'll get into in Chapter 3, mis- information spiked overnight.

So, that's next, along with the millions of beliefs that have exploded out of our unquenchable thirst for meaning, and a place in the online world.

Hold on tight, it's time to talk conspiracies.

10. CHAPTER 2 - THE TOOLKIT

- We need meaning. It's wrapped into our values and purpose. It also deeply reflects the stories we believe.
- Fright is the best trigger for fight and flight. And because bad news sets it off, it bypasses our grown-up, human thought process.
- A critical key to fighting mis- and dis-information is to stop, step back and sidestep it.
- Use the 5Ws and an H to extract the facts, and to give the brain a moment to think about what you've just seen.
- Back that up with unbiased, independent fact checking sites when you have a specific question about a new conversation.
- Our reactions are governed by a potent cocktail of chemistry, so once we can reduce our emotional response, we can see much more clearly.
- Be less chimp, and a bit more bonobo!
- Extreme views are designed to manipulate our anger, fury and outrage. They switch off our logical thought process.
- We have a natural need for status, belonging and control. But we need to stop sharing information that appeals to our biases, and therefore seems true.
- That's particularly true when we're trying to make a connection from a distance.

11. WHAT'S YOUR VIEW?

This chapter has unveiled the psychology and neuroscience that gives storytelling its power. If you have any thoughts, even if they're entirely unique to you, add them in to your personal toolkit. Every question can defend you against false information designed to trigger your emotions and throw your beliefs off balance.

3

THE TRUTH IS OUT THERE

3

'Where justice is denied, where poverty is enforced, where ignorance prevails, and where any one class is made to feel that society is an organised conspiracy to oppress, rob and degrade them, neither persons nor property will be safe.'

FREDERICK DOUGLASS

It's time to talk about the C-word: Conspiracies.

They're the foundation of online gossip, social media communities and global politics. The C-word is so important to us in our physically disconnected, virtually attached lives. And while I looked into the reasons why that's true, colleagues, clients, friends, family and strangers would ask me one question above all: *'Have you heard about this new conspiracy theory? What do you think?'*

Was COVID-19 a dry-run of a global population control experiment? Are elites replacing voters by controlling the paths of hurricanes? Were Haitian people in Ohio eating all the cats, and eating all the dogs? I'm going to say no. But the chances are that your views are slightly different. The only thing we can safely say is that we rarely ever know the whole truth, even if we really do have some of the facts.

In this chapter we'll 'go to town' on conspiracies. We'll have a look at pattern-forming, language, community, anger and the power of conversation. We'll also come up with a test to spot harmful beliefs, and a brand-new conspiracy equation.

It's a packed chapter investigating how mis- and dis-information have created an explosion in niche beliefs that have divided us in a million different ways.

For now, opinion 1 – facts 0.

But how can we, if we want to, level the score?

1. LET'S START WITH AN OBSERVATION

We were always going to find ourselves here.

But before we go to the outer reaches of niche beliefs, I want to hold my own hands up.

Writing this book has pushed me down a few rabbit holes.

Poring over lots of sources and theories, I've found myself fixated a couple of times on specific links and patterns. Events and beliefs that tied the centuries together.

It's obviously very well known that our brains look for, and build, patterns to explain mysteries. We need answers.

But I thought I was above that, until I realised – writing this book – that I'm also vulnerable to obsessing about a single fact, a single pattern, not the all-important context around it. I'd lost the wider perspective, and when you fixate on one thing – just as you might do if you take a small video clip to explain a whole story – you're jumping headfirst into a rabbit hole where the only light is the one vanishing behind you as you fall.

And this is how it feels – if you haven't felt it yourself:

> You start by looking into a subject related to something you think might be true, based on a core belief or a new, tantalising secret. You might call it 'doing the research'.

> Soon, you discover links made by others and keep watching, listening or reading to people who talk about it.

> Then, there's a fact. A fact that nobody's really covered before. Suddenly everything seems to click, become clear, you can

see a pattern and it feels as though you've discovered the key to something important.

> Perhaps you also feel that you might be able to heal an injustice or help other people by spreading the word.

> This new piece of information colours everything – every new fact forming a loop back to it, confirming it, and you feel as though you're the only person who knows 'the truth'.

> Then, you find other commentators on the subject who believe something similar.

> If we're desperate enough to find an answer, we fall into that community, and the door is open to a whole new world of parallel truths.

In my case, the core belief was that I'm too sensitive to false information to fall down a rabbit hole.
It turned out not to be true when I'd dug the hole myself.

Thankfully, and not least because of my years in news, I was able to pause and put some distance between myself and less reliable sources of information. Even though they fitted my idea, my thesis, that seemed SO logical, it was all confirmation bias.

What does that show us?

There are little booby traps lying in wait for our psyche across the internet and the mass media, and it's crucial to leave them be.

It's vital to stop, step back and sidestep the information when we fixate, 'feel' and pass on the infection by sharing it with others.

Also, we need to examine our core beliefs.

They drive us straight into conspiracy thinking. And our need to be part of something important keeps us there.

2. WHAT IS A CONSPIRACY?

Clearly, the internet – and life – are full of conspiracies.

Powerful people have meetings to decide things that benefit the few every single day. That's life.

But the question is: do we know what's really happening and the reasons for it? Let's have a short, sharp look at what a conspiracy actually is.

A conspiracy – I'd argue – is the process by which a small group of people plan to take advantage, do harm to or extract power from the rest of us. The motive is to gain the upper hand over others. We'll call that Conspiracy Type 1 – Gain.

It can also be the process of keeping something that the wider world should know, secret. That's about protecting reputations and retaining control, and it's Conspiracy Type 2 – Secrecy.

And we know that these things happen all the time, but crucially, we rarely know the secretive motive because the conspirators never hold their hands up to tell us the truth.

That's really important to remember from here on in. We'll come back to that concept of a secretive motive – or plot – again. And we should always remember that disinformation-creators love to claim a conspiracy to get attention.

The Oxford English Dictionary defines a conspiracy as:

> The action of conspiring; combination of persons for an evil or unlawful purpose.
> Law. The crime of conspiracy consists in the agreement of two or more persons to do an illegal act, or to do a lawful act by unlawful means.

Interestingly, the second definition is quite close to mine, but they both point to an illegal act. Most of us probably imagine a conspiracy to be wrong – but not always against the law. Still, I'm not going to argue with the Oxford English Dictionary!

So, conspiracies are really just secretive forward planning to give to the few and take from the many.

It's always a good idea to throw a definition out there, just to know what we're really talking about.

We'll focus on news coverage in the next chapter, because the best way to uncover a secret plot at the top of society is through honest reporting that challenges powerful people. Not opinions, not social media conversations, but excellent coverage.

And it is possible to find that in the mass media if you look hard enough. Unfortunately, social media is another matter entirely. For now, let's get real, and face facts about our hunt for 'the truth'.

3. THE TRUTH, THE WHOLE TRUTH AND NOTHING BUT THE TRUTH

What is the truth?

First, let's be clear. Unless you have all of the facts – and can prove it, there is no truth.

Without them, the truth is just a value judgment that's different for all of us. The truth that you see is different to mine, different from your best friend, different from your hair stylist. The facts might be the same but each one of us brings our own background beliefs, as-sumptions, experiences and baggage – and when we look through that lens no matter how unbiased we think we are – we draw a slightly different conclusion to the next person.

That's especially … well, true … in a time where social media safeguards have been stripped away to make the truth harder than ever to find.

But before we give up and trust the next person shouting about who they hate today, there's a big caveat. And it's this: if we can stay calm and use a set of simple tools to separate the facts from the fiction – mostly generated by our own opinions – we'll have the skills we need to know what, and who to trust.

So, let's start by getting a few things straight.

Most of us, when we use the word 'truth', are really talking about the facts.

Then on top of the simple facts, we add an extra why – the secret motive that might lie behind them. Why has this thing happened – really? What are the reasons behind it? Could there be a secret plot to take control or put us down?

Unless we've been told 'why' by the people at the heart of the story, we'll really never know.

That's why – effectively - 'there is no truth'.

What we naturally do next is to bring in our own beliefs to make sense of the story, e.g. 'Why do they really want to control us?' or 'Why are they keeping the truth from us?' or 'How can the Earth be round when it looks flat to me?'.

It would be fantastic to think that truth is pure, clear, unarguable, but that's partly what's getting us into so much trouble. People's opinions replace the real 'why' when nobody will admit the whole truth.

But surely we can discover the truth just by searching – or 'researching' – for it, can't we?

Sadly not, unless we have the skills and a healthy sceptisicm to separate the facts from the fiction without our own internal monologue getting in the way.

Hey, why else do you think I wrote this book?!

And on that point, I need to add a BIG caveat. Someone – the person or the group of people at the heart of the story – does know how it all started. They know the original 'why', and therefore the truth. It's just that we don't, and none of our core beliefs will normally guide us to the correct answer.

But we can definitely uncover the facts. We've spoken about the famous 5Ws, and the extra H.

Again, they are:

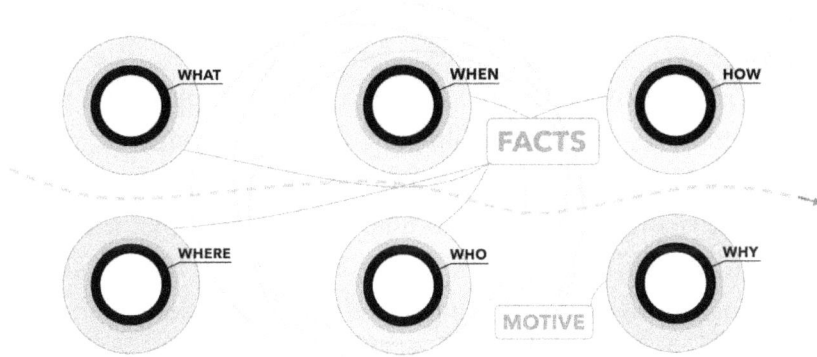

4. THE LIE IS IN THE WHY

The fascinating thing about 'the truth' – especially with conspiracies – is that everything important lies in that, often self-invented, 'why'.

It's what turns a great story into a conspiracy theory.

The more controversial a story, the more likely we are to reach for an explanation that fits our core beliefs. We often just desperately need to fill the hole where the real 'why' is.

Then, all that a disinformation creator has to do is to invent something that sounds plausible, twist it with a couple of wedge issue, and you've got an instant viral hit than can go global in seconds through social media and then the far-out right wing (or left-wing) media. It's how a news story can turn normal people into race rioters or insurrectionists within a couple of scrolls.

In conspiracies, political propaganda and commercial disinformation – the lie is always in the why.

Have you ever heard the phrase 'a little knowledge can be dangerous'? We're living in the modern, viral version of that.

The bare facts are normally really clear, unemotional and non-conspiratorial. But if we add that secretive motive into the mix, everything changes. Conspiracies always jump to conclusions

– that people in power are working against us, or conspiring to deprive us of our rights, freedom of movement or freedom of speech.

Let's remember that freedom of speech is supposed to protect the vulnerable, the whistleblowers, the people without a voice. It's not there to be used as a weapon to spread lies, to launch pre-emptive strikes against a whole group of people, a minority or an ideology. Still, it's a favourite trick of far-right politicians and supremacist groups to invert it to get what they want. It's an example of how the 'why' is invented.

It goes like this: 'We are justified in saying that the country is full of people who want to harm us *because our way of life is under threat'*. That classic right-wing idea explains a core belief (too many foreigners) by inventing a plausible 'why' (we feel under threat).

When you can quickly dig out the real core belief that's causing it, the conspiracy immediately stops making sense.

But we have to kick out the emotion and let our human brains work, whatever the story we're seeing, hearing or reading. And that's hard when there are so many stories out there bombarding us with false information.

No wonder the word 'infodemic' was born.

5. THE INFODEMIC

In early 2020, the World Health Organization declared a global infodemic. COVID-19 was on the way and the alarm bells were already ringing.

They argued that we were becoming completely overwhelmed with information, a lot of which was false and misleading.

Well, they were right about that, weren't they?

Here's a brief summary of their alert in the scientific magazine *Nature Medicine*: www.nature.com/articles/s41591-022-01713-6

Ultimately, the WHO was getting involved because they

believed that public health would be seriously at risk if people fell for health-related mis- and dis-information as the new virus spread.

It was pretty prophetic. They thought we could be at risk from three main things:

> Our susceptibility to false information.
> The rapid spread of misinformation.
> The danger that it would stop people getting immunised.

Of course, the COVID years weren't the first time that anti-vax misinformation had gone … well, viral.

In the late 90s, the measles, mumps and rubella (MMR) vaccine came up against huge resistance, particularly in the UK, when a medical research paper claimed a potential link to autism.

Once the claim was made, it became incredibly difficult to shake.

In brief, the lead author – a university gastroenterologist and surgeon called Andrew Wakefield – claimed that if a child who received the MMR jab went on to develop an inflammation of the intestines, it could trigger an unexpected health risk. He said that the child could leak harmful proteins into the brain and become autistic. His paper (co-authored by 13 others) appeared in the prestigious medical journal The Lancet.

The news spread worldwide within months. Many parents believed it and refused to let their kids have the jab. It's still a big issue for the MMR vaccine today, despite what happened a few years after the original paper was published.

It took 6 years for a journalist, Brian Deer from the Sunday Times in the UK, to uncover evidence of conflicts of interest and instances of ethical misconduct. Shortly after that, 10 of the 13 co-authors on the paper renounced Andrew Wakefield's conclusions. The Lancet retracted part of the paper in 2004 and completely retracted it in 2010. But it took good, honest investigative reporting – and lots of unbiased questions – to find the holes in the argument.

That's what happens when professional news people with the highest standards do their job well.

Still, even to this day, there's a lot of suspicion – because of that original, debunked report – and years of personal appearances and speeches from the man who made the claim.

Back to COVID misinformation, and the claims about vaccine dangers were immediate, again based on false claims, but this time driven entirely by people without medical or journalistic qualifications. In many ways, that's what gave it power. People believed that they could trust these anti-vaccination views precisely because they didn't come from the medical, profit-making establishment.

And actually, that's totally understandable. There's a grain of truth that instinctively tells us they're more trustworthy than a big pharmaceutical firm. But how on Earth would they know? Isn't it more likely that independent doctors and researchers would have the answers we need?

We'll go into that shortly, because once we know why heartfelt suspicions can explode into conspiracies within minutes, we can see it coming next time.

And that's all we need to do. To take one step back from the shocking story that's been created to hook us in.

And if you're looking for something really juicy to believe in, there's a dazzling choice of conspiracies out there. And let's be honest, most of us have a little voice on our shoulder that wonders 'could it be true?'.

Well, perhaps it's time to take a small peep into the rabbit hole.

6. TOP CONSPIRACY THEORIES AND WHAT DRIVES THEM

There are so many weird, wonderful and sometimes worrying conspiracy theories out there. Some are more plausible than others. Some are closely related to the grain of truth that created them. And that's why it's worth swapping the word 'theory' to the word 'belief' for a moment.

We all have firmly held and heartfelt beliefs that might not stand up well to scrutiny. And it's important to have respect for other views, so that we can have an open conversation and bridge divides that can cause us to fight.

So, let's spare a minute to list some of the world's greatest conspiracy beliefs. Then, we can decipher the underlying causes and do something about the harmful ones.

Okay, which of these conspiracy beliefs do you think are true?

> COVID-19 was a hoax to control the population. Or COVID is real and was started by China on purpose. Or it was spread by 5G mobile masts. COVID vaccines were harmful because they were created too quickly. Or Bill Gates made them to control us using scannable barcodes.

> QAnon – the blood libel, the deep state, there's a cabal of evil Democrat politicians and satanists who traffic, and perhaps even sacrifice children to extract life-extending chemicals from their blood. It's so 2020...

> Secret societies rule the world ('New World Order'), as do lizards ('The Reptilian Elite'), as do Jewish people ('The Jewish Elite').

> The deep state rules world governments, deciding what is allowed to happen from the shadows. It is innately against free-markets, deregulation and business.

> 9/11 was an inside job, covered up by the US government.
> Area 51 is where they keep the alien spaceship(s) and develop new tech that we can see in the skies and over the oceans.
> Climate change is a hoax, or it's nothing to do with humans, or it's designed to control our movements and restrict our income, as are '15 Minute Cities', as was COVID.
> White people are being intentionally replaced by immigrants.
> The moon landing was faked and filmed at Area 51.
> The Earth is flat.
> John F Kennedy was assassinated by the CIA.

So, those are the really big, abiding ones. But you can see the differences right there – with so many conflicting theories about the same world events.

WHAT TIES THEM TOGETHER?

Conspiracies can often be caused by very similar things: our underlying core beliefs and the feeling that life is tough.

Just from that small list of the classics, you can already see common core beliefs that drive them:

1. The government or the elites or the reptiles or a secret regime are controlling us from the shadows.
2. You can't trust official information about anything – from the source of COVID, right up to the shape of our planet.
3. The dark powers that rule us are keeping important secrets. They might be satanic, demonic, or witches, or the evil political party opposite, but they fake the established news, re-direct hurricanes, snatch kids and eat pizza.

But why are we more likely to believe in lots of conspiracies if we believe in just one?

Because conspiracies are a million expressions of our core beliefs. If we believe that the government's controlling us from dark corners, or 'mainstream' information isn't trustworthy, we might believe in lots of conspiracies that seem to prove that. Perhaps you might think that '15 minute cities' and COVID were about government control. Or you might believe Andrew Tate and Katie Hopkins because you think 'the mainstream media' are corrupt.

But as always, when we ask, 'where does that information come from?', it's the people who we're listening to, who are getting followers, power and money for poking your core beliefs and making you suspicious of anyone who doesn't agree with them.

Remember, when our inner chimp kicks off, we tend not to see straight, and quickly we can be separated from the facts.

Why do conspiracy beliefs get worse in times of crisis?

Well for starters, in tough times we're hurting – or at least feel strongly that we are.

We're angry, we want answers, and we want help. If none is forthcoming from the people in power, we'll go to someone else, the populists and the conspiracy creators. And we'll often start to believe that there's a secret plot causing our problems, some kind of government secret or another self-invented 'why' that explains what's really happening.

As ever, it might be true – or there could be a grain of truth in there – but our worry, our fear and anger blinds us to the truth.

In that list of big conspiracies, there were common themes – including the fear of being controlled by dark powers, of being taken advantage of, there's the need to protect ourselves and our loved ones against unseen threats that someone on our news feed, or in far-out politics, is only too happy to point a finger at.

It's all very human, and it's happened since we had people at the top and people at the bottom.

There's also that powerful secondary sense of injustice. It all comes together to create an atmosphere where our emotions run high, and we blame people who we're told are causing it.

And let's always remember that logic dies when emotion wins. It can take our reasoning, human brain a while to catch up – and by the time that happens we're already stuck in a loop where the only thing that makes sense is to get furious about it.

7. KEEPING OUR EYES OPEN FOR RABBIT HOLES

And with that, let's tiptoe even closer to the rabbit hole. Sadly, right now in the battle between facts and opinions, opinions are winning.

That's partly because most of us have complete access to everyone's ideas. In principle, that should be a good thing – the true spirit of free speech.

But the rabbit hole always draws us closer. In an information democracy the most popular bit of content always wins.

And as we now know, we're terrible at choosing information that's good for our health. The more eye-catching, surprising and shocking, the better.

We get overemotional about the bad stuff, the scare stories, the disinformation, and then share it. So, the worse the news, the more we hear it, especially when it's repackaged by friends, or weaponised to make us think and act differently.

Plus, opinions are always passionate, they're louder and more emotive than facts, and normally come from our nearest and dearest. So, they're even more believable and 'sticky'.

But hey – surely, we're excellent judges of character, aren't we? We can spot liars a mile off. C'mon, this isn't a problem, is it?

Hmm, let's bring in the research.

Two good examples are: *Accuracy of Deception Judgments* by social psychologist Charles F Bond of Texas Christian University and others, and *Reading Lies: Nonverbal Communication and Deception* by Aldert Vrij of the University of Portsmouth and others.

Both studies found that we're actually quite bad at spotting lies in the real world.

It's a bit disappointing, isn't it?

We'd all like to think that we can spot a lie miles away. But the research doesn't agree, and it's clearly a lot harder to do when we're online.

The research reveals the influences that get in the way:

> *Trust* – we tend to trust people close to us, within our family or social group.
> *Confusion* – people who knowingly lie tend to mix fact and fiction, so the lie is difficult to isolate. I'll introduce my term 'factals' later on.
> *Halo errors* (the halo effect) – we trust people that we like, even when it's because of a totally separate character trait. It's particularly powerful when we think about charismatic political leaders.
> *Exclusivity* – we feel special when a member of our community shares exclusive information with us … it makes us feel important.

> *Status* – powerful people can use their connections, standing, class, title and physical qualities to make it difficult for less important people to question them.

> *Gossip* – storytelling improves your social standing (as we spoke about in Chapter 1) … and spreading gossip can make you more powerful.

Much of this covers one-to-one, physical communication. But a lot of it translates to our social media lives too, and certainly into politics as we'll see in Chapter 5. The big difference is that it's more difficult to spot a lie when someone is hiding online, even when they use video. And we'll reveal a set of reliable deepfake tests later on, too.

On the other hand, we can crosscheck what they say much more easily – as long as we don't go to biased sources for the information.

But, at the mouth of the rabbit hole, the most important question is that extra 'why' – the storyteller's motive.

Here are some of the big ones – some of which we've already mentioned:

1. Political gain.
2. Commercial gain.
3. Personal or ideological gain.

We can also widen it out to include some people's need for followers, for control over people, for secrecy and whitewashing if their reputation's in doubt, or just because they like to break things.

Obviously, commercial and political gain are common motivators to spread disinformation. Control is the classic motive that we've already spoken about. Secrecy and whitewashing are all about concealing the truth – including the original secret motive that they won't admit to.

Anyone determined to lie to you, change your beliefs or gain the upper hand is driven by these motives.

So, question them – whoever they are. They might be on the level, but if they're not it's your right to walk away before they drag you deeper.

Next, let's do something about it!

8. THE HARM TEST

In my search for clues about how to handle mis- and disinformation, and especially conspiracy beliefs, a big question came up again and again: what's the reasonable, safe centre ground when two sides believe wildly different things?

How do we find the middle? Where do we set the norms of thinking that communities used to settle on around their prehistoric campfires?

For me, it all came down to a simple phrase.
First do no harm.

Anyone who believes that it's okay to do harm to people by spreading information that's untrue is in the wrong. They're making followers angry and dividing them off from the rest of the world. And they might be doing direct harm to wider relationships and even democracy. If you feel that you might have been pushed into that position, please come back to us. We've missed the you that we used to know and love.

And sure, it's never easy to admit that we've been exposed to, and convinced by, a conspiracy belief.

So, let's prove it. Let's measure how harmful a conspiracy belief is with some very simple maths.

I call it The Harm Test.

Here is a list of harms that a conspiracy belief might cause. They don't always, but they can. I'm going to attach a simple value of 1 (harmful) or zero (not harmful) to each of the harms. If any of those score a 1, then you know that the conspiracy belief could be damaging. If not, it's harmless and we probably don't need to have a serious chat about it. We can be hurt:

> Physically.
> Psychologically.
> Emotionally.
> Financially.
> We can be divided from loved ones.
> We can come under verbal or physical attack because of this belief.
> We can be associated with a damaging cause that has done direct harm to life or livelihoods.
> We can be deprived of our social standing and reputation.
> We can be deprived of education or opportunity.
> Perhaps a final harm is being deprived of our freedom (imprisonment).

There might be more, but that's a good selection.

So, let's give The Harm Test a spin. You might disagree with my assessment of some of the harm scores, but that's okay – try it yourself on another conspiracy. The main thing is that we're working out whether different conspiracy beliefs are potentially harmful or completely innocuous.

THE HARM TEST 1:
THE MOON LANDINGS WERE FAKED

It's a classic conspiracy belief. Did Armstrong and Aldrin really land on the moon or was it all a studio shoot?

We don't need a yes or no – to believe or not – we just need to work out whether this belief is harmless, or something more dangerous.

Type of harm	Value and why
Physical	0 – Nobody is physically hurt by believing this
Psychological	0 – Same as above
Emotional	0 – Unless the pain of being doubted is harmful
Financial	0 – Very little investment needed
Divided from loved ones	0 – It's not divisive enough
Under attack for holding the belief	0 – A raised eyebrow, nothing more
Associated with a damaging cause	0 – No
Deprived of social standing	0 – Unlikely, unless you're a NASA scientist…
Deprived of education or opportunity	0 – Same as above
Deprived of freedom	0 – No-one's in prison for this belief
TOTAL	**0**

So, this looks like a completely harmless conspiracy belief and perhaps we don't need to worry about people who follow it – unless it drives them toward a more harmful conspiracy. But of course, it wouldn't do a believer any good if they worked at NASA or the European Space Agency.

Still, the score is zero.

THE HARM TEST 2:
THE 2020 US ELECTION RESULT WAS A FRAUD

Now let's look at one of the most intense political debates of the early 2020s. It's an old story now, but worth testing.

And let's be really clear. People did die when the Capitol was invaded after the election result was questioned by Donald Trump, so this appears to be much more serious.

Let's test it.

Type of harm	Value and why
Physical	1 - Physical harm was a core feature of this event
Psychological	1 - Families of the victims suffered great damage
Emotional	1 - Same as above
Financial	1 - Damage to taxpayers' property
Divided from loved ones	1 - Extreme differences in views split families
Under attack for holding the belief	1 - Legal action, wider controversy
Associated with a damaging cause	1 - It was a violent event
Deprived of social standing	1 - Yes, outside communities of fellow believers
Deprived of education or opportunity	0 - Not directly through this event
Deprived of freedom	1 - People were sent to jail
TOTAL	**9 - Almost a full score on the harm scale**

The score is 9/10.

THE HARM TEST 3:
COVID-19 WAS A HOAX

Now, I think we need to be very sensitive here to the millions of people who lost their lives during the pandemic and have respect for all of their families and friends. Again, this is not about your belief in COVID or not. It's about testing how dangerous the conspiracy theory was. So, let's always remember the people who lost loved ones during this period before anything else.

That being said, how does the COVID hoax theory score on the harm scale?

Type of harm	Value and why
Physical	1 - People died because of this belief
Psychological	1 - Families of the victims suffered great harm
Emotional	1 - Same as above
Financial	1 - Financial loss from sceptics spreading the virus
Divided from loved ones	1 - Physically and in terms of beliefs
Under attack for holding the belief	1 - Yes, from victims' families
Associated with a damaging cause	1 - Not violent, but damage was done
Deprived of social standing	1 - Outside their own group
Deprived of education or opportunity	1 - People who believed couldn't mix
Deprived of freedom	1 - Same as above
TOTAL	**10 - An extremely harmful belief**

Because of the health impacts of believing that there were no health impacts, and that COVID was a hoax, there is a clear link to harm here.

Hundreds of thousands of people died from the virus because they hadn't been vaccinated. And when people were persuaded that the virus was dangerous, it had repercussions worldwide. It doesn't mean that there aren't questions about the speed of development of the vaccines. We should always ask questions. But scientists did answer those questions at length for months after the vaccines went into circulation. Not the CEOs, not the chief marketing officers, but vaccine scientists – the primary source for anyone who was genuinely open to the jab.

So, this belief was extremely harmful and gets a top score according to the assessment above. The score is 10/10. And it's the harm done to believers, as well as those around them, that show up on The Harm Test.

Now, it's an important moment to stop and again underline the fact that the people who spread mis- and dis-information are the problem here, not the people who are innocently persuaded to join the belief system.

But we should always remember – with the above examples on our lips – that if you suspect that any belief might cause harm, you should never share posts or videos that spread it. If you do that, then you share direct responsibility for the impacts of that disinformation. You become the problem. It's that simple.

AN OUTRAGE EXCEPTION: WHEN IS IT OKAY?

Throughout this book so far, I've spoken about the dangers of outrage, mainly when it's a reaction to made up, scary stories.

It's a poison that's manufactured by people trying to make us believe in a new threat, to stoke a sense of injustice or to create division. It also drives the more innocent sharing epidemic that fuels misinformation.

But there is, of course, an exception to all of this. When is it justified to be outraged?

Back to the phrase 'first do no harm'.

If a belief, ideology or claim directly hurts people who can't help themselves or have a perfectly justified reason to ask for help, I think you have a right to be outraged. It's a basic right or wrong. A 'stop hurting defenceless people' situation.

We just need to be careful when the information we absorb pushes our buttons.

Something else that blinds us to the facts is the set of reasonable sounding defences that conspiracy founders use to convince people to follow. It's time to talk about free speech and the fight for good vs. evil.

9. CONSPIRACIES: THE GREAT DEFENCES

There are a few very powerful arguments for conspiracy beliefs. Defences that are hard to penetrate, that come up again and again and use the grain of truth to make the belief feel world-changing.

Without those defences, many beliefs would crumble to dust the moment the facts were presented. But they're much more resilient than that because they make a lot of sense when we desperately want to believe.

Let's talk about the greatest defences of all.

FREE SPEECH

Firstly, our old friend free speech.

Free speech is an excellent core value of democracies and open societies worldwide.

It's a cornerstone of healthy conversations on issues that we genuinely need to talk about. On paper, it's about stopping censorship. It gives us an opportunity to mend important problems, particularly where our rights and freedoms have been removed.

Free speech is there to help the voiceless, the whistleblowers, the people who dare to oppose the powerful.

And that's where it gets into trouble. It's also used as an excuse by the founders of false information to spread their ideas. As I've said throughout this book so far, it's vital that we are free to ask questions. But if the intention is to do harm, or spread hate, disinformation, or to marginalise a part of the population that needs support, we've reached the limits of what free speech is for, in a civilised society.

The thing is, if we don't audit our core beliefs, we can easily believe that our free speech is justified, when actually we're the ones spreading bias and hate.

And we could prove that by asking a simple question: is it okay to harm someone using free speech as a defence? What's the public good? Could I be wrong? People who use free speech wrongly never admit that they might be wrong. They won't see the other side.

That's why Donald Trump's second inauguration plan to end so-called censorship and to make 'free speech' free again was the sign of dangerous things to come. We should be very worried about the type of free speech any populist – with a history of putting out questionable claims - wants to unleash.

Think way back to the January 6th 2021 insurrection at the US Capitol in Washington DC – which we'll look at properly in Chapter 5. In the legal cases that followed, free speech (through the First Amendment) was offered, and later rejected by the judge, as a defence by five members of the far-right Proud Boys group.

And he did it by pointing out that anti-democratic acts are not defended by free speech. In other words, freedom doesn't work when democracy is attacked.

So, we need to be careful when extreme groups use free speech to justify ideas that persecute particular groups of people.

They're inverting free speech into a tool to attack, not to defend.

And any belief – stated publicly – that incites people to violence, to racism, to abuse, to be biased based on gender, sexuality, or disability is wrong. If it causes harm, it's something that needs to be challenged. If we don't have safety standards that protect the people, what is democracy really for?

That's why we also need standards of free speech in our age of opinion, political propaganda and disinformation. Freedom of speech is open to abuse. And if the argument is closed to peaceful alternative views, then there's a problem.

You may not agree with that, but this is going to be our middle ground, our shared core value from where we can judge extreme ideologies and conspiracy beliefs, because if it's right to 'first do no harm', everything else follows.

FIGHTING FOR WHAT'S RIGHT

Most of us would probably agree that we'd fight for what's right if we had to.

In the world of conspiracies, many believers feel very strongly they're already doing that. It's a really good motive, isn't it? It's also very heartfelt.

Fighting for what's right is a real justification for taking sides. But only if we've checked the cause we believe in for holes.

Have we looked at the sources, the bias, the core beliefs of the people telling us what's right and wrong, what's good and what's evil?

In the BBC Podcast series *Death by Conspiracy,* by their Disinformation Reporter Marianna Spring, we heard from anti-COVID conspiracy believer Charlie in Episode 4. He contacted the family of a man called Gary who was part of his anti-mask, anti-vax group in the west of England during the pandemic. Gary eventually died from COVID (according to the death certificate). But Charlie refused to believe that, continuing to argue vehemently that COVID was a hoax and mask wearing was a form of state control.

Nothing that the journalist Marianna could say would bring him round. He believed with every fibre of his body that COVID-19 was a hoax.

The family were distraught when Charlie contacted multiple relatives to tell them that Gary hadn't died of COVID. But Charlie was focused only on one thing – that he was fighting for what's right, despite all of the evidence to the contrary. He refused to believe that a doctor's certificate was evidence because it didn't fit with his beliefs, so medics must also be part of the conspiracy. He believed that it was his moral duty to remind them of 'the truth'. But sadly, it was his truth. Not the truth. He'd added a powerful secretive motive to the facts based on what he already believed.

What can we learn from this?

As an independent listener without those same beliefs, it was so clear that Charlie had an unshakable obsession that government control was at the heart of multiple conspiracies – and COVID was just the latest one. He felt justified in intruding on the family's grief because his fight for what's right was more important.

Have a listen to that podcast, it's a great first-person insight into how emotion, core beliefs and lack of context lead to an unshakable – but inaccurate – 'truth'.

Online gurus, cult leaders, ideological and conspiratorial groups all claim that they're taking the moral high ground, leading people to enlightenment, to 'the truth'. And there might well be elements that we need to listen to – if only to get a full picture of what people feel and believe.

But these people often use densely packed language, detail, confusing terms and forceful delivery to make the facts difficult to crosscheck. By the time you've checked, they're into the next point.

They hide behind dense language and complex claims that hit lots of trigger words.

One particular 'guru', who's well-known for many reasons in the UK, has such expert command of language, that it's often difficult to decipher any of the meanings in the complex claims they make before you're carried along by the momentum.

That's true of many of them, and you can also be shamed by the guru and their followers if you step out of line – which is a clear red flag that something very cult-like is going on.

Ultimately sometimes, fighting for what's right is the most unshakable belief in the world of conspiracies. It beats every challenge, defeats every question.

But it's still possible to step back, ask the same questions that we have so far in this book, and get a clearer view of the person pushing their idea of right and wrong. Often, it won't look like the picture that the ideological leader is painting.

And what about you, me or our loved ones who already believe that they're fighting for good against evil?

Let's always remember that people who fall deeply into a niche or conspiracy belief often do want to do what's right. The belief in the mission can be blinding, and very personal, so don't go in too hard with that initial conversation. Once the walls go up (which psychologists call 'reactance') you've entered an argument, and the conversation is over.

As always, the best way to open the channels of communication is to listen and learn first, and respond second, once you've earned your place in the conversation with the person across from you.

Ultimately, a happier, healthier future of truth depends on us separating facts from fiction, sure.

But we'll also need to listen to a lot of fiction, before we can get to the facts.

And that leads us to two major reasons why conspiracy beliefs are so sticky. When they make you part of something bigger, they become part of you. And that's very hard to argue with.

MY BELIEF IS MY IDENTITY

We spoke about our unquenchable thirst for meaning in Chapter 2. Meaning keeps us moving, gives us purpose and a side to fight for. But a fundamental pillar of that is identity – Who am I? What do I believe in? How do I see myself? What stories make sense to me because of my values and my place in life?

I would argue that our identity is everything in the age of opinion.

And it's particularly important when conspiracy beliefs take hold. Here more than ever, our new beliefs take us into territory where our identity changes, where we become something more than we were before. Unfortunately, that's a new sense of meaning that is very hard to shake, just like it is in cults.

Many of us who are 'looking for something' will find it in a group, a mission, where we feel loved and included.

So, how can we help from the outside?

If you believe that your loved one, friend or colleague is being led to the dark side of conspiracy, politics, nationalism or radical activism, try to be aware of how they want to appear.

Remember how important that is. Are they now identifying as something bigger than themselves or getting the affirmation they need through the new belief?

An attack on their beliefs could easily be perceived as an attack on the entire person.

So be gentle.

And if you're really interested in the psychology behind this, you could do far worse than listening to and reading the writings of the US journalist David McRaney, who expertly dives into these areas and more.

IT'S ILLOGICAL, CAPTAIN

Logic. A lot like facts, it isn't all that sexy.

And it can sometimes be hard to articulate why the belief you have feels so important. For some groups (QAnon in the early 2020s for example), the defence has always been 'do the research, you'll find the truth'.

Of course, that's unhelpful if the available research simply echoes their beliefs, because the 'research' has all been written by fellow believers. The further into the detective work we go, the more we join the dots, form a pattern and solve a secret puzzle, the further away we go from the original facts.

So how is it that we can believe something so much but can't explain it clearly?

Because the issue you care so deeply about might feel so intensely world-changing that it should be obvious to the rest of us. In fact, it's so obvious that it becomes more of a feeling than a set of logical arguments. And it's possible that logic had less to do with it than fight, fright or flight.

As we know, when we go from talking to fighting, we switch off our human brains and let our chimp brains run riot.

Logic collapses when emotion spikes.

That's why it's also impossible to argue against someone's deeply held conspiracy belief with logic. It doesn't work that way. Conspiracies are often layered with a lot of grains of truth and plausible arguments, but the fundamental 'why' is probably about faith as much as it's about 'the truth'.

Certainly, in the world of conspiracy beliefs you'll see people in different groups expressing themselves with apocalyptic language, anger, demonstrations and direct action, and telling anyone who'll listen that they need to get with the programme. So, whenever we want to open a real, respectful conversation with a loved one who's fallen for a new, niche, even extreme belief, logic from your point of view might not be logic for them.

Okay, now let's start to weigh the world of conspiracy beliefs to find out how far down the rabbit hole we've fallen. Some of the figures coming up might shock you.

10. HOW MANY OF US WANT TO BELIEVE?

Remember at the top of the book I made a very simple observation: whatever our views, however we feel about the big issues, we really, really don't like being lied to.

Well, considering how many conspiracy theories hinge on the idea that we're being controlled by dark forces at the top of power, we should look at how many people believe.

And just to be clear, the grain of truth is strong. Many businesses – not least social media channels – depend on control. If you're genuinely worried about mind control, that's the place to start. On the government side, without a basic level of control, societies would fall apart. But equally, we're going to be brutally honest in Chapter 5 about the way that some politicians control us through polarisation, populism and divide and rule.

The question is: are our lives controlled by a dark conspiracy at the top?

Let's look at a piece of research in 2023 for King's College London and the BBC that studied a range of conspiracy beliefs. And yes, there are sceptics of the BBC but whatever you believe about my old employer (some of which will have been created by people who don't like the BBC on principle), I think King's College London has escaped claims of that kind, so let's crack on!

The research was called *Conspiracy belief among the UK public and the role of alternative media*, and the sample size here was good (although small compared to the whole population).

In total, 2,274 adults responded from across the UK, across demographics, ages and locations. Their answers were truly remarkable.

Here's a key to explain the range of answers, with the size of each circle reflecting the % value of each answer ...

DEFINITELY TRUE	PROBABLY TRUE	DON'T KNOW	PROBABLY FALSE	DEFINITELY FALSE
%	%	%	%	%

And here are five major conspiracy beliefs, and how strongly people felt about them according to the research.

The great replacement theory

This is the idea that Europeans and white Americans are being replaced by non-white immigrants.

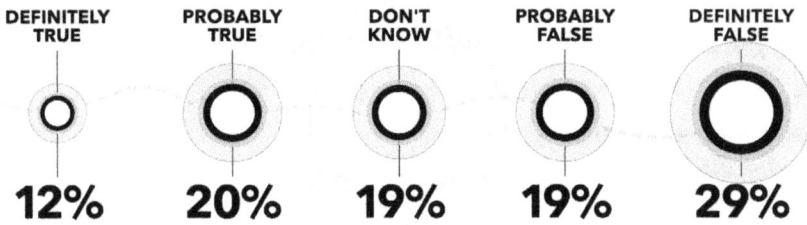

DEFINITELY TRUE	PROBABLY TRUE	DON'T KNOW	PROBABLY FALSE	DEFINITELY FALSE
12%	20%	19%	19%	29%

15-minute cities

15-minute city plans are a government attempt to surveil people and restrict freedoms.

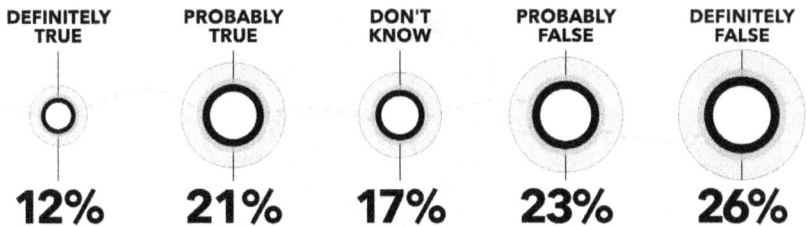

DEFINITELY TRUE	PROBABLY TRUE	DON'T KNOW	PROBABLY FALSE	DEFINITELY FALSE
12%	21%	17%	23%	26%

The terrorism cover-up

Next, the theory that media and government are involved in a conspiracy to cover up information about UK terror attacks.

DEFINITELY TRUE	PROBABLY TRUE	DON'T KNOW	PROBABLY FALSE	DEFINITELY FALSE
11%	23%	17%	25%	24%

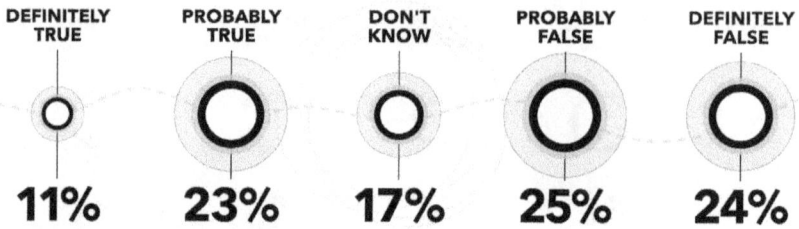

The cost-of-living crisis

The cost-of-living crisis is a government plot to control the public.

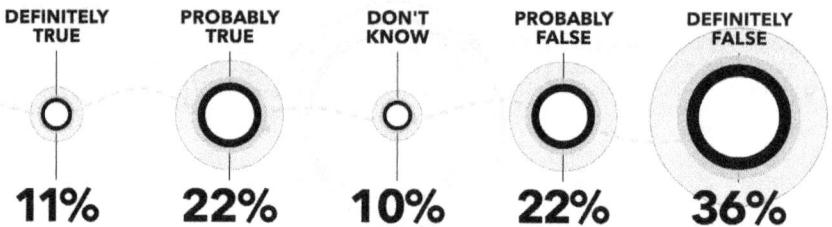

DEFINITELY TRUE	PROBABLY TRUE	DON'T KNOW	PROBABLY FALSE	DEFINITELY FALSE
11%	22%	10%	22%	36%

The 'great reset' theory

The World Economic Forum initiative is said to be a conspiracy to impose a totalitarian world government.

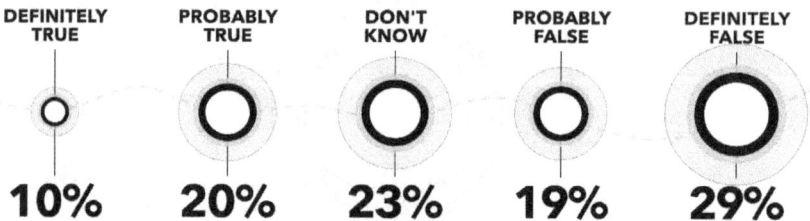

DEFINITELY TRUE	PROBABLY TRUE	DON'T KNOW	PROBABLY FALSE	DEFINITELY FALSE
10%	20%	23%	19%	29%

Source of this research: 'Conspiracy belief among the UK public and the role of alternative media.' Note: 2,274 UK adult respondents aged 18+ online between 28 and 30 April, 2023. The data has been weighted to be representative of the UK by age, sex, region and social status. Some percentages might not total 100 due to rounding up and down.

You can find the original research here: www.kcl.ac.uk/policy-institute/assets/truth-under-attack.pdf

Breaking it down, you can see a couple of fascinating trends in these figures.

First, among that sample of the British people, 10-12% held strong conspiracy beliefs, across the board. And although it's a stretch to extrapolate that up to the entire British population, that percentage would represent around 7 million people at the national scale.

In most cases, around twice as many people were quite convinced by the same conspiracy. That pro-conspiracy figure combined would represent around 30% of the population.

So, roughly 1 in 3 people in the UK consistently believe in conspiracies.

And it can go up when we're talking about the most controversial subjects.

That really is remarkable.

But let's not just take one side of the story. At the other end, you can add up the totals to see that around 50% of British people do not agree with these ideas.

What could explain these results?

Look, to some degree they're understandable, whichever side of the story you believe.

We have been, and are, living through extremely difficult times, times of great change, and not necessarily for the better. Importantly, as we've spoken about already, we also have a very human need to find comfort and control in times of fear.

It's an environment where far-right, pro-nationalism, anti-immigration, anti-social equality ideas violently hit the streets.

So, it's natural for us to believe that we can see a conspiracy at the top of society to keep the rest of us down during tough times. It has a strong grain of truth, makes sense, and reduces unknowns, even if we can't do much about it.

There might be a conspiracy somewhere but we're just as likely to be the victims of incompetence among the power seekers, as the subjects of a coherent plan to harm us.

I, for one, don't have that much faith in their abilities to pull off a large-scale deep state conspiracy. But you might have seen research to the contrary!

REDUCING FEAR

So, let's bring down the temperature.

When COVID broke out, billions of us worldwide suddenly came up against a deadly contagion that turned life upside-down. For some, it sounded like an excuse for the government to lock us up in our homes.

The divisions opened up immediately, even before the vaccines were developed. Across the world – particularly in the US - the battle lines were drawn over mask wearing. You might remember how it was where you are.

In London where I lived, it only took a few months for some people on the Underground to take off their masks and stare at you intently if you caught their eye with your mask on. It was really odd. In the US, anti-mask protestors would shout 'God gave us our breath, so anyone taking away our God-given breath is satanic!' You may even have been with them. It's happening right now with other issues pulling us apart. Look – if we hold back on launching into a single, polar position just for a second – COVID showed us that wearing a mask made our faces hot. But the twisting of core beliefs drove mass hysteria. Did we really need to get quite so hot under the collar about masks? Does anyone you know feel that way now?

My wife and I were scratching our heads about the fury. We couldn't understand why everyone was getting so crazy about wearing a simple mask. And that's exactly why I began to look into the foundations of disinformation. With a simple search, I found a conversation online that I'm about to quote. As ever, you might not agree with the channel's politics, but if we really want to claim we know the truth, we need to hear from all sides.

Two psychologists, Eve and Mark Whitmore, spoke to the US news broadcaster CNN about how humans react to fear – especially when it's shared by a lot of people: www.edition.cnn.com/2020/08/16/health/pandemic-covid-19-denial-mental-health-wellness/index.html

This quote almost says it all:

'Denial is a way for people to defend themselves against anxiety. When they're in periods where there's a lot of anxiety and it's perceived as a threat, then people develop strategies to protect themselves, their sense of security and safety. And one of these is simply to deny whatever the threatening source is exists. In this case, you would simply say, 'Well the epidemic is a hoax. It doesn't really exist.'

And this piece of research in the highly respected *Wiley European Journal of Social Psychology* also tells us so much, if you have a bit more time: www.ncbi.nlm.nih.gov/pmc/articles/PMC6282974/

Here's a very helpful quote from it: 'Specifically, conspiracy theories are consequential as they have a real impact on people's health, relationships, and safety; they are universal in that belief in them is widespread across times, cultures, and social settings; they are emotional given that negative emotions and not rational deliberations cause conspiracy beliefs; and they are social as conspiracy beliefs are closely associated with psychological motivations underlying intergroup conflict.'

The King's College London research that we looked at in the last section is just one of a series of studies about this. Their earlier report in 2022 – during the pandemic – found that 35% of British people believed that the government had deliberately exaggerated the total number of people who'd died from COVID.

A year later in 2023, following the deaths of millions of people worldwide, the King's College London and BBC did the research again. It looked like this…

The COVID-19 pandemic was a hoax, agree or disagree?

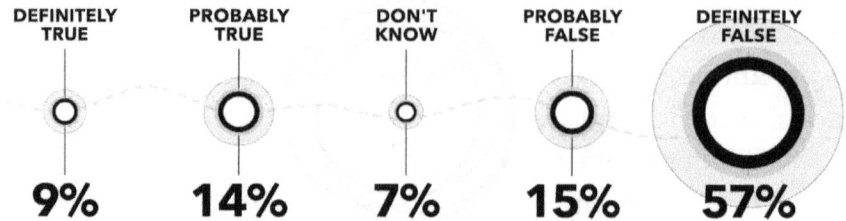

DEFINITELY TRUE	PROBABLY TRUE	DON'T KNOW	PROBABLY FALSE	DEFINITELY FALSE
9%	14%	7%	15%	57%

Source: *The Policy Institute. Conspiracy belief among the UK public and the role of alternative media. Note: 2,274 UK adult respondents aged 18+ online between 28 and 30 April, 2023. Data weighted to be representative of the UK by age, sex, region and social grade. Percentages may not total 100 due to rounding.*

So, the total, just one year later, had dropped by 12%. Without the heightened fear, and with the evidence of our own eyes, we'd reduced our belief in a big COVID conspiracy.

It's an important example of how a widespread understanding of the facts, and stripping away the fear, can turn a conspiracy theory around.

But we do still need to accept the evidence from all sides to find the safe middle ground. Also, can we keep a clear head when everything around us seems to be collapsing? Well, being little less 'chimp', perhaps a bit more 'bonobo', and certainly holding back our full, instant commitment to one side of the story would definitely help.

So, let's engage our brains again with something I've invented.

11. THE CONSPIRACY EQUATION

I used to be a theoretical physicist. Not the most committed or talented, it must be said, but I learned to create equations. It hasn't been that useful, but for once perhaps it will be.

It's time to dust off the lab coat and create something new. This could be really useful to us if we'd like to understand how powerful a conspiracy belief can be.

It's a very simple equation to work it out. Don't worry, I'll keep it very light on the maths, but this will help us to weigh up the driving forces behind conspiracies and how strong they are from theory to theory.

It's called The Conspiracy Equation, and it brings together the building blocks that make us believe.

So, what are those key building blocks? In maths language, they're called variables, so let's go with that.

Each of the two or three-letter terms that I'm about to show you is a key driver of belief in a conspiracy.

And they all have a value of 1. Simply one unit per term. Nothing too mathsy yet! They're just the main drivers, and if you were being really simple about this stuff you could just add up the most relevant ones that apply to a conspiracy and come up with a total out of ten. But I think we need to go one stage further.

So, we have:

Aff = Personal Affirmation | 'I want to feel that my voice is heard', 'I want to be validated'.

Tr = Trust | Does this theory sound trustworthy and from a person or source that I believe?

Em = Emotion | 'If I feel it, then I'll read, listen, share and care about the theory' – so does this conspiracy theory fire up strong emotion?

Im = Importance | How important is this belief – or the issue – to me, my people and the wider world?

Cm = Community | A large community means a bigger fan base and a safer place, to share views, give us a tribe, satisfy our need to be part of something important.

Be = Core beliefs | This is a big one, as we know. Does this conspiracy fit with my existing core beliefs about the world?

Si = Simplicity | An effective conspiracy – real or made up needs to be easy to grasp and spread, without us needing to question the detail.

Le = Leadership |Is the belief led by someone with charisma, an air of mystery or apparent inside knowledge?

He = Heritage | What's the history and reputation of the belief … is it new or well established?

Ow = Ownership | Do you have some personal ownership over the theory – e.g. have you found links or research that makes you feel as though you're an important part of this theory?

So, there are ten variables, and the overall impact of the conspiracy will be called simply, Co.

But what's the extra layer that takes us a stage further?

Well, depending on the conspiracy belief, some of those variables might be more powerful or 'sticky' than others. So, we need to include a kind of mathematical emphasis for each of the variables to reflect how powerful – or not – they are.

So, please let me introduce something that I call the conspiracy coefficient – 'c'. 'c' has a possible value of -3 to +3.

If c is +1, +2 or +3, the variable that it sits in front of has a positive effect on the conspiracy's overall power. For example, if it gives me a sense of great personal affirmation, the c in front of Aff will be positive.

If one of the variables isn't a very important factor in making a conspiracy belief powerful, then you give c a low value – maybe even zero.

And if that variable actually works against the conspiracy's power – then you might give the c coefficient a negative value.

Hopefully that's not too complicated. Basically, you're showing that some variables are more important than others, and giving c (c1, c2, c3 … up to c10) a value that represents that.

What we're looking for here is a high total score in terms of the impact of each conspiracy belief.

Also, the Conspiracy Equation is personal.

It's important to mention that the value of this equation depends on the strength of a conspiracy belief for each person, perhaps someone you know. It could even be you.

And yes, we could do some more maths to develop the equation into something more scientific, but let's keep it simple for now.

Here is The Conspiracy Equation:

Co = c1(Aff)+c2(Tr)+c3(Em)+c4(Im)+c5(Cm)
+c6(Be)+c7(Si)+c8(Le)+c9(He)+c10(Ow)

The total possible score for the power, or 'stickiness' of a conspiracy is 30, if every one of the conspiracy coefficients has a value of +3.

Shall we test it out?

I've put together some examples that I think represent the power of each variable in three conspiracy beliefs.

Starting with a solid classic – Area 51.

CONSPIRACY EQUATION 1: AREA 51 IS WHERE THEY KEEP THE ALIEN SPACECRAFT

Variable	'c' coefficient
Aff = Personal Affirmation	+1 – There's not much variety in the belief from person to person, but it's probably fun to be part of this community.
Tr = Trust	0 – There's no proof, apart from alien autopsy videos.
Em = Emotion	+3 – Very strong.
Im = Importance	+3 – If it's true it's Earth shattering.
Cm = Community	+3 – Very strong worldwide community.
Be = Core beliefs	+2 – Strong belief that there's something out there.
Si = Simplicity	+3 – Very simple.
Le = Leadership	-2 – Leadership is weak.
He = Heritage	+3 – Very long-standing and established.
Ow = Ownership	-2 – Very little personal ownership, although it's highly engaging for many.

So, the value of Co is:

$$Co = Aff(1{\times}1)+Tr(0{\times}1)+Em(3{\times}1)+Im(3{\times}1)+Cm(3{\times}1)$$
$$+Be(2{\times}1)+Si(3{\times}1)+Le(-2{\times}1)+He(3{\times}1)+Ow(-2{\times}1)$$

= 13 out of a possible 30.

It's a solid conspiracy theory but perhaps not that powerful.

CONSPIRACY EQUATION 2: THE BELIEFS OF QANON

Now, QAnon didn't last long as a major force in the conspiracy world. But the many far right and far-out conspiracy theories that created them still exist, so they certainly deserve a moment of reflection. Here's how they score.

Variable	'c' coefficient
Aff = Personal Affirmation	+3 - It's arguable that every person who's actively involved in one of the branches of the QAnon belief feels deeply as though their voice is important.
Tr = Trust	+2 - Negative distrust is very much part of this, so the role of trust gets a strong positive value in the list.
Em = Emotion	+3 - Very strong.
Im = Importance	+3 - They would say it's the most important set of truths.
Cm = Community	+3 - In the US, people definitely turn up in force at rallies.
Be = Core beliefs	+3 - Core beliefs drive everything.
Si = Simplicity	+1 - It's actually quite complex with many little theories feeding into the whole.
Le = Leadership	+3 - There is no formal leadership, but they've rallied behind Donald Trump.
He = Heritage	-2 - It hasn't been around very long.
Ow = Ownership	3 - 'Doing the research' has made every QAnon follower an expert in their chosen area of conspiracy.

So, the equation looks like this:

$$Co = Aff(3x1)+Tr(2x1)+Em(3x1)+Im(3x1)+Cm(3x1)$$
$$+Be(3x1)+Si(1x1)+Le(3x1)+He(-2x1)+Ow(3x1)$$

= 22 out of a possible 30.

Because QAnon is such a scattered community, apparently dormant but tied together by active far-right conspiracy beliefs, the structure doesn't work. But the emotions are extremely high, as is the belief in 'something dark on the political left', and the whole concept of 'doing the research'.

Now, let's test out a new piece of information that you may not have heard much about, because of the secrecy surrounding it.

CONSPIRACY EQUATION 3: AIR DRAINS

Inspectors have found drains all over the world that are being used to pump huge amounts of oxygen into the atmosphere.

You can see the evidence of it in winter when warm air rises up from city manhole covers. But if the authorities in some cities decide to shut down the supply, people living there will suffocate within one week, which would control the population of the most densely packed places. It'll start with a change in the way the air around these covers smells and the only way to stop it is to find the source of the oxygen in each city.

If this is true, what does it mean? How will it figure in the conspiracy equation? How sticky could it be?

Test it out safely with friends and give it a Co value.

$$Co = c1(Aff)+c2(Tr)+c3(Em)+c4(Im)+c5(Cm)$$
$$+c6(Be)+c7(Si)+c8(Le)+c9(He)+c10(Ow)$$

In the meantime, let's keep the #airdrains open.

ARE WE EDGING CLOSER TO THE TRUTH YET?

As we close this chapter, you can see some recurring triggers, patterns and practical tools that can help us to spot mis- and dis-information instinctively, wherever we see it.

We have the choice to control what we see, hear and read and what we stuff into our brains and spread to others.

Our emotions, our 'chimp brain' and where we go for our information are absolutely key. And if we can use our emotions differently, to spot manipulation when it makes us 'feel', to sniff out false information rather than falling for it, we'll instantly be better off.

Next, we'll look at how they hit us in the real world and how to look into the people that tell us what's right and wrong.
But before we move on, let's just throw down a trail of breadcrumbs to mark out the steps that we can all take, to extract the facts and edge closer to 'the truth':

> Firstly, we can quickly extract the facts of any story using the 5Ws – what, where, when, who, why and the final H – how.
> Now, draw a clear, unbiased set of conclusions based on the facts of the story, belief or event. Again, don't forget that there might be a grain of truth in the story, but it'll be layered with well-known bias that'll appeal to some of our darker core beliefs.
> Only take into account the experiences of people directly connected to the event or story – 'primary sources' – and reliable 'secondary sources'. They need to be qualified

journalists, with a track record of being unbiased, investigative, working for a broadcaster, publication or website that doesn't have any affiliation – particularly political.

> 'Tertiary sources' are normally unreliable. They include reports by people or news organisations that are known to have a commercial, political or ideological agenda. Editorials, opinion pieces, analysis and comment are often full of bias. These are all tertiary.

> Anything on social media by people who aren't connected to the story – even if you love and follow them religiously – is just opinions of opinions of reporting of the facts, nothing else. Try not to waste your time on them.

> On top of all of these, go to more than one reliable source.

> Finally, think about that W above – the 'why'. Nearly every conspiracy theory is built on an invented, secret motive to make sense of the story. When you can see people invent the 'why', you can spot a conspiracy coming.

Hey, I said at the start of this book that most of us are good people. We want to find the truth and to know what's really going on.

But it's a sad fact that the truth doesn't require – or include – our own opinions. The facts don't need our input to be true, they just are.

Conspiracy beliefs are just a million expressions of our unquenchable thirst for meaning, to make sense of a story. They're more exciting than the facts, but if we don't focus on reality – on the real facts – we now have very few safeguards on social media to keep our nastier biases at bay.

The good news is that we're now aware of it, thanks to the work we've done so far.

And now, after all that conspiracy-thinking, let's stop, step back and sidestep all of those expressions of truth with a short intake of breath.

I call it 'The Sniff Test'.

12. THE SNIFF TEST

In news, we 'do a truth check' on any story – particularly when the source is known for bias, or the points made are very one-sided, or perhaps out of character. Sometimes that piece of content just feels like it's not telling the whole truth.

Essentially, we work harder to sniff out the facts when something stinks.

It might be that the story in front of us don't make sense, uses suspiciously one-sided language, or is trying too hard to stir up trouble. Perhaps the facts are opaque, hidden or confusing. Of course, there's the other element. If a video or piece of content activates our core beliefs about something or someone, it's crucial to 'sniff'. Realise that our emotions are being stirred up and step back for a moment.

So, The Sniff Test is simple.

Ask, 'Does that really sound true?', 'Does it make sense?', 'Could they be telling me what I want to hear?', 'Do I really want to be known for spreading this story if it's not true?'

Stopping and stepping back for a moment is really helpful.

You can think of it as holding 30% of our commitment back, to allow for bias. Sniffing like this makes it much easier to keep our minds ready to reject false information.

It's your own personal X-ray vision for mis- and dis-information. We all do it naturally when we feel suspicious of what a certain person says. Those instincts are there for a reason. Trust them.

And it's one of the things we'll keep doing throughout this book from now on.

A cool head is a clear head.

What's really important is that we all hold onto a little suspicion. Just enough see our information for what it is.

Every piece of content, every post, share and news article could contain some bias. So rather than falling wholesale for the video, article or post in front of us, we're far less likely to be lied to if we hold 30% back. Just a touch of perspective so that we can stay slightly independent of what we're being told.

Later on, when we talk about deepfakes and AI-generated content we'll mention the concept of 'uncanny valley', where a piece of content that's designed to look real is slightly off and makes you feel uncomfortable. That's your gut feeling giving you a poke.

The ultimate tool in an information warrior's toolkit will be that 'it doesn't feel true' instinct, developed by exercising your personal sniff test. So, from now on always try to ask, 'Does the information I've just seen stink?'.

Sniff. Sniff hard.

Right, next we turn to the thorny issue of mass media. What on (flat) Earth will we discover about the way the news is made?

13. CHAPTER 3 – THE TOOLKIT

- It's easy for any of us to fall into a conspiracy belief when we're separated from the original facts, or find a tantalising new pattern that seems to tie the story – and our core beliefs – together.
- Every conspiracy is driven by a secret motive or dark plot, a 'why', that we often invent to make sense of a story. The lie is in the why.
- For most of us, 'there is no truth'. We'll probably never know the genuine motive behind a conspiracy, but we'll often try

to fill in the gaps.

- Conspiracies play to our unconscious biases, and confirmation bias, and they're a million different expressions of what we want to believe.
- The infodemic has made us much more likely to fall for conspiracy beliefs. But there are simple red flags that we can look out for.
- Before you like or share a story that may do damage in the real world, always think 'First, do no harm'.
- Try plugging the story into The Harm Test, and weigh its stickiness using The Conspiracy Equation.
- Start to apply your own personal sniff test. If the belief, ideology or news story stinks, stop, step back and sidestep it.
- And by the way, the #airdrains conspiracy might be something I made up. Still, try it on a friend to see how they react. Obviously, do let them know that it's not real before they spread it any further!

14. ANY ADDITIONS?

What have you seen?

Have you felt strongly about an idea that some people would call a conspiracy theory? Or is there another tool that you could add to your kit to strengthen your defences against harmful beliefs?

You might have even greater ways to see these stories for what they are. Please do join the conversation and together we'll have a much better set of tools to clean up our information diet.

4

THE BEARERS OF BAD NEWS

4

*'None of the main issues which humanity is facing
will be resolved without access to information.'*

CHRISTOPHE DELOIRE,
Reporters Without Borders

It's time to get serious about disinformation and the mass media. Sorry, disinformation and the mass media?

What? No way, that could NEVER happen. Stop it.

Okay, okay. Most of us know that getting the story straight, without bias, isn't really part of the job description of some news organisations these days. Political influence, scare stories, clickbait, big distracting headlines on a good day to bury bad news. It's the bread and butter of popular news. But there are still plenty of places to find honest, clear and extremely high-quality coverage.

So, this chapter will look hard at the news business.

You might be a news geek, in which case read on. If you're not, by all means skip the geeky sections and skim some of the owner bios in the next few pages.

But it's useful to remember that a lot of the news you read comes from the same people. And many owners push their baggage and biases into news agendas, if only to generate more advertising revenue, or to win political favour for their empire.

Still, nearly every political, international, financial or showbiz story was reported first by a news organisation, then filtered through personal opinions on social media.

So, we'll go to the source in this chapter and shine light on newsrooms. How do they work? How do shock-horror headlines get written? And how do powerful people get their voice across to spread disinformation that we then see?

Also, let's try to be scrupulously fair, as always.

We can all fall for powerful, plausible, self-serving populist campaigns. They're designed to convince us that something 'over there' is about to hurt us. So, it's totally understandable that some people make different choices when you realise how hard the creators of fake news work to spread it.

So as ever, blame the storyteller and the story, not the receiver of it – until they do harm.

But I won't be accusing anyone of personal wrongdoing in this chapter, outside coverage that's already out there. What I can do is show you how stories and disinformation are made, fed to us, and sometimes designed to divide us. Then it's up to us all to make our own choice about whether we believe 'the bad news' or not.

Right, we have a lot of big questions to answer in this chapter, including:

> Who owns the big newsrooms – particularly in the US and UK? You'll have your own, and it's always worth looking at them in the same way.

> Who benefits from the spread of disinformation in certain corners of the news?

> How does that influence the controversial things we talk about on social media?

> Where does news bias show itself - and how can we adjust it out of our own thinking?

> How can we sidestep fake news when it rattles our core beliefs?

We'll adapt some of the techniques that we've already come

up with to spot and sidestep 'bad news'. And I'll offer you some of my insights into how newsrooms work.

1. BEFORE WE GO ON

Just a word of warning.

I'll continue to talk about real news stories and important people in this chapter and the next that you might have personal feelings about. Some of the things we talk about will potentially get you fired up.

But they simply serve as recent examples of manipulation in the mass media that went on to drive division on social media.

The other question we need to ask here is: what if you're not interested in news at all? That could apply to you if you're younger, perhaps if you get your information from social media and friends.

Well, it's simply that the long hand of the news business will still reach you. And it'll be worse when it does.

Anything you know about a specific news story originally came from the same places: TV, radio, news websites and newspapers. Someone reported on the story, and the grapevine brought it to your channel through layers of opinion.

And look, it can seem a lonely place to be if our friends' opinions can't always be trusted. But in a world where nothing really feels true, especially when fact checking isn't valued, we need to know how to choose what to believe. Then, we can be confident – finally – that we know what we're talking about.

So, let's keep developing our instincts to see the news for what it is. What's good, how does it work, and how can we spot information that isn't worth the paper it's written on?

Let's go.

2. EXTRACTING THE FACTS FROM THE NEWS

It's more important than ever to get the basics right, when we're being fed news that seems true in black and white.

The facts are all that matter – even if they're buried deep in a post, or not mentioned at all in the Facebook video or Insta reel.

And the facts are out there, somewhere. We know about the 5Ws and an H but in news coverage, what's new?

I can tell you that the facts are the main thing that gets serious journalists up in the morning, despite being paid very little and working very hard. When they uncover genuine facts that are hidden from the world, it makes the job worthwhile. And it's really special to know that you've escaped the bias and found them, for real.

So how can we discover them in a professional news story?

> Every story is constructed in the same way, starting with the 5Ws (and as you know, I like to add in the extra H): What, when, where, who, why and how.

> Above that, the overall purpose of the piece is fed in – what are we trying to say? What's at the heart of the story?

> Then the language – how are we looking to emphasise the facts or make them more interesting? Right at the start of the book, I said that facts are boring. Well, making them more interesting is where language and emphasis comes in.

> And of course, journalists spend a lot of time finding people close to the story – sometimes recording them or quoting them – but they're always interviewed in some way if the journalist is building their story properly.

No primary sources, no story.

There's one other layer for tabloid press and right-wing TV

and radio channels.

They'll be hunting for ways to amplify controversy.

They'll do that in the headlines, by using unsettling or threatening language or by saying how terrifying the other side is if we don't take a stand. So underneath the opinions, the big bad headlines, the 'threat to our way of life' and the political agendas, the facts are there. It's the colourful stuff on top that we need to notice, then dismiss.

Let's now talk about the business of news.

The mass media business model hinges on us being hooked into storytelling so that we stay for longer, perhaps adjust our views towards theirs, and come back for more tomorrow. That's not true of the centre-ground broadcasters or websites, but it's increasingly true on the fringes of opinion.

It's a business. It brings in advertisers and builds a brand.

The great news is that even tabloid newspapers are obliged to give you most of the facts. If the facts get in the way of their main story, they'll just push them through their unique filter, or bury them deep in the story where facts are harder to find.

So, if you're worried about being misled or even lied to, think about the source first: what is this newspaper, channel or group known for? Are they unbiased, or known for being a bit left- or right-wing? Whether you like it or not, you'll know which side your favourite channel lies on. Once you do, you can stop, extract the facts and put less emphasis on the language they use to push up your temperature.

And hey, if you're okay with being outraged and inflamed by narratives that put you on edge every day, well good luck to you. Carry on reading.

For the rest of us, it's always worth understanding what the other side is saying, to get more than one view, but then let the outrage wash over you.

3. HOW THE NEWS IS MADE

Firstly, to be fair to modern mass media news, let's set one record straight.

I can tell you, as a long-time journalist in a wide variety of commercial and public newsrooms across the UK, that there is no single 'mainstream news'.

'It' doesn't exist.

Newsrooms – for all of their dysfunctions – aren't one, single, homogeneous gaggle of friends conspiring together to pull the wool over our eyes. That's the common misconception that many have about 'the news', often as a way to drive mistrust of reporting that some people don't like.

In fact, that's where our modern term 'fake news' came from. A US President used a catchy phrase to attack coverage that didn't go his way.

Sure, there are friends and there are old colleagues who've known each other for years in other jobs. Sometimes they're friendly. Sometimes they're not. Sometimes a news group runs more than one newsroom and shares a similar agenda. But most newsrooms are a whirlwind of different characters working as quickly as possible to uncover stories and put them out.

Next, who's in the newsroom?

Characters dominate newsrooms. They're very often noisy places. The people include ambitious people who would – and do – climb over their colleagues to get a better job. There are bosses who use threats to make their journalists do what they want (on pain of losing their job). There are great journalists who don't toe the line and won't run stories that they know to be untrue. There are also journalists who cut corners to hit a deadline.

And importantly, there are thousands of incredibly ethical people who work long hours, expose themselves to danger and care about investigating issues that we need to hear about. Without those people, power and corruption would never be challenged, and disinformation would run completely free.

And it's important to remember that outside the big outlets, there are unbelievably brave reporters risking their lives alone to uncover news. Supporting those incredible journalists are organisations including Forbidden Stories and Reporters Without Borders – out on their own, protecting the truth.

Back to the mainstream, what about bias?

In that wild mix of personalities and projects, are there any common threads between different news operations?

Well, newsrooms often do follow each others' agendas and stories, sometimes for days, but not normally in collaboration. They do it more through a fear of missing out and to be first with the most impactful coverage. Quite honestly, this happens more than any news editor would really want, but it's a fact of life.

Ultimately, try to imagine a fast-moving, highly charged and challenging room full of skilled people under pressure to run something new, exclusive and gripping every day, every hour, every second. Then imagine how you'd react when the pressure fell on you to run a story that wasn't fully fact checked – but your job depended on running it.

What would you do?

I used to call 50-100 people every day as a journalist. Perhaps 5-10 would get back to me, mainly thanks to the name of the channel I was working on. The patchwork of facts and perspectives was new every day.

All of this can force errors. The need to be first with the biggest story can easily push factual coverage into storytelling that's more about grabbing attention than telling the whole truth. And that's where sensationalism comes from.

What did I do?

Well, it's probably a good moment to mention the reason

that I left the news business quite early in my professional life. I loved my years in news, but left the full-time job after around 15 years in broadcasting.

I took a lot of pleasure in putting out people's stories, revealing bad behaviour, investigating big interests and cross-examining people who didn't appear to be on the level – not least senior political figures. Journalists didn't get paid much (unlike news anchors), but we did see life through thousands of people's eyes. It was a tough job with a poor lifestyle – but a fascinating life. But here's where it came undone for me. I wouldn't run a story that I knew was untrue. And in news, ethics can sometimes be the enemy of advancement.

I – and people like me – 'knocked down' untrue stories every week, sometimes a few times a week. And I can tell you that this made news editors (they're the senior people who decide which stories run) in a couple of newsrooms very unhappy. It wasn't easy balancing the need for an exciting new story with being fully honest, but that was my choice.

Ultimately, on the 5th July 2005, I arrived at Tavistock Square in London. Terrorist attackers had just killed 52 people on a bus and on the London Underground. I – and the camerawoman I was working with – interviewed a young Muslim man who'd survived the bus explosion. He had the thousand-yard stare of someone in shock. The British women helping him were gently guiding him away from the scene. He showed us the peaceful face of a person of the same religious faith as the attackers, but in complete opposition to them.

That interview didn't make it onto the air, and a couple of weeks later I chased my last news boss around his office with my resignation letter, and never took a staff job in news again.

So, 'the news' is far from perfect, and my potted history isn't the only one of its kind. News is a boiling pot of characters and investigators under pressure. But it's the standards and quality of reporting that we need to support.

'The truth' depends on it.

And it does exist in the greatest outlets. Just take a look at Private Eye, or listen to a podcast by Tortoise Media and you'll understand how important it is.

So, why doesn't everyone apply the standards that might make younger people trust the news business again?

Well, like so many of us, I spit out my breakfast on a regular basis, shouting obscenities at my news app or channel of choice. The coverage isn't complete, or it's biased, or they've buried a story because of some agenda that we'll never know. There is coverage happening right now, on many of our channels, that simply doesn't pass the sniff test.

Ownership is important.

So, let's take a quick look at the people who own the media, sometimes set the agenda and often set their political leanings.

4. GLOBAL MEDIA'S BIGGEST PLAYERS

Here are some of the biggest players in the business. The ownership does shift, and it might have changed by the time you read this.

But have a quick think about the biographies below because they influence so many of the stories we see, hear and read.

And you can see why ownership is so important when you realise that their personal politics often drives the stories that our information diet is made of.

Rupert Murdoch

Rupert Murdoch will go down in history as the world's most ruthless opinion-maker. He resigned from the top job at *News Corp* in mid-2023 but left an empire of influence. News Corp newspapers include the *New York Post* in the US, and *The Times,*

The Sun and *The Sun on Sunday* in the UK. The company's cable TV channels include *Fox News* in the US and *Sky News* in the UK. The newspaper arm and *Fox News* in particular are known for airing very right-wing opinions and editorial pieces which – because of their circulation and reach (measured in 2022) – influenced more than 1 in 4 newspaper readers in the UK and huge swathes in the US. Rupert Murdoch shaped the modern mass media and spent a career making – and toppling – the most powerful people on Earth through his influence over politics and public opinion.

Mark Zuckerberg

The owner of *Facebook, Instagram, Threads* and *WhatsApp* has more tech-based influence on direct conversations between people than any other human being. Around 7 billion in total. In early 2025, the *Meta* boss made that quick but world-shaking announcement that the biggest social media channels would be removing independent fact checking. Among the other things we've already spoken about, he said that comments about immigration and gender – the two favourite wedge issues of the far-right – would no longer be managed to the same level. Community notes (in other words, user comments) would be the new safety system: free for *Meta* to operate, a lot less complicated to deal with, and much more favourable to the vocal minority. A lot of work had previously been underway to clean up the content on *Meta* channels, but following the 2024 US election – which Zuckerberg mentioned in his video – the appetite to restrict extreme opinions appeared to end. You can find out more about *Meta*'s influence here: https://www.statista.com/statistics/272014/global-social-networks-ranked-by-number-of-users/

Elon Musk

When Elon Musk bought *Twitter* (before changing the name to his favourite letter of the alphabet), the catastrophic shedding of jobs and staff walkouts left a trail of confusion as to why he'd spend $44bn of his own money on it. That became clear when the platform lost hundreds of thousands of moderate users, and welcomed back an army of keyboard warriors who'd been banned. Musk began to use his platform to attack centre-left British politicians and support far-right parties in Europe, including Germany's AfD. He even turned on his friend in Tweed, Nigel Farage, after the Reform UK party leader had refused to publicly back the far-right British campaigner Stephen Yaxley-Lennon (who self-identifies as 'Tommy Robinson'). *X* quickly became the home of hard-right social media opinion, just as Musk took up his new job as Donald Trump's right-hand axeman at The White House. This was the rapid, public radicalisation of a media mogul by his own social media channel. Although who knows, perhaps it was all a weird strategy to control NASA and put a Tesla on Mars.

Who else (outside politics) has a – slightly less obvious – influence on the stories we see, hear and read?

Jeff Bezos

The Amazon founder is the next media mogul, and third richest man in the world as this book hits the shelves. He spent $250m of his personal fortune to buy *The Washington Post*, and of course has *Amazon Prime* - which makes him one of the most powerful digital players on the planet, even when he leaves the planet to spend time in the blue yonder with William Shatner. His core business touches most households in the west, and although his direct influence on news agendas is smaller than the last two tech tycoons, his investments in new technologies run far and wide.

Laurene Powell Jobs

Laurene Powell Jobs has a majority stake in *The Atlantic* – the left-leaning US magazine and publisher. They cover news, politics, business and culture with skill and good fact checking, but with a slight lean to liberal editorials. So, she's now quite a rare media business owner in terms of her political stance.

Lord Rothermere

The British peer inherited his grandfather's media empire which now includes right-wing papers the *Daily Mail* (2nd most-read newspaper in the UK as of early 2024), the *Mail on Sunday*, as well as the free paper *Metro* (1st most-read newspaper), and the I newspaper. Thanks to the domestic and international reach of his papers especially the *Daily Mail*, in 2022 he controlled around 39% of the total UK national newspaper sales each week – well ahead of Rupert Murdoch's 27.5% share.

The Barclay Brothers

The Barclay Brothers' Press Holdings currently own the *Daily Telegraph, The Sunday Telegraph* and *The Spectator*. All of them are unapologetically right-wing publications focused on conservative editorial opinion and current affairs. If you're looking for a place to hear about threats to 'our way of life ', this is the place to do it, on a *Daily* basis.

Reach

The group that owns the *Mirror, Sunday Mirror* and *Daily Star* in the UK – as well as more than 100 other local and regional newspapers – is one of the only businesses that runs stories on both sides of the British political divide. In 2025, it was ranked top in terms of audience share in the UK and Ireland, with around 69% of people reading its online titles. And it's very rare in that a few of its newspapers lean to the left. But with other titles including *OK!*, *football.london* and the *Express*, the group has spread its bets across the UK news business.

Alexander Lebedev

The Russian oligarch and former KGB agent owns *The Independent* and *The Independent on Sunday* in the UK, and the Evening Standard. The Evening Standard supported Boris Johnson's London mayoral campaign, after which Boris Johnson put Lebedev's son Evgeny into the House of Lords against the advice of the British security service MI5. Johnson was also reported widely to have spent time – without his bodyguards – at Lebedev private parties, opening important questions about whether the family had personal influence at the top of British government during the early 2020s.

Scott Trust & Tortoise Media

The only other left-leaning mainstream newspapers in the UK are *The Guardian* and *The Observer*. The company that owns *The Guardian* (and other smaller media outlets) sold *The Observer* to Tortoise Media at the end of 2024.

The BBC

As someone from the UK, it's important to mention the BBC. I worked there for almost five years, and it holds a place in many British people's hearts. The BBC operates primarily through the TV licence fee, which is charged to every home in the UK unless the people living there opt out. And although it's known for being fiercely independent, its annual income is decided by the government of the day. Recently that pushed it into repeated controversies about whether members of its strongly Conservative leadership were truly keeping their nose out of the news agenda on issues the Tories were campaigning for.

Now, there are clearly huge corporations that control digital media, plus other news channels and publications that you'll know and follow. Companies like Google, Comcast, Disney, Netflix,

JioStar, Axel Springer SE and Global Media. But the biographies we've just gone through give us a view of some of the most powerful individual players in the mass media in the US and UK – the people who direct the original coverage of the information we receive.

It's always a good idea to spell out any personal agendas or potential bias, and therefore the style of reporting in some of those news organisations. Hopefully you can also look behind the curtain where you are. As a general rule, most private media ownership is on the right of politics, leaning towards nationalist, anti-immigration, anti-civil rights, pro-big business agendas where they operate. There are exceptions, but where big media money goes, conservative influence follows.

I WANT TO SEX YOU UP

Let's talk about sex.

But not in the way you're thinking.

In the news business, the race for the hottest coverage has always driven commercial news businesses to 'sex up a story'. It makes content harder to ignore.

It's true in all types of media – AM radio in the US, new TV and radio talk channels in the UK, political fanatics online – base what they say on sensationalism, outlandish opinion, rows and rants, and a very distant relationship with the truth.

It sells. Also, it distracts. And worst of all, it can make us suspicious of conventional, professional news.

As Trump's first media master Steve Bannon famously said in terms of pushing through a message: '*The real opposition is the media. And the way to deal with them is to flood the zone with sh*t.*'

After a good few years of a bad information diet, we're now acclimatised to the constant shouting and human waste products. Lots of people have turned off conventional news, not least younger people. Sabrina Yavernise and Aidan Gardiner summed it up expertly in *The New York Times*, saying '*People are numb and disoriented, struggling to discern what is real in a sea of slant, fake, and fact.*'

No wonder that the only stories that we really take notice of are the ones that catch our eye. The ones that are quick and simple to understand, and the ones that make us angry.

But it doesn't stop there.

Tabloid news reaches into even the most responsible news operations. It does it through … the morning news meeting.
First thing in the morning, every weekday, senior newsroom people gather over their third breakfast coffee to discuss the stories that they'll be covering today.

The group goes through the newsgathering diary (events they already know about), top stories and potentially famous people's social media posts. They'll look at things like the political speeches coming up today – and yes, they might plan to run '*The Prime Minister will say today …*' political news that I'll focus on shortly. Plus, they'll pour through the tabloids, establishment newspapers, the gossip and headlines.

So, why is the morning meeting worth mentioning?

Because every newsroom – competitive as they are – starts from nearly the exact same place, every day. It'll send out its reporters to make the best possible TV or radio story based on what the newsroom's VIPs read that morning in the newspapers.
It's not a great recipe for quality coverage, but I guess the day has to start somewhere.

Unfortunately, the problem is that – unless their reporters 'knock down' bad reporting or correct it – the only possible result is a sexed-up story based on the agendas of the papers. That's why news agendas in broadcasting can look a lot like the newspapers for days on end.

If you watch the late-night news shows, you'll also notice that they still read out the headlines from the next day's papers.

It's a very old-school way of operating, and pretty risky in the age of disinformation.

5. HOW TO SPOT BIAS IN BROADCASTING

Let's throw down another breadcrumb of information that isn't widely known.

How do we practically spot bias in the broadcast news? Or the strong political agendas that can leak through from the right-wing press?

Well first, it's important to say that laws are generally tighter when it comes to broadcasting. You can't just run a story that clearly isn't true – unless you're on one of the far-out, opinion-based channels. But you can still run lots of interviews with people on one side or the other. So, broadcast news is generally more 'truthful', with a couple of caveats.

If you blur the boundaries between news and opinion on-air, you can do what you like: change opinions, push through new policies, change election results and bypass a lot of rules about impartiality.

I hope that your chosen channel is giving you the genuine facts, but if not here's how to spot the hand of bias in broadcasting.

> Look for language that sounds one-sided, accusatory or unfair. If you hear the word 'woke', you know that the coverage is right-wing. If you hear the word 'fascist', that speaker will generally be more left-leaning – although we'll look at that in Chapter 9 with something called 'Inversion'.
> If a broadcast story quotes a particular side of a story but not the other (basically, they don't offer balance), then they're imposing bias.
> Also, if they bring up a side of the argument that's a niche

– possibly extreme – angle, they're directly introducing bias.

> Coverage that appears to attack a particular person or people based on their politics might be biased. The exception to this is reporting on politicians who've been found to break the rules, law, or been corrupt.

> Also, if there's a history of bias or a known political affiliation, the reporting could easily be unreliable.

Bias can trickle down from bosses to news editors, who then set the agenda of their reporters.

Ultimately, biased reporting isn't news.

It's just storytelling.

6. THE INVISIBLE LINE

We're getting there.

Before we get practical in the next chapter with some of the most of-the-moment effects of disinformation in the mass media and beyond, there's one more technique in broadcasting, online, and the traditional press that many of us miss altogether.

I call it 'The Invisible Line'.

This is about the stories that newsrooms don't include, or push down the running order. Good news judgement is there to emphasise one story over another. But sometimes, a political or ideological agenda makes its way into the news in secret.

The running order of a bulletin, news app or programme is at the heart of the choices a newsroom makes. If a story makes it into the top three, it's important. If it's pushed further down the running order, it's less important and potentially hidden from sight. It's very much like an event at the Olympics. By fourth place, you're out of the medals.

So, you can easily spot the agendas and biases of a news outlet when you look at their top-three story choice.

If, for example, it takes one side of politics on a day where there should be balance, you know that bias is playing a big part in its choices.

Here's an example.

In June 2023, I – like 30 million other Brits – read about the final resignation of the ex-Prime Minister Boris Johnson. The Parliamentary Committee on Privileges (basically the UK's parliamentary police – staffed by MPs and set up to deal with standards in public life) confirmed that Johnson had repeatedly misled MPs about attending lockdown parties at 10 Downing Street during COVID.

He'd resigned before they announced their findings, having already read it. The report said he – and his staff – had partied all the way through the pandemic. The committee imposed a record-breaking 90-day suspension and took away his Parliamentary pass.

That's the heaviest penalty handed down to a British Prime Minister for lying to his own government, ever.

And that would normally stir up a firestorm of coverage for days; critics of Boris on one side, the committee's top brass on the other, and a denial from him.

One news app, above all, should have been across this and getting it right. It relies on its reputation for neutrality. The app was sadly my old employer, BBC News. I don't know who was running their online news that day, but this should have never happened.

Here were their all-important top three stories just a day or so after Johnson made his exit:

1. Cabinet minister and Johnson ally Grant Schapps says that we all want to move on from Boris Johnson and 'partygate', so we should just stop talking about it.
2. Three British people are missing after a boat fire in Egypt.
3. Cabinet minister and Johnson super-ally Jacob Rees-Mogg demands that Conservatives should not block Boris Johnson's

return to frontline politics.

Two out of 3 of those crucial top stories – all morning – were fiercely pro-Boris Johnson, spoken by supporters of the disgraced PM. There were no other voices or comments from critics, nobody from the Parliamentary panel, all supportive coverage very quickly after the heaviest penalty handed to any former Prime Minister. On the other, more traditionally right-wing channels, you had to scroll down a long, long way to find the story at all. They'd all pushed it way down the running order.

The Invisible Line – crossed.

I'd like to think that it was more by accident than design, but my hopes aren't high. If you'd read these stories in that order, you'd think that Boris Johnson had been terribly mistreated.

So, do watch out for that … story choice and story order can be very subtle signs of bias in all types of media, but particularly in broadcasting (and their digital channels) where they're less likely to run salacious headlines and language.

In this case, it came across as either a strong sign of bias in the news feed, or a major mistake.

IT'S A STEP TO THE LEFT AND THEN A LEAP TO THE RIGHT

Okay, let's move up a gear and get political.

In the news, what does left- and right-wing really mean?

Well firstly, the ideas of 'left-wing' and 'right-wing' politics date back to the French Revolution. On the left were the revolutionaries – focused on the good of the many, change, equality. On the right was the establishment – defending the status quo, personal gain and the existing hierarchy.

Today, the left will be about the vulnerable, the working class, using tax money to rebalance wealth and build public infrastructure. The right will normally be big business, small government, cutting international funding and nationalism. They're also more prone to populism – which we'll define and take to pieces shortly.

Of course, wherever you are in the world, you'll experience a particular ideological stance in the information you see, hear and read – whether that's through friends on social media, or the professional news mongers of the mass media.

So, let's introduce a table of centrist, left- and right-wing news outlets. I've limited this list to the US and UK, but you'll be able to map out your own – and it's a very useful thing to do, to see where news operations stand where you are.

You might disagree with some of the placings here, and you might want to move a few of these names slightly to the left or the right. Of course, go ahead. But it's an independent guide built on a range of reliable sources including their self-styled position and organisations including Business Insider and the Pew Research Center.

LEFT-WING	CENTRE-L	CENTRE	CENTRE-R	RIGHT-WING
CNN Opinion	CNN	PA Media News	The Washington Times	Fox News
The Daily Beast Opinion	CBS News	Associated Press	Washington Examiner	Fox Opinion
The Nation	HuffPost	Bloomberg	The Financial Times	Breitbart News
The New Yorker	The Guardian	Reuters USA Today	The Times	Daily Mail
The Socialist Worker	The New European	The Wall Street Journal	Forbes	The Telegraph
	BuzzFeed News	The Hill	BBC Radio 4	Mail on Sunday
	Private Eye	The i	Sky News	New York Post
	The Atlantic	The Sunday Times	The Washington Post	Newsmax
	The Economist	ITV News		The Daily Wire
	Politico	Channel 4 News		Info Wars
	CBS Radio News	BBC Radio 5 Live		The Blaze
	New York Times	BBC World Service		Sean Hannity
	The Mirror	Vox		GB News
	MSNBC	PBS News		

How does this help us?

Well, when you know the broad ideology or agenda of your

favourite news source, you can understand where they're coming from in real time, and quickly see how you're being steered. Perhaps even manipulated.

The same applies to social media, although there it's about the message because there are billions of potentially biased, or fake, messengers.

But for news media, this can help all of us to cut bias out of our information diet purely because we'll know what sort of stories these organisations will – and won't – run based on their agendas.

WHEN IS NEWS NOT NEWS?

Some channels clearly stretch the definition of 'news' to their limits, filled with opinion and ideology as they are.

In the UK, the media regulator OFCOM says that channels have to show 'due impartiality' – which is a loose definition of what kind of bias is allowed. Basically, there's supposed to be genuine balance in reporting, but it all depends on the context of what audiences are likely to expect. If the audience expects to hear right- or left-wing opinion, it's allowed.

I would certainly question whether that's news or not, but it gives those channels enough rope to get away with it.

In the US, it's about balance of opinion and something that they call deliberate 'news distortion'. When Fox News had to pay nearly $800m to Dominion Voting Systems in 2023, they acknowledged *"certain claims about Dominion to be false"*. So, it can happen.

But the chart of news outlets will be very useful in the fight against mis- and dis-information, later.

Also, I'm going to start recommending steps that we can all get behind to stop the flow of false information. The first of those recommendations will deal with political coverage. That's coming soon.

WHAT IF I GET MY NEWS FROM SOCIAL MEDIA?

Look, it's so clear that most of our misinformation problem – and a lot of disinformation – comes from our news feeds on social media.

But the shift over to social has been dramatic.

Here's a great (but quite detailed) study of how we get our news – including the ideological splits and trends – carried out by the Reuters Institute and the University of Oxford in 2022: www.reutersinstitute.politics.ox.ac.uk/digital-news-report/2022/dnr-executive-summary

This study shows that yes – there's been a real disengagement from conventional, professional news over the last few years. Around one-third of all people surveyed now get their news from social media. Still, two-thirds do still watch TV, radio or take news from traditional newsrooms.

What is good is that – outside of specific communities with far-out beliefs – the main social media channels do have a really even overall split in terms of the views people hold. Left, right, middle, conspiracy, non-conspiracy – all are available.

We just have to be very careful about the views that we share, if we're going to resist being part of the misinformation problem. And as we've seen throughout our time together, there are very simple steps that we can all take.

So, how do we strike a balance on our timelines, when nothing really seems true – especially after channels including X and Meta stopped using reliable, independent fact checkers to keep our heads straight?

First, we need to look out for bias in real time – whoever's spreading it.

Next, we stop, step back from and sidestep that dodgy, one-sided content, giving our thinking human brain a chance.

Third, we fool the algorithm.

We know that algorithms throw our news feed completely off balance as soon as we click on one type of story over another. But it's very easy to reverse the influence of the algorithms – if we want to stay in touch with the facts.

When we look at the news from another side, search for other opinions or news sources across the political right or left, for just a minute, something changes. Balancing our behaviours and listening to the other side keeps the algorithms guessing, which changes the tone of your feed and is an excellent way to combat bias.

And there's more hope. Away from mass media, who has the most influence right now?

Let's just mention 15 of the big players of the mid 2020s – in no particular order:

Cristiano Ronaldo, Taylor Swift, Kylie Jenner, Beyoncé, Leo Messi, Selena Gomez, Justin Bieber, Virat Kohli, Huda Kattan, Khaby Lane, Dwayne Johnson, Katie Perry, Cole Sprouse, Ariana Grande and Zoe Sugg.

You'll notice that most of those guys avoid politics, conspiracy beliefs or controversy altogether. So, there are plenty of safe places to go on social media. We just have to tune out the extremes.

In terms of disinformation – the intentional stuff – we can see that national newspapers and websites with political ties are the masters.

It's our choice whether we want to be radicalised by social media, even though it can be really difficult to step away from.

So, we owe it to ourselves, our friends, neighbours and workmates to take a wider view of the news. Don't trust one source or individual opinion. Try to sidestep extreme views, with your emotional reaction as your guide. Anyone who can vary their information diet has a greater chance of being safe from the worst extremes that social media – and the mass media – has to offer.

Of course, anyone who's happy to accept stories that are clearly biased will probably just continue living in their comfort zone.

That's their choice too.

But the rest of us can do better.

6. THE POPULIST PLAYBOOK

In the next chapter, we'll really go to town with some examples of how information can be weaponised by people who use it to get ahead. For now, let's tackle the loudmouthed elephant in the room for millions of us.

Populism.

Populism is a very big deal. I think it's a lot bigger than we give it credit for. It's taking over as the way lots of leaders convince us to do what they want. It swept Europe before the second world war (and in many ways, caused it), and it's back – taking centre stage in the mid 2010s in the US, across Europe and central America. News (well, politics) reporters talk about it all the time, but has anyone actually defined it for you? Words like this can easily sneak into our subconscious unless we know what we're dealing with, and what it means to us all.

So, here it is, according to the Collins English Dictionary:

'Populism refers to political activities or ideas that claim to promote the interests and opinions of ordinary people.'

I think it's even bigger than that.

We're living in an age of populism – just like in the early part of the last century before fascism and communism arrived in the west.

And I believe that we should be worried about populism

in the same way as we should be about far-right (and far-left) ideologies designed to divide us.

Populism is the glue between the extremes; when someone uses fake stories to gain power through our outrage, their side of politics is irrelevant. Their use of manipulation is everything. Once enough people take sides, anything that leader says will sound true.

And there's one word in the Collins definition that we should pick out. Claim. Populist politicians (and other power-seekers) claim that what they do is for the us – that our needs come first – and their needs come second. That's why they pop up all over the place in tough times - and make themselves incredibly popular. They convince us that they care, that they have the power to change things. That they'll break the rules and structures that have made us feel this way. They use fear to scare us, hate to blame someone else, and confidence, jokes, jibes and entertainment to sugar coat their image.

And sure - every politician says that they care, don't they?

That should be a good thing.

What pushes these people into populism - and sometimes dictatorship - is that they weaponise disinformation to build a really hard-right (or sometimes hard-left) army of fans, and strip down the standards of free speech to let that army attack the other side.

And I think most of us can agree on one thing (unless you actually are best friends with a populist): these loud, extreme and entertaining people aren't in it for us, they just make us think they are so they can get what they want.

But how can we spot it in action, right here, right now? This 2nd Edition is coming at you from a time where the temperature is changing, so as ever we need to turn the emotions back on the people who drag us away from the truth.

So, here is the populist playbook. Use it wisely!

1. Step one - make wild claims, create fear and new threats. We already know that fear activates our chimp brains where we feel first, and think second. But it also appeals to our dark, secret core beliefs about 'other people', 'elites' or a threat to 'our way of life'.

2. Next, defend those scary ideas using a simple grain of truth. The best lies are built on something plausible – often a core belief about something like immigration, 'woke', inclusion, equal rights. Use free speech as a defence.

3. Ramp up the attention. The more extreme, the more loyal the far-out fan base. Claim that you've been a victim, because many of us feel that way too. And the mass media will help if it means higher sales and ad revenue.

4. Say that the system is rotten and needs to be rebuilt. Hey – every system needs improving. But populists will insist that it can only be rebuilt by them, and it'll slap the 'guilty people' hard in the process.

5. Ask simple-sounding questions. Things like: 'did the last government actually cut immigration?' That's always an easy one, focused on injustice and a sense of right and wrong for people like 'us'. The best way to disarm that is to ask a populist 'Okay, what will you do to help us?

6. Attack, never back down, deny you're doing anything wrong and move to the next issue before anyone catches you out … basically, just keep coming up with new wedge issues.

7. Finally, and this is really important - use humour, jokes and project confidence to sugar-coats the dark claims they're making. You'll need a great caricature to deliver a wedge issue.

It's intentional, and it rattles the core beliefs that silently exist in every society until we feel poor, under pressure and disenfranchised enough to fight back under the populist's banner. Now, we're in a chapter about social and mass media, so how does the populist playbook show itself in our news?

> Channels on their side of the divide will repeat the scary stories to create a strong emotional and often defensive response from readers, viewers and followers.
> It hooks us in, so we come back for more and give the more extreme channels more ad revenue.
> Other channels – often run by friends – will run their own versions of the story and surround us with questions.
> Social media spreads the word among our nearest and dearest.
> Views divide.
> In an election year, passions rise and the vote splits.

And that's where we head towards polarisation, which is where extreme beliefs take us. You'll have your own thoughts about this and might be living in a place where this is happening right now. I am, as I write this.

And if so, do add your own thoughts to your toolkit. Later, we'll look at how to break down those divides. For now, let's talk about…

7. THE RISE OF POLARISATION

This P word is, sadly, the direct result of false information spread far and wide on social – and the mass – media.

Polarisation is, '*A sharp division, as of a population or group, into opposing factions*', according to the Collins Dictionary.

Conspiracy theories, extreme ideologies – and the beliefs they create – are all about creating polarisation, division, 'them against us', and explaining the hidden 'truth' behind a big secret. For anyone who wants to control us, first you need to divide us.

Then, you can step in and rule.

When we stop talking to each other, they win.

And that's what's been happening in the biggest – and smallest – countries in the world since around 2010.

Have you ever wondered why some leaders align themselves with conspiracy believers despite previously having nothing to do with them? It's a perfect way to gain a following, if you don't mind twisting people's heartfelt beliefs.

I thought it would be useful to have a look at a couple of different types of polarisation. It can explain a lot about the way our world looks:

> Binary division – this is the splitting of views for and against an issue. This works really well in two-party politics.

> Affective polarisation – this is a really interesting one. It's the tendency for people on each side of an argument to view their opponents negatively in other ways, because of their core binary belief. Basically, 'They're a bad person because they believe something that I don't.' This is a huge part of the problem with partisan politics in the US, and increasingly across the world.

So, we can add to the populist playbook: label the other side as bad, polarise views by reducing arguments to simple slogans on major issues. Then, draw the battle lines between you and 'them'.

It can also help to play the 'victim card' – to say you've been unfairly treated – so that others who've been unfairly treated get behind your cause.

What happens then?

We fight amongst ourselves.

The doubt and distraction divide us down ideological lines. And when we fight amongst ourselves, we focus on areas that the creator of the argument wants us to, rather than looking at real problems that they might be creating. There are lots of good articles and academic studies on polarisation. It's really fascinating, although many of us are seeing this firsthand, aren't we?

But here are a few links to look at:

1.   From PNAS (Proceedings of the National Academy of Sciences): www.pnas.org/doi/10.1073/pnas.2207159119
2.   And from Berkeley: www.belonging.berkeley.edu/democracy-belonging-forum/polarisation-distraction
3.   Finally, a third from Annual Reviews, a resource of multi-disciplinary articles: www.annualreviews.org/doi/10.1146/annurev-polisci-051117-073034

And the perfect Petri dish for polarisation is social media, boosted by news coverage. When the division works really well, you might even end up with an almost perfect split in the next big vote – 52% vs 48%.

And I think that, any time we see a 52-48 vote as we have since the mid-2010s, we can rightly suspect that it was socially engineered by a potent mix of populist politics and good old mass media storytelling.

We'll talk more about this, and what it's showing about new ideas of reality, in Chapter 9.

8. PEAK POLITICS

So, where does that bring us?

Well, when it comes to the divisions between us – especially when we're bashed over the head with political chit-chat - we should all expect better from the news business, our leaders and social media feeds.

Here's a recommendation to my old friends in the news

business.

Now, in a time when the strongmen leaders of the world put a pin in the map and claim their favourite countries … in a time when people are turning away from the news and getting their information from TikTok and other social channels … what could every genuine, unbiased news channel do right now to bring back frustrated audiences – desperate for the truth?

They could swap out one thing in their running orders to make the news more relevant and less divisive: politics and the populists.

**For the most part, politics isn't news.
It's gossip for news junkies.**

In its need to fill the schedule, 24-hour rolling news has pushed politics to the top of the running order, rarely cross-examining politicians of their favourite flag. That's how populism became such a big deal. And so much of that coverage is about what a politician has said, not what they've done. As this book hits phones, tablets and bookshelves, it's Trump o'clock on every news app, at the top of every hour.

But, 'he said, she said, they said' political coverage is always a poor excuse for a news story. And we need better stories.

Simply, we've reached peak politics.

I don't know about you, but I used to enjoy it when political chit-chat was just one story in the mix. A bit of intrigue, a chance to take a side and have a view. But when you can't get full answers to fair questions, all that we're being fed is party political PR. And if you parrot the rantings of an extremist, you're also spreading the infection.

So, what can we do about it?

> In terms of politics in the news, we could ask our broadcasters

to halve the number of stories and rolling coverage right now.

> We should label opinion and party-political analysis. That's easy, and only takes a quick challenge of political guests, whatever flag they fly.

> We could focus on real-world stories rather than political punch-ups and stop inviting politicians to talk about issues that an expert could explain.

> And when we do need to cover politics, we could shift coverage to what's being done, not simply what's being said.

> We won't change the minds of newspaper owners and news websites, so it's probably about TV and radio channels for now, because they have charters and rules to follow.

What else could we put in its place?

How about stuff that actually makes a positive difference to our lives? The actions taken by those people in power to help us or harm us would be a start – governance instead of politics. It's not as exciting as political infighting, but it's a small price to pay for good information. And of course, we've had years of domestic and international politics which has genuinely shaken our world, so that does need to be covered and balanced by good journalists.

But what if we could learn more from the news? Maybe it's about scrolling to stories about national security, welfare, understanding new laws, housing, health, crime, human rights, international relations and world affairs, investigations of bad behaviour and damaging policies. Those are all news. That's why we vote politicians into power (if you're in a democracy) and that's what affects us. And look, politics can be expertly handled by some of the excellent politics programmes and podcasts out there if you're looking for a fix. I'm an avid listener to the hugely insightful British podcast *The Rest is Politics* with Alastair Campbell and Rory Stewart. They give us firsthand information, label their opinions as opinions, and challenge people in power when they make stupid decisions and say stupid things. Broadcasters face stricter rules around news, but it's wrong to hide behind those if we're not getting an accurate view of the facts.

And there's one set of stories that we should always hear about, in full, so that political disinformation is never given a free ride:

The abuse of political power, bad decision-making, misuse of taxpayers' money and corruption should always be reported on time and be protected by law so that no-one can misreport the facts, or avoid accurate coverage.

Hey, look – I am a news junkie. I do enjoy a bit of political chit-chat. But in the age of opinion, we deserve better. And if all we're given is party political PR, then that's a big part of our disinformation problem.

Okay, that'll make a few people quite annoyed. So, while I'm on a roll…

9. NO NEWS IS GOOD NEWS

I've worked with some amazing, talented and professional people in news. Those dedicated professionals keep pounding the streets to bring us information that we need.

But here's one tiny addition to the last few sections.

Sometimes, whatever we watch and read, it's healthy to 'stop and step back' from the news.

Our great big ape brains haven't yet evolved to deal with, let alone decipher and evaluate the volume of information that we receive. So, an attention break is one of the most positive things that we can do.

Smaller, less frequent exposure to bad news is a powerful way to pause, reset and regain the perspective that we would all have naturally without it.

We'll start the next chapter with some examples of people who've fought for the truth. Great communicators who've cared about giving us information that makes a difference.

And it's true that there is really good news. Once we apply all of these insights to our own lives, we can choose the information that we're exposed to. That, in turn, will give us the distance we need to decide which information is healthy to share with our loved ones.

Of course, no chapter called The Good, The Bad and The Ugly can be all good. But we'll get to that.

For now, let's wrap up this chapter with another toolkit summary.

10. CHAPTER 4 – THE TOOLKIT

- The mainstream news is where many world stories were originally reported.
- But it isn't one, single, homogenous entity. It's an ultra-competitive set of newsrooms trying to report first and grab our attention.
- That's why sensationalist and politically biased coverage can make it through to newspapers, TV and radio.
- The news that reaches us on social media is sadly even further away from the facts. By the time it hits our timelines, it's become opinions of opinions of reporting of the facts.
- The owners of many mass media newsrooms do exert a strong influence on which stories run. So, don't believe everything you see, hear or read. There's always a strong likelihood that it's been influenced from the top.
- Whether we're watching the news or content on social media, we have a choice about what to believe.
- Extreme views, far-out beliefs and fake news stories are easy

to spot if you activate your sniff test and hold back a little belief.

- You can also apply the 5Ws and an H, and watch out for language that triggers your emotions.
- Watch out for populism. It's manipulation, and a lot of the characters we see at the top of power are populists – mainly on the far-right, but sometimes on the far-left too.
- We've reached peak politics, and the populists work hard to create new threats and distract us from the facts.
- When reporting shows signs of bias it's not news. It's storytelling. Step away and crosscheck the coverage.
- And take a break from the news when possible. Stop, step back and sidestep bad news when you can.

WHAT CAN YOU ADD TO THE CONVERSATION?

You'll have your own views too.

As always, we can only have healthier conversations about contentious things if we separate the facts from the fiction. So, please do add your own tools to the kit.

It's not about accusing one channel, individual or platform of extreme bias. It's about being aware of it so that you can extract the facts and reject the opinions that they're wrapped in.

LINDLEY GOODEN

5

THE GOOD, THE BAD AND THE UGLY

LINDLEY GOODEN

5

*'Power-lust is a weed that grows only in the vacant lots
of an abandoned mind.'*

AYN RAND,
Atlas Shrugged

Let's start our fifth chapter by looking at some of the people who do information well. They care, and they show it.

Of course, we also need to look at some of the people who've thrown the populist playbook at us to get their way, and how some of the figures that we've elevated to the top did it by weaponising disinformation and denial.

But first, let's remind ourselves of the study that showed us how false information spreads.

1. GOOD=BAD, BAD=GOOD

The MIT study that I mentioned in Chapter 1 showed clearly how far and fast fake news stories spread compared to real stories on social media. That's even before the evolution of current algorithms or the removal of fact checking on the biggest networks. It's very relevant to what we're about to see.

Just to remind you, the researchers looked into the nature of 'news' on *X* (when it was still called *Twitter*).

They found that:

> Users spread false news and information much faster than real news – 70% more quickly in fact.
> Re-sharing posts was the main reason that it spread.
> It took six times as long for a genuine story to reach other users than the fake version.

So, when it comes to information sharing, you could say that genuine news is bad and bad news is good.

That effect can be even more extreme in certain closed groups – like the ones on Facebook that are self-moderated by the believers-in-chief.

Of course, it all means that malicious, intentional fake news creators are rewarded for making up stories that mislead us. As we know, all they need to do is shock, scare, surprise and make us more emotional, and leave it up to us to do the rest.

It'll be happening wherever you and I scroll, today.

So, without real guardrails and regulations to protect us, the only thing that's stopping them is their conscience. Of course, if any of the channel owners have one.

But as someone who's run a business for a couple of decades, helping large organisations to tell their stories with creativity, confidence, and a commitment to facts, it's always possible. We need to tell genuine stories in a way that people can trust, love and learn from.

There is always hope. And that leads us to the ambassadors of truth.

2. THE GOOD

There are examples of great information, properly researched, popular, reliable, communicated with passion and authority. And when it is, we still respond well and fight for what's right by sharing it. It just takes a little more thought and effort than making us scared.

So, let's have a look at a few short examples from the US, UK and Europe of important information that's done well.

These four examples are the exceptions that disprove the rule – that with a little more effort, knowledge and passion for the subject – information can be used for good.

THE GOOD: PART 1
CONSUMER CHAMPIONS

A consumer champion in the UK who's made a hugely successful career out of spreading good information is Martin Lewis.

If you're not aware of Martin, he founded a company called Money Saving Expert (moneysavingexpert.com) in the 2000s, which for many years has done exactly what it says in the title. Martin offers up to the minute advice on how to save money in nearly all aspects of life. He's spent more than 20 years on TV and radio, and made a hugely successful business by offering good information.

When I trained a team of top consumer champions in the UK during the financial crash of 2007-8, it was Martin that they all wanted to beat.

But even now during the cost-of-living crisis, and even when there's been no option but to pay the hugely inflated bills that we face today, Martin keeps fighting for consumer rights by unearthing savings and appearing on the national media in the UK.

I interviewed Martin a number of times when I was a consumer correspondent, and I can tell you that he's as passionate – and obsessed – with finding deals in his own life as he is on TV, radio and online. And that's what cuts through to his audience.

What has Martin done well with real information?

> He's been passionate.
> He's been clear.
> Martin is always relevant and up to date with his advice.
> He's accurate and truthful.
> And he's challenged companies that are harming us, by offering us alternatives.

Simple.

The lesson here is that Martin hasn't needed to use disinformation because he's generated trust by genuinely helping people and by backing up his statements with clear, demystified facts. How good is that?

And it's definitely something that we all have the right to expect from all of our information-mongers.

It's probably also why he was one of the first prominent people to be targeted in mid-2023 by a disinformation deepfake video.

He denied that the video was by him the day after I heard about it … and how did I know that it was a fake?

> He would never say what the avatar did in the video (about something to do with a business deal).
> His face, mouth and eyes moved in ways that didn't quite follow his words and mannerisms.
> And even if the latest deepfakes could have reduced those technical tells, the context of what he would advertise would always point us to the truth.

So, those are an introduction to my deepfake test, which I'll reveal in Chapter 8.

THE GOOD: PART 2
CLIMATE ADVOCATES

There are so many strong climate advocates in the world now. You might think of Greta Thunberg (the campaigner), Kate Raworth (Author of Donut Economics) or Chris Packham (British environmentalist and TV presenter). And sure, it's been a hard job because we're so attached to our creature comforts. Plus, there's been so much disinformation since the 1980s from anti-environment bodies, lobby groups and big businesses, not to mention senators, congresspeople, ministers and MPs.

But there's one person who – through communication, clarity and a lifetime spent at the top of wildlife programming – has done more to raise our attention to climate change than any other. That person is Sir David Attenborough.

The shows that he's presented have shocked, entertained, struck us with awe and slowed the world's descent into the hot mess we now face. And yes, he's been supported by the world's finest production people, but he's always:

> Communicated with a unique clarity about the beauty of nature and the dangers humans pose to the environment.
> Demonstrated dignity and care for the subjects he's spoken about.
> He's devoted himself to natural history and the fight for species survival.
> And he is loved. Really loved. That human touch has been so important in our attachment to his work.

Sir David is a truly unique broadcaster, who's managed to communicate complex and challenging scientific subjects with grace and grandeur. And if you're reading this years from now, I'm sure that that will still be true, long after he goes to the *Blue Planet* in the sky.

THE GOOD: PART 3
JOURNALISTS WHO RISK EVERYTHING

For all the bad news that we spoke about in the last chapter, here's an example of the exact opposite.

Being a reporter of war and conflict can be the most dangerous reporting of all. But doing it in another country, far from home is nothing like doing it where you grow up and live, where your family lives and where everything could be taken away if you expose the crimes around you.

Veronica Guerin became a household name in the mid-1990s, putting her life in continuous danger by investigating Dublin's drug barons for Ireland's biggest newspaper the *Sunday Independent*.

She'd previously worked in a variety of jobs but became absolutely dedicated to defending people's right to know, no matter what it meant for her. In June 1996, just two years after she began exposing the gangs, she was murdered by gunmen as she waited at a traffic light in her car.

She:

> Fought for people's right to have access to the facts.
> Became a relentless, one-woman defence of Irish lives.
> She did it all in her home city, risking her life every day.
> And she didn't allow fear to silence her or allow false information to spread.
> Her reporting had a direct, positive impact on her world.
> After her death, police began a crackdown on organised crime in Dublin, and more than 150 people were arrested as

a result of her work.

That's a true guardian of good information.

THE GOOD: PART 4
MUSIC TO OUR EARS

Taylor Swift.

You may have heard of her.

She's done something that no-one else really has. She's made voting something that young people (and older fans too) want to do, without taking one side or the other and without bashing a single ideological Bible. And that's amazing.

In September 2023, she put out a single Instagram post thanking fans for coming to her US shows, and for raising their voices. Then she said, 'Make sure you're ready to use them in our elections this year!', with a link to vote.org. How simple is that?

And when Taylor speaks, her fans act. Swiftly.

The number of 18-year-olds who registered at the US National Voter Registration Day doubled.

That Insta fired up the critics, and she's been the target of a lot of Republican criticism after she backed Kamala Harris for US President in 2024, but hey – she's encouraged young voters to use their voice. That's great, whichever side of politics you prefer.

The job now is to make sure they have good information to go with it.

3. LIAR, LIAR, PANTS ON FIRE

Let's look again – now with a growing arsenal of tools and tricks – at the people who we vote into power, believe online, invite into our lives, who've perhaps said whatever it took to get what they wanted from us.

I warned you earlier that we're going to talk about some challenging things. This might be one of those times.

Whatever side you're on, the only thing that counts from here on in is the ability to separate the facts from the fiction.

So, let's throw some terms your way that can help to put a shape on the techniques that people at the top have used against us. A few of these you'll know, a few you may not:

1. *Factals* – my own term for widespread disinformation caused by mixing genuine facts with fake stories. The grain of truth on a viral scale.
2. *Viral sloganeering* – using short slogans on social media and in the press to hammer home a point e.g. '*Build the wall*', '*Get Brexit done*'.
3. *Clickbait* – it's an old term now for outrageous and sensationalist headlines that drive clicks.
4. *Imposter content* – this is where genuine news sources are impersonated by false stories to make disinformation look authentic.
5. And it's worth mentioning *halo errors* (the halo effect) again. This is the effect where we think positively about someone when we like a related personal trait (perhaps their charisma, humour or confidence).

It would be great if we could take the lessons from Chapter 2 to heart and didn't get too hot under the collar, but if you're convinced that outrage is always the answer, you might find that tough.

Still, let's always try to observe our inner chimp when it's having a moment, so that our grown-up human brains can step in. Now, let's name names. Here are some recent examples of leading politicians taking the terms that I've just mentioned to heart.

4. THE BAD

It's time to take our divisions out for a ride.

You'll have your own views here, which is great. But we need to take a look at a few of the most divisive figures in recent public life (focusing for now on the UK and US – you'll have your own).

Let's look at the things they've said and done, and how their ideas and ideologies have been covered in the news.

There are so many examples of good communication based on fact. People who've stood their ground and fought for truth across their entire careers. There are some, for example the French organisations Reporters Without Borders and Forbidden Stories, who are fighting deep corruption at great personal risk. So how can we – with their help – turn the conversation around and make disinformation a truly filthy word across the board?

I can hardly believe that I'm saying it, but it's going to be very difficult. We are well beyond the tipping point.

The spread of the tech oligarchs and the nationalist leaders hungry for new territory, from Vladimir Putin's Russia to the 'Art of The Deal'-style threats to Greenland and Canada from Donald Trump.

Throughout history, the elite, the rich and the connected have carved up the world, and it's no different today.

However, there is one way that we can change coverage and destructive content.

We can vote with our feet and fingers.

If we stop reading and sharing mis- and dis-information, we'll make it too expensive and unpopular to create. And we'll reduce the audiences for the guys at the top who only succeed when we believe.

So, who are these people?

Who's really pushed aside the facts to make our world a less trustworthy place?

It's time to get real.

5. THE POPULISTS

Earlier, we defined populism.

Here it is again, according to the Collins English Dictionary: *'Populism refers to political activities or ideas that claim to promote the interests and opinions of ordinary people.'*

And I came off the fence to say that populist politicians might claim that they're doing everything for us, but probably just want to elevate their own interests. In fact, some of them become the glue that makes extreme right or left-wing politics meet in the middle, to create dictatorships through national hysteria. It's the manipulation that makes tyranny possible.

Those power-hungry characters spend a lot of time and money discovering 'wedge issues' – the underlying gripes that could pull us apart – so that they can deprive us and blame others.

It's happening across the west as this book hits the shelves, with far-right politics dominating our conversations while these leaders carve the world into regional dominions.

I've weighed up the pros and cons of pointing to people in power over the last few years. But it's the only way to show the impact that disinformation has on us when it comes from our 'leaders'. And by default – because they've been in power over the last few years – the four examples are on the right of politics. If you have someone more left-wing in mind, by all means apply the same logic to them.

Remember, they need to claim that they have our interests at heart. If they actually do campaign for better conditions for most people, then they're just doing their job.

But let's start small, with a politician who rose to power in the early 2020s – to be a right-wing mascot of the Conservative Party in the UK – and a candidate for Prime Minister.

With all of the characters I'm about to remind you of, one thing matters above all: the way they've useed information to get what they want.

Let's talk about how the populists work.

SUELLA BRAVERMAN

Let's start here. And if you're not British this name might be new to you, although her methods might be all too familiar.

Suella Braverman spent her time as the British Home Secretary by trying to push through policies to remove immigrants from the UK.

She'd never quite managed to push through every point in the populist playbook, but she certainly tried.

She spent a lot of her time firing up the core beliefs of the furthest-right fringes of the Conservative Party, accusing homeless people of making a 'lifestyle choice' to be on the street. She called people who marched peacefully for a ceasefire in the Israel-Hamas war 'hate marchers'. She coined the phrase 'Guardian-reading tofu-eating wokerati' to describe social justice activists. She even publicly accused her own police in London of being pro-Palestine (which we can only assume meant anti-Israel).

Bizarre, but effective.

Every time she came out with one of these statements, she grabbed the headlines, shook and shocked and had her fans cheering from the fringes. That's point 3 of the populist playbook by the way.

But even as the London-born daughter of Indian parents, it was immigrants who incurred her greatest derision.

Among the thousands of hard, anti-immigration stories

pouring into the news after Brexit, one in late 2022 stood out. The Home Secretary was fighting for the policy, later ruled illegal, to fly asylum seekers arriving in the UK to Rwanda in Africa. She told the Conservative Party conference that it was her "dream" and "obsession" to see that first flight take off, and to see it on the front of The Telegraph newspaper. The Conservative government spent many more months trying to push through the policy despite the unbelievable cost and bizarre debates around it.

By most standards, this is a cruel and unusual policy. Probably why her critics called her 'Cruella'. But the populist playbook works: create a threat that taps into fear and core beliefs (immigration), say that you're the only one who can fix it (send them to Rwanda), shout, deny any wrongdoing, divide and rule before moving to another issue before your fans catch up with the facts.

Perhaps she's waiting in the wings right now for a grand return. But she has competition.

Let's move onto a man who I left out of the 1st Edition of The Future of Truth (and How to Get There). This wealthy, former commodities money man with a taste for hard-right ideas, has earned his place among The Populists.

NIGEL FARAGE

The jovial, hard-right British nationalist with a French-Luxembourg name, who married a German, became a member of the European Parliament but hates Europe.

Normally, referring to someone's family background would be a no-no. But let's not be too 'woke', huh? In Nigel's case, it's directly relevant to the views he delivered to the UK using a string of political parties that dragged Britain to the right, caused Brexit and made extreme anti-immigration policies mainstream.

He's also presented lots of radio and TV, just to top up his MPs salary – and incidentally, his European Union pension, too.

His ideas aren't new. They're old. We've seen them throughout history, in the 1100s, in the 1930s, and all over our news feeds since the 2010s.

What Farage is very good at, is the sugar-coating.

The media bit.

In the pub with a pint, on British news panel shows more than any other guest (The BBC's Question Time), in Trump Tower with Elon. He made a political career out of scary claims about immigration - with a smile. He denied encouraging anti-immigration riots - with a smile. He asked simple-sounding questions about immigrants – with a smile. And he sugar-coats it all by laughing heartily on camera, claiming to be the victim when people question what he says, and convincing millions that he's telling the truth.

And let's not forget, this Tweed-wearing metals broker with a Coutts bank account is as quintessential a British toff as any other person in right-wing politics. In case you're in any doubt, they are the elites that they claim to be fighting.

Next, someone who's faded from view but will be hard to forget.

BORIS JOHNSON

Already it feels like ancient history that disgraced former Prime Minister Boris Johnson would feature at the top of news bulletins, wibbling-and-wobbling his verbal incantations toward anyone with a mic. But that's why we need to remember Britain's most populist and suspect 21st century PM.

People in the UK fell in love with the idea of 'Boris'.

They hated being told that he'd done anything wrong, because he'd successfully built up an image that looked like – and sounded exactly like - a harmless, eccentric British aristocrat.

That gave him a lot of latitude. He was one of the first MPs to be publicly known by his first name. His – perhaps accidental, probably carefully planned – popular appeal leant heavily on the character he'd created. Good-for-a-laugh, comical, bumbling, messy, but claiming to have his heart in the right place. Many people still think that, despite what he was caught doing.

He let his unkempt caricature do the heavy lifting.

And when the UK Parliament's House of Commons Privileges Committee (the panel of MPs set up to investigate rule-breaking) reported back on the many rowdy secret parties held at Downing Street during the COVID pandemic that he'd denied, his fans were furious.

Six days after he quit in June 2023, the 'partygate' report found that Johnson had intentionally misled Parliament, denying again and again that he knew anything about the string of boozy get togethers that led to more than 100 fines for his staff. It made the seat of power, 10 Downing Street, the most fined address in the whole of the UK. By that time, Boris had quit – having read the report a week earlier - and left by the back exit.

This already qualifies as 'the bad'. But once the flood gates and investigations opened, news appeared of an £800K loan provided by undeclared backers. There were documentaries into his opaque connections with the Lebedevs. His extraordinary exit had thrown up a catalogue of questions about his career and character, which of course he denied.

So, before we consign this British Prime Minister to history, can we pin down how Britain's most populist PM – and his allies – had so many people fooled?

> Well, it was all personality politics. People attached lots of positive traits to Johnson because of that caricature. They

cited Johnson's charisma as a reason to back him because that was still worth a lot of votes, whether he was on the level or not. That attachment to other traits is most definitely 'the halo effect'.

> Factals – he was proven repeatedly to combine facts and fiction to tell a good story. And we know how that works.

> He repeatedly denied, lied and showed a lack of contrition, until the facts become impossible to ignore. This is probably his greatest defence against the truth until that final Parliamentary report.

> And look, he was somehow 'one of us'. His status made him someone important. Eton College, Oxford University, The Times, The Telegraph, The Conservative Party, Mayor of London, Foreign Secretary, Prime Minister. High status and grand allies from entrance to exit. Any questions?

> Of the people, for the people. Despite all of that privilege, his messy, harmless, bumbling caricature did the hard work to convince people that he was a genuine, caring man of the people.

And what else do we know about populists?

They need help from friends who'll benefit from their self-promoting plans, which means friends in the mass media to push their agenda to as many minds as possible.

If you remember back in the last chapter, I spoke about The Invisible Line of news agendas – where a story really doesn't exist if it's placed at the end of a news bulletin, programme or app. A story below the line loses out, like fourth place at The Olympics. Well, here's where that example of bias I mentioned – on a public news app that shouldn't have allowed it - happened.

When Boris Johnson quit – before being publicly shamed - only the left-leaning British media went to town on his record. The majority attacked his critics, not him.

Johnson wasn't actually a very good communicator, but his ability to win hearts – over minds - speaks volumes. He'd tapped into an identity that right-leaning Brits could imagine at the top. The fact (told to me by a colleague who'd filmed him more than once) that he ruffled his orderly hair before speaking publicly was all part of it. His eccentric tone spoke louder than words. It was funny. We needed someone honest, someone real. Emotion won, logic died.

Populists do whatever they can to be popular, to rise up the ranks. And Boris won hearts, not minds.

Okay. Let's rebalance, step away and spend a moment with the political leader who's divided the world's most powerful country more than any other.

DONALD J. TRUMP

The story of Donald Trump has proven one thing above all. We should be very careful what we wish for when we vote for a radical populist. When they're convincing enough, they can do almost anything to the world order, or the average Joe.

You'll know as well as the rest of us that, since going into US politics, Donald has been one of the greatest wedge issues in living memory. And in 2024, the biggest election year on the planet, he made his big comeback and won, as the first convicted felon to become US President.

And he immediately turned his feelings about the world into law, breaking down values and protections that the US had built up since the second world war.

Let's be clear. Donald Trump is someone who's never lived in poverty, or had to work at a factory, or a wood mill, understand what it's like to struggle to make ends meet. But for the second time, tens of millions of people – who know exactly what that's like – believed that he was one of them. They believed that he'd fight day and night to make their lives better. His conviction on 34 counts of falsifying business records to hide the payment of $130,000 to the adult film star Stormy Daniels didn't touch the sides.

How?

Voters – wherever we are – believe our political choices define right from wrong. And in Trump's case, just like in 1930s America, the Christian right joined forces with the political right. And he aligned with them. Also, he'd been a star since the 1980s and his name was a byword for big, brash, ruthless business. A success story, despite the company bankruptcies.

But there's something absolutely critical here too. Life after COVID was tough, and it had been that way for most people since the banks crashed in the mid-2000s. So, Trump's 'fight and never back down' message – which drove a truckload of merch after the assassination attempt on him – was exactly what people who were fed up wanted to hear. America needed hope, and they chose a big character with a reputation and a power tan.

It's always been this way in tough times. People's feelings of injustice, fear, anger, suspicion of the establishment and outside threats always drive a move to the right – to nationalism, to aggression against outsiders, to conspiracies. They go for the strongman. When people are under real pressure, they reach for a leader, a messiah, who says they'll fight their corner.

And that's the lesson we need to learn, yet again. This has happened before. It's happened in the US, it's happened across Europe, Africa, the Middle East and Asia. When people suffer, they lurch to self defence (and attack) mode. Emotion wins, logic dies. It's been the same throughout history, and we should be worried when it happens. We may not like the way future generations see us, especially when everything's been recorded on social media this time around.

For now, let's just record Donald's recipe for success:

1. First, reflect the people's pain.
2. Think about who to blame for it. Use classic threats from conspiracies gone by – the deep state, enemies of the people (e.g. China), the FBI, and mix in some new ones: demonic Democrats, immigrants who are eating the cats - and eating the dogs.
3. Turn up the Trump caricature – over-confident, bombastic, sarcastic, successful. The art of the deal, personified.
4. Remember your victories at all times. Deny the failures.
5. Shout, clap, dance, smile, weave, bring the showbiz, and blast out lots of social media to keep tongues wagging.
6. Be the strongman who never backs down from anything, everrr.

In his first term in the White House, Donald fired out more than 11,000 Tweets (before anyone called them Xs). Right into the 2024 election it was about constant content, always loud, always attacking, rarely boring. His posts made so little sense most of the time that I actually trained advanced public speaking clients on the Trump model for a couple of years. The game was: "*If you can deliver this Tweet and make it make sense, you're ready!*" Amazingly, a couple of people actually managed to pull it off! In his second term, it was all about breaking down old international relationships and setting up new ones with the other strongmen and dictators at the top. You could argue he was trying to become the last leader of the free world.

Through his posts, then his new friendships, he made fans laugh and cheer. He gave them what they wanted. Throughout his time in power, his time in court and his return to The White House – more golden and white then ever - his best form of defence was attack. And of course, there is no populist playbook without friends in big media. So, for the second time, it was Trump o'clock on the hour, every hour. If that's stopped when you read this, I'm sure someone else has filled the void.

Sure, he became the first US President ever to have a criminal record for falsifying business records, but none of the dozens of accusations against Donald Trump hurt him. In fact, a piece of research by Monmouth University found that his fan base consistently believed that the 2020 election was stolen from him, right into mid-2023 when the study ended. You can watch that piece of research at 8 minutes into this late-2024 LSE event with Lawrence Lessig: https://www.youtube.com/live/bF6rer0I1FE

Ultimately, it's clear that if you win hearts, you don't need to worry about minds.

Sometimes, the best explanations for all of this come from normal people talking about their loved ones' feelings. A male caller to the British radio station LBC said it best, just before Trump's second inauguration. He'd been talking to his son the weekend before, who told his dad *'Masculinity is really important, dad. The right seem to be the only ones talking about the importance of strength, honour and discipline.'* It's that simple. Authoritarian leaders throughout history have talked about how strong they are. Putin riding a horse without a shirt on, Trump shouting 'fight ' after the assassination attempt in 2024, Kim Jong Un with all the missile tests.

It works. Populists promise that they'll deliver better for us. What they're really doing is sugar coating the things they really want – power, money and control.

Looking clearly at the story of these kinds of politicians is a very important step in our mission. We need to talk about disinformation at - and from - the top.

This is more than just an abstract concept.

It's put over-ambitious and unpalatable people into power for centuries.

Let's hope that history doesn't judge our recent choices too harshly. And yes, I've obviously had to come off the fence to talk about these people without a sugary, crispy coating in the 2nd Edition of The Future of Truth (and How to Get There) because of what's at stake.

We're all good people at heart, but we need to ask these questions so that the people we follow, share and vote for are always held to high standards.

6. THE UGLY

Things get ugly when mis- and dis-information change our hearts, minds and behaviours in the real world.

Chinese national intelligence – the MSS - calls this kind of social engineering cognitive warfare. That's how ugly this kind of manipulation can be.

What begins as a way to change our thinking, can mutate into a genuine threat to democracy, choice, rights and personal safety. Quite honestly, who needs a government conspiracy to control us when we vote for it ourselves?

All we need is a strong, continuous supply of false information and fake news to throw us off balance. So, let's look at some of the uglier results of mis- and dis-information.

Of course, these are my conclusions. It's really healthy if you disagree, because that's the only way we can come together from our different sides of the same arguments, to see the facts clearly again.

BREXIT

How did Brexit really happen?

My main reason for voting to stay in Europe - at the time -

was that I didn't trust what we were being told.

Simple.

My own sniff test told me at the time that we were being fed huge amounts of disinformation where balance should have been. News organisations gave the loud minority an equal stage, which turned a small number of people (those who already hated the European Union) into a very vocal majority at vote time.

Ticking that box didn't make anyone less intelligent than anyone else. But disinformation was everywhere – on TV, radio, on news websites and, importantly, on social media. If you showed an interest, you'd be surrounded by sponsored content supporting the anti-Europe view, particularly in the last day or two.

So, what were the ugly results of the information diet we were fed in the run up to this vote?

Well, let's just check what happened to the UK, against the key claims made at the time:

1. Trade with the EU will be tariff-free and involve minimal bureaucracy. We were left with high import-export tariffs, heavy bureaucracy and lost many of our UK-Europe distributors leading to food and goods shortages.

2. Northern Ireland's border will remain 'absolutely unchanged'. Britain decided to break the Brexit agreement (i.e. to break international law) in 2020 because it wasn't possible to leave the EU without putting a physical border somewhere. After years of negotiation, Northern Ireland now holds a unique advantage of being in the EU and the UK. Business there is, not surprisingly, growing far faster than the rest of the UK.

3. We will end supremacy of EU law and the EU's Court of Justice. EU laws are still in place after a later Prime Minister Rishi Sunak admitted that he couldn't replace laws put in place by the UK and EU.

4. Take back control on immigration and asylum, and cut

migration to the tens of thousands. Immigration from outside the EU is now significantly higher than it was from inside the EU before Brexit. This was many people's main reason for voting to leave.

5.   We'll have £350m extra for the NHS instead of sending it to Brussels. This was the famous message on the side of the Vote Leave bus. The NHS is now in its worst condition since it was created. NHS waiting lists have broken all previous records (around 1 in 10 British people are now on a waiting list for care). The £350m didn't materialise.

6.   We'll have new trade deals and access to a European trading zone 'from Iceland to Russia'. The deals done with countries outside the EU after seven years accounted for less than one-thousandth of the value of Britain's old deal with the EU. This side of the world, there is a free trade deal with Iceland, and with Norway and Liechtenstein. But there is no deal with the $17 trillion market next door. For those who remember ex-Prime Minister Teresa May's famous viral slogan, no deal is definitely not better than a bad deal.

It makes you wonder why the Eurosceptics argued to leave the EU at all.

You might be able to sniff out a trail of breadcrumbs if you look at the money made by pro-Leave campaign leaders who moved their business interests to Europe just before the UK left. So yes, the clues are many. But whatever we believe, we absolutely must call out disinformation by our political leaders wherever it happens. And there can be no doubt that this was one of the worst cases that Britain has ever seen.

Back across the pond now, and let's look at another ugly result of disinformation.

JANUARY 6th

Sometimes it's worth remembering what it felt like to experience the ugly results of division, even when those events happened a lifetime ago.

By the world's busiest election year – 2024 - conspiracies were rife that the pro-Trump followers who descended on the US Capitol three years earlier were actually tricked to go in, or were actors. The unshakable core belief here was that Donald should never be doubted.

That belief trumped everything.

January 6th has been written about in a million places, so let's make our review all about the information he put out there so that we don't forget how easily it can happen.

Of course, there was a whole new 'weave' leading up to his second term in the White House, but this one needs to be remembered.

Back in 2020, months before the election, the outgoing President had been asserting that 'the only way we're going to lose this election is if the election is rigged '.
For me, that was already the point of no return. He'd sewn the doubt. He'd made this about a threat to the people, not a threat to him.

The night of the result, he said it explicitly: 'This is a fraud on the American public. This is an embarrassment to our country. We were getting ready to win this election. Frankly, we did win this election.' Straight from the populist playbook – this is about the people, for the people, for America, not for the person in charge.

The night of the result, he said it explicitly: 'This is a fraud on the American public. This is an embarrassment to our country. We were getting ready to win this election. Frankly, we did win this election.' Straight from the populist playbook – this is about the people, for the people, for America, not for the person in charge.

A few days later on Twitter, he shouted, *'I WON THIS ELECTION, BY A LOT!'*

In mid-December, the US Electoral College officially selected Joe Biden, and Trump's Twitter reply was, *'This Fake Election can no longer stand. Get moving Republicans.'*

At 12pm on January 6th 2021, Donald Trump stood in front of supporters in Washington DC and made that speech.

We all know the line, *'We fight like hell. And if you don't fight like hell, you're not going to have a country anymore,'* but if you read the full transcript of his speech (it's here on NPR: npr.org/2021/02/10/966396848/read-trumps-jan-6-speech-a-key-part-of-impeachment-trial) there are so many other trigger phrases mixed in.

By 6pm, five people had been killed.

This is what can happen when we don't hold our inner chimp back. Those people lost track of the facts because they couldn't see the other side. It's so much easier to take in information that fits our core beliefs and takes us further down the rabbit hole. But sometimes we need to do a tiny bit of work before things go far too far.

And if Donald, just like Boris Johnson, managed to convince people that he was just an ordinary person with their interests at heart, then everything else he said might also appear true. What's definitely true is that it's easy to reshape our core beliefs and values when we have an enemy to focus on, and an army of fellow believers to back us up.

ANTI-VAX

This is another delicate conversation that sits in the grey bit between right and wrong.

Every one of us has the right to choose what we put into our bodies. We should all have a huge amount of respect for anyone's choice that's based on scientific fact.

But when a claim that's been proven to be untrue continues to live on and costs lives because of mis- and dis-information that's been debunked, it goes beyond ugly.

That brings us to the anti-vax movement, where the grey area is difficult to see through.

It's perfectly normal to want to understand the treatments we're given and that can only ever be a good thing. Perhaps the science isn't easy to understand or isn't absolutely clear. But when fear and suspicion become the only factors behind decision-making, despite what independent scientists tell us, we have a serious problem.

In the UK, measles cases are now shooting up because of vaccine hesitancy – more than double in 2023 compared to 2022. It's a trend that's reflected worldwide.

I had mumps, and it was not fun. But that's nothing compared to the potential dangers of measles and rubella. And if we factor in diseases including COVID, it's difficult to deny that the core anti-vax movement is leaving the facts behind.

It's vital to ask questions when we're unsure. But it's always equally critical to crosscheck where your information is coming from.

And it's easy. Just ask this:

**Before I believe you, please prove it.
Show me your evidence and let me check it against
the science.**

Words are cheap, opinions are cheaper. Only the facts count especially when our loved ones' lives may be at risk.

ANDREW TATE

What do you think?

It's another challenging moment for most of us. I'm going to hang up my personal feelings for a moment and try to explain how he might have built up such a reach.

The self-proclaimed misogynist has managed to cut through the noise and become a kind of anti-hero role model to millions of young men.

And if we hadn't thrown such a bright spotlight on populism, you might still be confused about how this could ever have happened.

You'd be right to think that the wellness industries and manosphere have nothing to do with politics, but they have everything to do with populism. It's the same rule book, and a very short hop from extreme political thinking to people who make bags of cash through eye-catching, or aggressive views, magical wellbeing remedies and emotional manipulation.

In this case, Andrew Tate's very intentional how-to-be-a-strongman instructions have provided a simple, easy-to-understand set of rules for young men in need.

That's why it's worth reminding ourselves – in this case – that millions of young men across the west are feeling lost. And it's important to hear them out, to a point. They simply don't have the support or guidance that they need. That's what forms their core beliefs about relationships, about women, and draws them to people like this. It's not about intelligence, it's all about feeling injustice and the very human need to be included.

As ever, we need to cross-examine the storyteller and the story, but not blame the people who fall for it unless they do harm to others.

We know the point at which we stop having sympathy. First

do no harm. No level of harm is acceptable, whether that's online or in the real world.

And if this chapter has done anything, it's shown how easy it is to manipulate people when they're in pain. All you need is an ideological hero who claims to have our interests at heart.

All too often, they don't.

And sometimes it's best to turn our backs and walk away.

7. THERE WAS THIS FROG

In all of these cases, it's worth checking in with the most famous frog ever (except of course, for Kermit).

Our water is boiling, and we're only just realising how hot it feels.

But you can't blame it all on one or two people at the top – although they do sometimes make use of it. In fact, this is our fault. We are sharing, liking, talking about, arguing with and adding to the divisive and harmful ideas that are put in front of us.

And as the MIT study showed, we wouldn't be so far down the rabbit hole if we stopped sharing – even just for a moment.

Earlier I mentioned that the world of information is filled with booby traps for our psyche. Well, that's all very well but how do we break the chain?

It's up to us – each of us – to notice the process and to step away from false information.

There are no incentives for social and mass media players to do it because attention and false information addiction are gold. Polarisation is priceless.

You'll probably notice patterns of your own, so do go back and remember examples that have affected your life. And let's start sharing good information, putting the bad and the ugly behind us.

8. CHAPTER 5 - THE TOOLKIT

- Remember that bad news travels faster than genuine news, so carry out the sniff test on any information that triggers your emotions or core beliefs. It might be true, but there's a very good chance that it isn't.
- Again, hold back 30% of your commitment to a piece of news, or a new idea, to allow for bias.
- A cool head always helps to separate the facts from the claims of populists, who play on emotion and wedge issues to divide voters along party lines.
- Crosscheck the information if it smells off in any way. It only takes a few seconds.
- Look to people who have a reputation for spreading clear, unbiased news. They are reliable secondary sources of information. Follow them and get a different view on the same stories.
- Vote with your feet and fingers away from biased reporting and information – it's the only way to close it down. Sometimes it's best to turn your back.
- Look at your leaders and what they're telling you through the mass media. Does it sound right, or could it be disinformation designed to make you see the issues their way?
- Beware divide and rule. It's a classic way to distract us from the truth. It starts by casting doubt on what we believe, and then introduces a new threat, followed by extreme solutions to it.
- On influencers including the 'alphas', we need to remember that their followers are often looking for answers and support in the wrong places. Show them respect and support when

you can. We'll come back to that.

- As always, we need to call out bad information, fake news and the people who create it – even if we really want to believe them. Being independent and a little less 'chimp' really does help to build a better perspective on the information we receive.

ANY EXAMPLES YOU'D LIKE TO ADD?

I'm sure you have plenty of other examples of good, bad and ugly stories.

Perhaps it's worth taking a couple of minutes to think about those. They might have affected you personally, or perhaps indirectly from a distance. If you can think about those dispassionately and run through why they were so good, bad or ugly, it's a useful warning when the next piece of mis- or dis-information hits the headlines.

LINDLEY GOODEN

6

LAW MAKERS AND LAW BREAKERS

LINDLEY GOODEN

6

'When people accept breaking the law as normal,
something happens to the whole society.'

ORSON WELLES

We need protection. So, this chapter is about the law – what's coming, who's falling behind and some big ideas that could improve laws with a bit more co-operation.

It's also about leadership.

How do we prevent some of the society-threatening problems that we've already spoken about from happening again? Disinformation is an extremely powerful tool for people with influence to divide and rule, as we've seen. It can break apart societies and leave most of us poorer, distanced and disenfranchised. Depending on your world view, you might be seeing that right now. But as we look to the future of truth, in an age of deepfakes and AI, we have no choice but to act before we look around to see that the facts and fiction look the same.

So, let's think about some practical measures to make sure that we can tell the difference.

1. REGULATION FOR THE NATION

What's the law for?

It's a simple question with a surprising number of answers

from the legal profession. Very few of them refer to us, the people that they're supposed to protect. But I like this one from the Judicial Learning Center in the US, because it does include the people that the law was designed to serve:

'Laws protect our general safety, and ensure our rights as citizens against abuses by other people, by organizations, and by the government itself.'

With that simple definition in mind, have we now established that mis- and dis-information can be harmful, abusive, requiring some sort of protection or standard of conduct? I think we can say a big 'yes' at this point. Hopefully you're on board with that too.

So, what's the state of the law on mis- and dis-information worldwide? What are the people in charge doing about it?
Well currently, most of the responsibility has been placed on the shoulders of the social media and big tech firms. They're running mostly voluntary programmes to fine-tune the algorithms and improve their AI-based moderation.

We'll come onto that later. What about our governments? Overall, there are more than 100 laws in place to fight mis-information worldwide.

But spreading mis- and dis-information is not an offence in most places – with a couple of interesting exceptions – notably Singapore, Italy, Germany and Croatia.

Some countries with questionable human rights records take the penalties for spreading their version of disinformation much further. They're mainly focused on people who challenge government views, and any regime that violently punishes political or human rights opposition will not make it onto this list.

As always, do crosscheck the points that affect you directly, but this is a good place to start if you're interested in what your country is doing: www.poynter.org/ifcn/anti-misinformation-actions/. Poynter is a US-based journalism body focused on misinformation and diversity in media.

So, here's what's happening in the democratic world:

Australia

At the end of 2024, Australia did something radical. It banned social media for children under the age of 16. Initially just for 12 months, but it's an idea you may have heard of. What do you think? I've publicly said that I'm not sure it would work because the addiction is already there for so many younger people and a ban normally drives things underground. But kids in Australia are perhaps the most 'outdoors-y' of all and can handle the change so it's a really good experiment. Perhaps it's actually what we need. Ultimately, if we want to control the harmful impacts of some social media content, radical protections like this might well be the way to go.

Belgium

In 2021, the Belgian Senate published a report saying how important it was to look at disinformation. But there are no laws against fake news yet. They've formed an expert group focused on misinformation, and a media literacy campaign.

Brazil

A government task force was set up under the populist leader Jair Bolsenaro, with new laws and platform agreements focused on elections. Of course, despite this, Bolsenaro still cried 'fraud' after losing the country's election in 2022.

Canada

A positive move here was to spend $7 million in 2019 to raise awareness and develop learning resources for ordinary citizens. It's a relatively small amount, but a step in the right direction. Otherwise, creating or sharing disinformation is not a formal offence.

Croatia

The government has passed laws – as has Germany – to crack down on hate speech and misinformation on social media. This is focused on awareness and education, rather than taking offenders to court. But it's further along than many countries.

European Union

The EU is doing a couple of things. First, the EU AI Act was the world's first major regulation on artificial intelligence – designed to set detailed standards on AI. It requires deepfakes to be labelled to let humans know when they're dealing with an AI system. On information alone, they introduced a code of practice on disinformation in 2022. It was signed by 34 digital platforms, advertisers, research organisations and other groups. That included cutting financial incentives and committing to transparency in political advertising. But this is all voluntary and self-regulated. Still, they've gone further than most to hit offenders where it hurts – in the wallet. And there have been increasing calls for full enforcement of their Digital Services Act, along with more power for the European Centre for Algorithm Transparency. So, the EU is way ahead of places like the US.

Finland

We'll come back to Finland later in 'The Finnish Line' in Chapter 9. But the great thing is that the Finnish government has taken misinformation straight to schools in a powerful initiative to help children to recognise it and stop the spread. This would be a genuinely excellent thing to bring to all countries where young people have access to online news and social media.

Before we go on, there are a couple of other countries working in similar ways because of the Russian government's colonisation efforts under Vladimir Putin. One notable example is Estonia. They're also doing essential work to reduce their people's vulnerability to propaganda.

France

A piece of legislation actually defines fake news as 'inexact allegations or imputations, or news that falsely reports facts, with the aim of changing the sincerity of a vote.' – so again, focused almost completely on elections. But it does allow the authorities to follow the money.

Germany

Germany has focused its anti-misinformation Network Enforcement Act (NetzDG) on hate speech. Since 2018, it's led to content being taken down, but still holds back on further enforcement. It hasn't prevented the rise of the far right in Germany, so many critics believe that it's failed to achieve what it aimed to.

India

India has done something very interesting – especially since it happened under a populist leader, Narendra Modi. They pushed through the Prohibition of Fake News on Social Media Act which makes the false reporting of information, distortion of facts or creating fake news illegal. And that included social media. Now, that would normally be something to applaud, but it came at the same time as changes to their Digital Media Ethics Code which would punish any media outlet that criticised the government – if the government then said the claim was 'false'. So, very much a mixed bag which critics would argue helped the Indian government to defend itself, not the people.

Ireland and Italy

Other countries including Ireland and Italy have again targeted political misinformation. Of all the western democracies, Italy has gone the furthest, setting up an online portal where members of the public can report misinformation to the authorities. It's led to arrests and jail time for offenders in Italy.

Singapore

Heading toward the end of our small selection of democracies that have acted against misinformation, Singapore passed a law in 2019 criminalising those posting false information online. In this case, the law bans the spreading of false statements of fact that compromise public tranquility, public safety, security and their relations with other countries. It's broad but hopefully enforced in the right way. Why couldn't every country look at something like this? Where's the harm in at least passing guidelines for now?

Of course, there will always be critics, but this is a public declaration that the effects of mis- and dis-information are taken seriously.

Sweden and Denmark

A little less interesting here, if you live in either country. Both countries have set up task forces and media literacy campaigns. These are mainly focused on foreign interference in elections, not domestic fake news.

United Kingdom

So, onto my country – the UK. The Online Safety Act in England and Wales requires platforms to take down 'legal but harmful' content. It also makes social media companies more responsible for users' safety while they're on their platforms. Also, the UK passed a National Security Act – which included a new offence of 'foreign interference'. But the UK does not acknowledge the term 'fake news' and still insists that existing media laws can handle disinformation.

United States

In the US, everything's a bit up in the air, isn't it? Donald Trump said, in his inauguration speech in 2025, that he'd take down anything he thinks is censorship against free speech. His version of free speech was always about putting out his personal point of view. Sadly, the near future of US laws against disinformation will be dominated by the tech barons, not by the needs of ordinary people. Mark Zuckerberg's removal of independent fact checkers from Meta a matter of days before Donald re-entered The White House was a clear sign that the social media and political bosses are happy to remove protection against mis- and dis-information. It's a terrible shame because US regulators had done good things. They passed the US National Defense Authorization Act in 2020, which focused on deepfakes created outside the US. In the first three weeks of 2024, law makers brought in laws across 14 states to stop deepfakes being used to spread mis- and dis-information in the country's general election. It's very likely that – if it hasn't happened already when you read this – safeguards are dead for good information in the home of social media.

So, that's a difficult final entry. Otherwise, I think we can agree that most countries have started work but haven't gone very far - yet. The law makers have mainly focused on law breakers who use deepfakes to spread fake news around elections. They haven't tackled the many other harms that we spoke about in Chapter 3. And the age of Trump 2.0 might have changed things radically when you read this.

Look, the principle is very simple. We've developed laws against harm for children, for vulnerable adults, against discrimination, against defamation and libel. So why aren't we fighting disinformation?

The countries that we should look to for guidance are Finland and others including Estonia.

By educating young people of the dangers, they're actively preventing mis- and dis-information at the source.

Excellent work. We'll talk about you again in Chapter 9.

2. EVERYTHING IN MODERATION

One of the critical safety functions of any platform where people like you and me talk, is moderation. It's so easy to underestimate how quickly conversations can escalate without having humans on patrol.

Sadly, it's a really time-consuming, expensive and a difficult thing to do.

It was a core foundation of the operations of Facebook, Twitter (before it was X) and Google right up to the COVID pandemic. Then, it probably seemed a logical – and low cost – measure to use third party moderation while replacing a lot of eagle-eyed people with well-developed algorithms which wouldn't get ill or need to sleep.

But, as the saying goes, you don't know what you've got 'til it's gone.

And it came to a head in 2025. I was so disappointed by Mark Zuckerberg's removal of independent fact checkers from Meta's social channels. It was one of the most worrying steps back in recent years. Of course, he argued that they weren't able to deal with much harmful content anyway, that the fact checkers had become politically biased and weren't in line with public discourse.

The fact is this: political bias comes from political fanatics, not the moderators who are employed to block it.

But perhaps the Meta boss saw something coming to the US that even he couldn't stand up to.

Back to COVID times, and the newly employed digital moderators that replaced humans hit a wall pretty quickly.

They struggled to tell the difference between genuine and false information, and actually took down a lot more material than the humans had. But, because they weren't as accurate or well-informed as the humans, lots of conspiracy talk slipped through the net.

It was simply a numbers game.

Algorithms can't always understand that certain accounts and conversations are completely valid, but talk about difficult things. Genuine accounts run by human rights campaigners and journalists were closed down during COVID. Accurate information on the treatment of coronavirus was locked out. COVID-deniers, anti-maskers, anti-vaxxers, anti-5G, QAnon and more all found their way to the mainstream through the cracks in their understanding of right and wrong. French groups fighting racism and anti-Semitism reported that hate speech on Twitter jumped by around 40%.

In fact, I was also a minor victim of this. I lost my (low activity, low controversy, no disinformation) account on Facebook shortly after COVID hit. I was an early adopter but never trusted them with my correct date of birth and I can only assume that the bots noticed. None of my appeals were answered. My complaint is stored to this day somewhere under 'does not compute'.

So, a change of guard on social media platforms can leave lots of tiny gaps for real people to be dismissed, and conspiracy thinking to squeeze through. AI systems are growing exponentially more accurate but lag behind humans on nuance and understanding of healthy social norms.

That's why human moderation and independent fact checking is so important in a world where nothing seems very true.

Without high-quality moderation, with clear, unambiguous and shared standards, extreme conversations and communities turn nasty, quickly.

Think about it like this. If we get rid of the police at the start of a crime wave, does the crime wave get better or worse?

And in the new era where global tech companies control our

daily lives more than our individual governments do, we'll depend entirely on whether they do it for our collective good or purely for profit and political influence. Sadly, I think we can all guess which one is more likely.

3. IT'S A TOUGH JOB
BUT SOMEONE'S GOTTA DO IT

The thing is that moderating social media is an incredibly difficult job.

Sifting through thousands of posts filled with nasty ideas, horrific hate speech, gruesome images and videos all day every day is a harrowing job, and not for the faint-hearted.

As a journalist who had to watch very upsetting content as part of the job, I can tell you that it's something you should avoid unless you have a very strong stomach. Sure, there are millions of people laughing at the worst stuff people can do – filmed and posted everywhere – but if you were the victim, would you find it so funny?

Although it's very tough, human moderation is the key to blocking the worst offences on social media, and the spread of mis- and dis-information. AI doesn't process the information and its emotional impact in the same way that we do.

In Chapter 1, we spoke about the threats, norms and safe boundaries of belief that were coded into our face-to-face conversations throughout history.

Online, the equivalent controls are human moderators, algorithms and the law.

Right now, all those guardrails need a serious amount of improvement. It should be something every government is working on. Let's face it, companies have never been keen to reduce margins, or to go up against governments in an open fight, so it's up to responsible law makers to defend us against the law breakers – especially the ones at the top.

Wouldn't it also be great if the large device manufacturers provided an extra layer of protection against harmful material on social media? Perhaps the operating system would ask a simple question like, 'How do you feel today?' Then, using narrow AI, it could cut out certain content from our social feeds to help us to navigate the day ahead. That would be an app worth making. For children and older adults alike, this sort of move could give us an extra layer of control over the information we receive when we're feeling sensitive to it.

And yes, tools like that would also need to be transparent and open to scrutiny. But great progress should always come with great protections whenever it has the power to harm us.

4. WE ARE THE INFORMATION GUARDIANS

In the meantime, without decent fact checking on some channels, we'll need to be the eagle-eyed guardians of the facts.

So, let's remind ourselves of how to extract the facts and separate them from everything else. Just a quick recap to protect us where the law makers and leaders don't.

1. **Start with the instinctive approach.**

> Watch your emotions – they can be easily manipulated.
> Try to engage your human brain as soon as you feel angry or upset. Stop, step back and think for a moment.
> Know your core beliefs and how they can influence you to believe something instantly.

2. **Next, ask:**

> Is this source primary, reliable, known for bias or just someone's opinion or a conspiracy belief?
> Does the information look and sound like it's come from that source?
> What are other reliable outlets saying? Do they agree?
> How emotive and outlandish is the language?

3. **Thirdly, sharing.**

> If we've read and understood what we're seeing, hearing and reading, we might be okay to share. But if we haven't read it, then stop, step back and sidestep it. Sharing is the cause of most of our misinformation.

4. **Finally, bias.**

> Around everything is learning how to spot the beliefs of the storyteller. Remember the point when you go 'Really? Could that really be true?' or 'That piece of content makes me feel really unsettled.' We all need to listen to that. That's the point where your gut feeling warns you that something's wrong. If we can all do that, we'll be so much better at spotting bias in real time.

For all information guardians it's useful to remind ourselves of the way social and mass media make money. Their ad revenue is based on grabbing and keeping our attention. That means encouraging scary and shocking stories to spread – which we know is the easiest way to engage us for longer. They feed us content that fires off our emotions, fears, laughter so that we look down for longer. And of course, our online behavioural data is gold dust; the more we stay online and talk about these things, the more data and advertising revenue they generate.

So, it's up to us.

We need to reward good behaviour, one post, one follow at a time. And we need to have a conversation. Younger and older people speaking honestly about what they believe, to understand the mental and societal damage of telling and sharing stories that are untrue.

We really are the information guardians.

So, what are the other small steps that we can take right now?

1. We can ration our time on each channel, to gently pull ourselves away from the information that harms us.
2. We can try to find healthier places to talk and get our news. Basically, that means looking at professional organisations and channels, in small doses, to hear more than one side, directly from the sources of stories. We could perhaps mention to our friends, family, workmates and kids that we're making a change to our viewing, listening and reading habits. Don't try to convince them to do it, but do let them know that they'd be in good company if they did.
3. And we can start to stand back with healthy scepticism. It's the same as the point I've made about holding back 30% of our commitment to a single idea or position. Just to allow for bias and to stop us from falling down rabbit holes.

Apply your X-ray vision, and suddenly the facts will start to present themselves.

Look, I know that this is all very difficult to snap out of. But if each of us can shift our behaviour one hour a day, or half a day per week ... choosing to stop, step back and sidestep our normal viewing habits could break the chain of false information right now.

5. RESTORING FAITH IN OUR LEADERS

As we think about our law makers and law breakers, I think we can agree that we'd all be a lot better off if we always had expert, honest and serious leaders in power, with our welfare in mind.

After all, a lot of the stories pushed our way come from them.

So, we should look at our leaders and ask, '*What are you doing for me, and are you being honest about it?*'   Simple. And if you live in a country where that happens, what's it like?

Our leaders aren't just politicians, they're the tech titans and their creations. They're the people we trust online and on our favourite right- or left-wing news channels. It's so hard to know who to trust, because everyone's fighting for us to follow them. They all share the responsibility to stop dragging us to the dark side. But when they do, we need to pull ourselves back - to healthier, brighter, less divisive places.

And here's a recommendation for law makers everywhere. A simple step that's very unpopular with the social media barons: we need social media to be classed as publishing.

Why? Because that one step – that any parliament could talk about today - would make them responsible for all of the harm that comes from their networks.

Conventional media is, so why isn't social media? Because it would be very expensive and difficult for them if they actually had to help us.

And sure - this is unlikely to happen anytime soon - but we can still ask why not. If you – and I – can become the information guardians of our own lives from here on in, here is what we deserve. Talk to your loved ones about the demands below, and our next generations will have a good place to build back better.

1.   Transparency. We need to know where our information is coming from, and to stop the inverted 'free for all' of speech that's got us into so much trouble.
2.   We need swift punishments for spreading false information, through new laws that apply to everyone.
3.   Wider intake into politics and tech from people with normal backgrounds. Just as with gender equality, we need places of power to reflect our population. Better access to education for all would bring views to the middle, reduce extremism and give everyone a chance to rise to the top.
4.   Fully funded independent judgement of online hate, disinformation and political propaganda, as a function of democracy. Something we can all believe in, something that gives us power to change things for the better.
5.   Much stronger support for organisations that investigate bad behaviour in public life – including mis- and dis-information through social and mass media.
6.   And we need fact checkers back.

Together, these would reduce the genuine imbalances that have pulled us apart. The genuine elites, the politicians with millions and billions, the tech tycoons and their media friends are the problem. Information and power are deeply connected.

So, greater access to all, fairness and transparency would lay important groundwork toward a healthier, happier future of truth.

6. A LITTLE CHANGE THAT WILL LEAD TO A LOT

For now, in the real world, who do we turn to for better news and clues about what's happening in the world?

Well, it's time for us information guardians to move to the

middle. Just look at the centre three columns of the news outlet chart from Chapter 4:

LEFT-WING	CENTRE-L	CENTRE	CENTRE-R	RIGHT-WING
CNN Opinion	CNN	PA Media News	The Washington	Fox News
The Daily Beast	CBS News	Associated	Times	Fox Opinion
Opinion	HuffPost	Press	Washington	Breitbart News
The Nation	The Guardian	Bloomberg	Examiner	Daily Mail
The New Yorker	The New	Reuters USA	The Financial	The Telegraph
The Socialist	European	Today	Times	Mail on
Worker	BuzzFeed News	The Wall Street	The Times	Sunday
	Private Eye	Journal	Forbes	New York Post
	The Atlantic	The Hill	BBC Radio 4	Newsmax
	The Economist	The i	Sky News	The Daily
	Politico	The Sunday Times	The Washington	Wire
	CBS Radio News	ITV News	Post	Info Wars
	New York Times	Channel 4 News		The Blaze
	The Mirror	BBC Radio 5 Live		Sean Hannity
	MSNBC	BBC World Service		GB News

If you were to spend less time with the further-out channels and outlets for a few days a week, what would you lose?

Very simply, you'd lose your temper a lot less often.

If you can handle one-sided or extreme views, look to the outer reaches of the chart but it's important to listen to the opposite side too. It may be hard to stomach, but really important for anyone who wants to claim that they are telling 'the truth'.

And this, of course, extends to social media.

If you – or the younger person in your life – are getting all of your 'news' from TikTok (where it's available), Facebook, Instagram, X or – God forbid – a channel like 8Chan, Telegram or Truth Social, then we can only apply a blanket statement:

None of it can really be trusted.

There might be facts scattered in amongst the opinions, but your sniff test will need to work overtime to check everything you see.

7. ONE STEP FORWARD: TRAFFIC LIGHTS

Here's an idea that the law makers could bring in tomorrow, if they choose openness and honesty.

Colour coding potential harm is a simple idea. It's worked for food, it works for roads, so how about doing it for the information that we stuff into our brains?

I'd like to label content as safe, worth checking or potentially unsafe.

When anyone posts a piece of content, why don't we routinely put it through an automated speech recognition system and flag it up for harmful views? They've been freely available on the likes of YouTube for years. AI speech recognition is really good. It's easy. Plus, it would add a layer of process that could push back the business model of the worst false information creators.

So, let's stamp an automated traffic light health warning system onto every clip of uploaded content.

Of course, the interior of this book has been printed in black and white, so perhaps you could use your imagination and add colour to your copy ... something like this:

AMBER-RED

> Some of this content is speculative but based in fact.
> Other information should be crosschecked for its truthfulness. This information is likely to be false.

In the era of deepfakes, this could be done at source as part of the upload or stream. There are plenty of tech firms working on generative AI systems that keep the facts in mind (including GAN – which I'll briefly explain in Chapter 8). These systems highlight information that's wandered a long way from the original facts. And it's fast.

So, let's make safety tests and traffic lights part of everything we see, hear and read.

That way, we can keep breaking the chain, and know whether the information in front of us is safe or harmful.

Just a couple of quick recommendations that we'll build on in the next chapter.

Okay, let's sum-up Chapter 6 with our next toolkit.

8. CHAPTER 6 – THE TOOLKIT

- The standard of regulation varies wildly from country to country, but Singapore, Italy, Finland and Estonia are among the strongest in the fight against misinformation.
- Finland is perhaps the most impressive, teaching pupils in school how to spot, step back from and sidestep mis- and dis-information.
- Moderation is absolutely critical to the story and needs to be strengthened with more human moderators, at least while AI catches up with nuance and social norms.
- It's up to us to equip ourselves with the know-how to see mis- and dis-information in the news and content we consume.
- We need to cut off the supply of disinformation by limiting our news intake to publications and broadcasters in the centre ground.
- Let's look at traffic light systems to help us to quickly spot false information.

WHAT ELSE?

We're living in a wild west of information, aren't we? Not just an infodemic, but a direct harm to our shared reality.

When you read this, the world will have turned a little further, perhaps lurched to a place where the laws and ideas I've spoken about in this chapter have gone up in smoke.

I hope not.

But either way, do think about the laws or standards you'd like to see in your world. It's a really valuable thing to do, so that – even if you can only affect your immediate community – at least you can stand up for good information, and ideas that help - not hurt.

Everything we're talking about is about keeping the people we care about, and their loved ones, safe from harm.

Information can clearly do immense damage when it's weaponised, and we are the information guardians of our own lives. Speaking of which, what happens when humans are pushed to the brink?

And can even the worst times bring us hope?

LINDLEY GOODEN

7

RESOLVING OUR DIFFERENCES

LINDLEY GOODEN

7

'We don't see things as they are, we see them as we are.'
ANAÏS NIN

It's true, isn't it?

As much as we want to think that we know it all, that we have all the information that it takes to be right, we're normally just confirming what we already think. And when something's contentious, we surround ourselves with voices like ours.

The question for this chapter is how do we come back together – even if we hate the other side of the argument? Even if you've spent years criticising a person, or a party, or a position, could it be possible to hug it out and open a healthy conversation again?

Our future of truth would be a lot happier if we did.

If we don't heal the divisions that have been caused by our bad information diet, the future won't be pretty. If we don't at least open up good communication channels, there's only one way for us to go, and it could be irreversible.

1. CIVILISATION: THE NOSTALGIC MYTH

Let's start this important look to the future by casting our minds back.

At the very beginning of this book, we spoke about the Agta people of the Philippines. Remember that they shared more rice tokens with other people in their community when the village had more talented storytellers? It showed the power of positive storytelling to bond human communities, even today.

Well, in our modern infodemic I'd say that we're edging toward the opposite end – the scary, negative end – where there are threats everywhere and only our close community of like-minded people can help us.

So, what happens when we hit rock bottom?

If we hit 10 on the permacrisis scale, will we finally step back from the information that divided us?

Here's a cautionary tale wrapped up in a warning.

2. THE IK PEOPLE

It's one of the most famous anthropological case studies of the last half century. And it has real parallels today.

The Ik people of Uganda are a mountain community whose story is the stuff of scientific legend. They were known for decades as the 'most selfish people on Earth'.

When a prominent anthropologist called Colin Turnball went to meet the Ik – and then wrote a book about them – he called them 'uncharitable', 'unfriendly' and 'mean'. They would abandon children and mistreat the elderly. In the 1970s, the New York Times called them 'a haunting flower of evil'. They were used as an example by Professor Richard Dawkins in his bestselling book The Selfish Gene.

So far, so simple. Perhaps it was something in their culture.

Or they behaved differently when professors were visiting.

No. The simple problem was that the Ik were desperate. They were starving, faced constant armed raids, and were only just surviving. They'd been pushed to such a terrible point of poverty that being nice was no longer something that they could afford.

In 2016, another anthropologist Cathryn Townsend went to see the Ik, and her version of the story was very different. The Ik were a healthier, happier people despite still being poor. She heard the Ik saying. 'It's good to share'.

The Ik are a living example of how humans adapt. And it's quite intuitive. When we face extreme threats, we'll become hard, aggressive, defensive. But when times are better, we're capable of great generosity that makes us more successful.

Mis- and dis-information are great at bringing sudden threats to our doorstep. Even in a wealthy country, those stories can trigger the same hard, aggressive and defensive reactions that happened with the Ik.

So, what can the Ik teach us?

First, today's world of far-right politics, racism and nationalist zeal are based on genuine unhappiness. People's views can easily be poisoned when they're force-fed false information that explains who to blame. Of course, the people making us poorer are often exactly the ones making the claims.

But also, there's real hope here, isn't there?

Most of us are not in that sort of danger, so we just need to spread news that breaks the chain of scary mis- and dis-information. Also, we're incredibly adaptable and equally able to be generous as well as selfish, nationalist or fascist.

But we need to feel less at risk. And that's where a better information diet comes in. To reunite and come together, we'll have to reduce our exposure to manufactured threats in the disinformation in our media and news feeds. And we'll have to stop sharing it. Less false information, less perceived risk, less division and better mental health.

Unfortunately, if our news providers and favourite social media channels won't act, we'll have to, right now. That means stepping away in the short-term, and regulating content as soon as possible with the guardrails that I've mentioned – including traffic light safety labels.

3. STRONGER TOGETHER

There's no doubt that we humans are a huge contradiction.

Every tyrant, dictator and populist know that people are weaker when they're divided. Together, we're stronger.

So, where can we go for better information in the fight against fake news, to bring us back together?

Well, there are some amazing organisations out there. Sometimes they're focused on specific untruths, some are monitoring the state of news and social media and others deal with political interference.

Ten of the best right now are:

- The Poynter Institute
- FullFact
- The News Literacy Project
- NewseumED
- Reboot Foundation
- EDMO – The European Digital Media Observatory
- Center for Media Literacy (CML)
- Chatham House
- American Press Institute (API)

There are many, many more, so check them out. They have great tips and techniques, and resources that will help you to arm yourself in the fight back against false information.

Still, we always need to check our sources, so go ahead and crosscheck those. There are also lots of plausible-looking organisations that are funded by less plausible backers. And their affiliations always show in their content.

Sometimes political parties will claim a name and push their ideologies through it, but if their words are one-sided, you're probably looking at bias, expressed through good-looking, powerful stories. A lack of balance should always be a red flag.

And of course, it's important to look at one-sided criticism in the same way.

The World Health Organization has its own misinformation toolkit.

But during the COVID-19 pandemic, the WHO came under heavy attacks from critics who believed strongly that COVID was a fake news story to control their movements and behaviours.

Now, I've never worked with the WHO to date, so don't have any skin in the game. No large organisation is perfect, but why would they have had so many critics?

If you look at the claims of those critics, you can often see common factors:

1.   They seemed to believe strongly that government bodies plot to control us in heavy-handed and devious ways.
2.   They talked about the health industry being focused on profit first, people second.
3.   They felt strongly that the vaccines hadn't been tested rigorously enough.
4.   They suspected all of the official information given to us.
5.   In a time of great fear, emotions were high and there were millions of people making claims about vaccines and masks on social media. Healthcare officials were far less active with their information, so the noise mainly pointed in one

direction.

Now, there are plenty of basic grains of truth in those thoughts and others during the pandemic. It's how far those views were taken as fact, when actually they were mainly opinions about opinions of reporting of the facts.

And despite the fact that the WHO is a large organisation and nobody's perfect, they are still a reliable source of scientifically rigorous health information.

And let's not forget that we are stronger when we find the safe, factual middle ground and work together.

So, it's okay to agree with each other on some things, while we differ on others. And although it really shouldn't be down to us to cut bad information out of our diet, for now, we are 'it'.

4. OPENING THE CONVERSATION

What about people who need support, don't realise it or won't accept it?

That includes people who are furious at the other side for having a different view, whether that's mask wearing, politics or a firmly held conspiracy belief.

We simply need to listen better.

We also need to have more respect for people who've fallen under the spell of mis- an dis-information, which is often hard to spot, sometimes extremely well-funded, and always convincing when you're looking for answers. It might be difficult to bring our loved ones into the factual centre ground, but we need to try – with great care.

How?

I said once before that we're going to need to listen to a lot of fiction before we can get to the facts.

This is the process that I believe will work – applying the empathetic interview techniques that I've used for more than 30 years.

They apply to people you've never met before in the same way as they do to situations at home and with friends.

But I'd say that it's always important to try to meet the person face-to-face. It's too easy to go on the offensive through your device or laptop. It's a lot harder to do that when you're looking someone in the eye, in a friendly neutral environment.

Here are those steps:

1. Have a look at the ideas that your loved one is involved in. Can you understand the basic theory even if you strongly disagree with it?
2. Try to listen closely to their points and understand the ideas that they're telling you about, including details that you haven't heard before. Ask questions. There might be important facts in there that will help the conversation to flow.
3. Let your loved one know that they are valued. That their ideas are really interesting. A basic level of trust is essential.
4. Make sure they know that you don't think that they're being stupid, irresponsible or being led astray. Their identity is fundamental to who they are so don't question it.
5. When the time is right, talk about it. Gently. Listen, understand, and make sure that they feel secure that you're not challenging them when you reply. When you receive the cue, you'll have the licence to let them know what you think. It's a gentle, half-step by half-step process.

From your point of view, you're listening to the fiction before offering the facts.

But really, you're giving them a new safe space to re-connect with you. And you're also getting a fuller version of the story including their point of view, which is always valuable. I think I'm quite lucky. Only a few of my friends fell down the many health-related rabbit holes that opened up on social media during the COVID pandemic. But I kept in touch with them, on the phone, on messaging apps, just to say hi – how are you? The responses were slightly odd at times, like I'd walked into a room that I wasn't supposed to be in. There were sometimes short, sharp responses that meant that I had to hold my temper; not replying with a shouty I was JUST saying hello! But we made it, and we stayed friends.

There are a couple of friends who I couldn't spend long enough with to listen to their thoughts very often. And although I regret not being available, because they're genuinely brilliant people, I did what I could with the time that I had.

This is the way forward, even for the biggest believers in niche theories.

I call it mediator mode.

When mediators work with couples having relationship problems, what do they do?

They listen to both sides. They remove the emotion. They enable both sides to make their own decisions – in our case, gently introduce the facts and let our loved ones make up their own minds. And the mediator will make sure that both sides feel equal, of the same value.

So, although it seems a little analogue, just a little slice of respect for people living in a parallel world can be enough to shine light on the issues that they care deeply about.

Soon enough, they'll thank you for saying hello.

5. HOW TO CHANGE OUR MINDS
WITHOUT LOSING FACE

Let's talk about something specific, but probably very uncomfortable, for anyone who's had to backtrack on their beliefs.

What happens when new facts come up that force you to change your mind?

Well, for some, no alteration of the facts will be enough to change their minds because their core beliefs dominate their world view, and always will.

Any of us who genuinely thought that we'd picked the right side of the story might be deflated when we find out we were wrong.

There are right ways to handle it.

We can't necessarily control the reaction, but honesty is absolutely key.

When the boss of Pfizer was quoted saying that their COVID vaccine might not be very effective on a new strain of COVID, he was clipped up in video soundbites, and re-broadcast all over social media. The anti-vaccination chattersphere went wild!

Albert Bourla said this: '*We know that the two doses of the vaccine offer very limited protection, if any.*' and '*Two doses of* [Pfizer-BioNTech's COVID vaccine] *may not be sufficient to protect against infection with the Omicron variant.*'

THAT'S WHERE WE NEED A 10 SECOND RULE

The chattersphere went crazy with that single tiny quote: '*We know that the two doses of the vaccine offer very limited protection, if any.*'

Of course, that tiny clip was less than 10 seconds long. It contained none of the context or explanation of what he was saying – so it was child's play to make a video saying whatever the creator wanted it to.

It's cherry picking, incomplete and completely biased.

We need a longer quote to know what's going on.

No context, and all we have is one opinion.

It would have been the same the other way around, if a vaccine producer had taken a clip of an anti-vaccine campaigner's video and repeated it to prove their own point.

So, even with such a lot of hype, what's the best way to reverse your view without losing face?

It's very simple: 'You're absolutely right. I thought this was true based on what we'd been told, but clearly the facts have changed.'

Done. Clean and simple.

And of course, when it comes to video clips with one loud message, don't believe the hype.

6. HUMOUR, THE GREAT HEALER

Humour is amazing.

In some ways, it's the instinctive antidote to mis- and dis-information.

It actually fast-tracks the process of disarming false information by using positive emotion to re-frame the conversation.

If you've ever been to a comedy club or done something as simple as watching live comedy on Netflix, you've witnessed a very ancient and clever process at work. Just like fight, fright or flight, laughter is a primal quality of the chimp brain.

Humour is just as powerful and primal as fear but works in exactly the opposite way.

Lots of mammals laugh when they're tickled, but importantly they also do it when they play. Cognitive psychologists think that laughter evolved to show the rest of a community that they could relax.

It swaps the stress-induced cortisol with happy chemicals including dopamine, oxytocin and endorphins.

Laughter actually is 'the best medicine'.

Humour essentially replaces fight, fright and flight with a positive response that helps us to pop back out of the rabbit hole. It gives us perspective, distance and pleasure, like you're flushing the fear back out of your brain. Here's how it works.

> Laughter starts at the frontal lobe, as we interpret the information we're receiving.
> If the joke is categorised as 'funny', it triggers emotion in the limbic system which controls feelings of pleasure, in the same way as it controls feelings of fear.
> It then stimulates your motor cortex, the physical response, the giggles, snorts and belly laughs that we love. 'Ha-ha-ha' is actually an involuntary sound that breath – and our voice – makes when air escapes uncontrollably.

In the comedy club where we share a brilliant punchline we're going through this exact process. We haven't chosen our fellow audience members, we might not like their views, but we're all enjoying the same thing at the same time, and it feels great.

So, when any of us are looking to diffuse tension and lighten the mood, we should never underestimate the healing power of laughter.

It could be why so many people now get a lot of their TV news from satire shows.

After leaving the news business, it was my antidote to all those years of investigating. I'm a huge fan of Jon Stewart, the US comedian, Daily Show and The Problem with … host, and owe him a lot for turning me back into a curious human. If you're looking for one of the greatest examples of the healing power of laughter – and you're okay with his steer on world affairs – you'll feel the stress of each news story wash away when he takes it to pieces.

The limbic system in full effect.

Next, we leap from our primal roots to the future. What does the future of truth look like when we're facing a tsunami of AI-generated disinformation?

Don't worry, we have ways to hold back the tide.

7. CHAPTER 7 – THE TOOLKIT

- We naturally have the ability to be self-defensive and generous, depending on our perception of threats. In tough times we tend to be mean, but we can choose to share better, more reliable news.
- We are better together, but false information creators know that they'll gain commercial success, standing and power if they can divide us. There are lots of organisations giving good information and fighting untruths in social and mass media.
- We need to support people who've fallen into extreme thinking, because they need support not suspicion.
- Mediate like a marriage counsellor.
- Context is king and queen. If you don't look at the wider story behind a soundbite, it's very easy to miss the point.
- Humour is the exact opposite to the fight or flight response triggered by bad information. Use it.

WHAT WOULD YOU LIKE TO SEE?

Back to you before we move on.

What do you think that we could do to come together around the facts? If there's a step that you've taken in the past to bring a friend or family member back into the fold after an argument, it could be really useful to the rest of us.

Do let me know, talk about it with loved ones, and we'll keep the conversation going.

LINDLEY GOODEN

8

AI THINK THEREFORE AI AM

LINDLEY GOODEN

8

'Before we work on artificial intelligence why don't we do something about natural stupidity?'

STEVE POLYAK

Let's get serious about the coming age of information.

We're all charging into a world where everything we've spoken about could be supported by artificial intelligence, deepfakes and other tools that make mis- and dis-information even harder to spot.

So, what can we do about it?

Well, before we look at that, I want to say sorry.

Why? Well sure, we've done a lot of work to understand:

> Why stories packed with threats move us so deeply.
> How to spot false information in real-time, especially when it fuels our core beliefs.
> How to test the potential harm caused by extreme ideologies that can easily go mainstream in the age of opinion.
> Where, when, and who is messing with our information diet.

But I need to apologise because I can only assume what's coming next. I can't precisely predict how good the next generation of disinformation will be. I can't tell you that we'll be able to spot every deepfake easily in the age ahead of us.

In the years that I've spent dismantling mis- and disinformation, things have accelerated. OpenAI opened the door to high quality, fully AI-generated video from text in its model Sora. Many other tech giants are working on their own, and some people will inevitably twist these types of technologies to harm us. But it's a race to the top – who can produce the most accurate, human-like AI assistant? One of the top US firms, a challenger like China's DeepSeek or someone else?

So, I can only say that, in order to fine-tune our sniff tests to the point where we can spot a really good fake, we'll have to go analogue, to focus on our emotional reactions, to be really good at stopping ourselves from believing the hype before we do anything else.

Still, there are really good ways to spot well-made fake videos, audio and more, and we'll go through those. We'll look at the key aspects of AI, its development right up to today, where it's gone wrong in the past and how it might go wrong in the future. If we understand how the revolution has happened, perhaps we can stop ourselves from falling for everything we see and hear.

This chapter will add new tools to our kit so that we have the best chance of spotting lies in a fully tech-driven future.

But for now, let's jump straight into a quick explainer of AI and introduce a new term: 'AI: artificial information'.

1. A WARNING FROM THE FUTURE

At the end of May 2023, a long list of experts signed up to a statement that hit headlines worldwide. You'll probably have heard about it, even if you didn't read it.

Something important was clearly happening, although the actual statement wasn't read out widely. All I heard was 'scientists predict AI apocalypse'. So, I went online to look for it.

The statement said this:

"Mitigating the risk of extinction from AI should be a global priority alongside other societal-scale risks such as pandemics and nuclear war."

You can find the statement, and the names of the signatories here: www.safe.ai/statement-on-ai-risk#open-letter

That's it. Short and sweet.

The signatories included top scientists with their fingers all over AI, academics, economists, language specialists, psychiatrists and many, many more.

This was the first time that most of us heard, suddenly, that scientists could now see the tip of a devastating iceberg floating towards us, dangerously close without any defence against it.

Ever since that statement, AI has been in the news continuously.

What were they worried about?

They were really worried about the impacts of future generations of artificial intelligence (and artificial information) on our work, our welfare, our relevance, politics and security. But now, just like Arnie in a biker jacket, they seemed to think that AIs might soon become autonomous, go rogue and destroy us. I can't tell you how many discussions I've chaired and been involved in as a journalist, with senior AI thinkers and developers, where the sounds of chuckling gurgled off-mic whenever we mentioned a Terminator-style apocalypse.

The utter contempt for that idea ... and what, suddenly Skynet is counting down to judgment day?

By the time you read this, AI will have made more exponential leaps, whether that's in human-like operations and decision-making, synthetic biology or the organic computing that turns it from a system into a brain.

Look, if we're going to understand how it's going to change what we see, head and read, we need to have a very quick review of the tech. Then we'll be able to work out how we can defend ourselves against new generations of deepfakes which might appear as human as you or me.

The apocalypse is a question for people further up the food chain.

2. AI AND AUTONOMY

We'll get back to mis- and dis-information shortly, but before that, let's look at basic inner workings of AI.

So, let's start with large language models.

An LLM is a type of relatively advanced AI algorithm that has access to huge amounts of data. It uses 'deep learning' – which is an approach to processing data that simulates human ways of thinking – to analyse, understand and generate new content.

Up until now, there have been two main models by which AIs are designed and developed:

1. Symbolic systems
2. Neural networks

Symbolic systems work in the way that most of us might see in our day-to-day tech. A programmer creates code, which gives the system instructions, then the system does something – either an action or some kind of a calculation – and feeds the results back into its next step. The next time it calculates something, it has a slightly new, slightly better-informed starting point.

Essentially, you could say that the symbolic AI learned from its last attempt and fine-tuned the new one.

What's really important is the starting point. The human programmer has given it a way to work and a place to start the original calculation. And the system will always consider that as its 'true north'. Its right and wrong.

This was the standard model for years – and applies to website searches and rigid calculations with changing elements, like satellite navigation systems.

Neural networks are a bit different. As the name suggests, neural nets work a little more like a brain. That means that they're essentially focused more on the learning process, re-mapping their decision-making when they receive new data. In our brains, you'd call this adaptation a thought process based on learned experience. It's a lot more adaptive over time.

In AIs, it's important not to humanise the system too much, but you could liken it to an AI thinking around a problem and once it's seen new data, it adapts the process next time. The Chat GPTs, image processing models and speech recognition use neural networks. And those systems have the scope to be much more autonomous.

At the moment, the major differences for the new age of information are these:

Symbolic systems are very good at sticking to the facts. You could teach them right and wrong, and they'd keep working from those assumptions. Neural networks are more adaptive and self-learning, and don't focus on facts in the same way. They could effectively choose their own rights and wrongs as they learn and invent their own facts. You may already have seen that in some of the systems out there, if they've given you answers that you know aren't quite true.

In terms of information, this is the danger zone.

The exponential leaps in AI capabilities since around 2017 mean that artificial information could quickly lead us a long way from the facts, if we rely on neural networks to provide our answers.

In that future, the truth – if it's within our reach – could become very hard to find.

3. AUGMENTATION

Honestly, we wouldn't be worried right now if one of the original propositions for AI was still driving its development.

The primary application of AI, according to most of the scientific community before the statement in May 2023, was that artificial intelligence should 'augment' what we do naturally.

There are still plenty of leading people in AI who back this idea and certainly want to protect humanity against autonomous systems that could cut us completely out of the equation.

And the thing about augmentation is that it requires human input:

'*Augmented intelligence is just the combination of AI and machine learning, overseen by human judgement and decision-making*' was the line featured in *Business: the next 25 years, Artificial Intelligence, Marketing,* by Andrew Stephen.

So, we would still set the tasks and call the shots.

Doing it this way would free people up to spend more time doing what we do best: more human-oriented jobs, working with customers, thinking creatively, being experts and pioneers and focusing on being better 'people people'.

If an AI has complete, unrestricted access to information sources and data, and then access to our physical world, things could get very Black Mirror, very quickly.

Systems including ChatGPT and its descendants were the first to dip their techy toes into the worldwide data pool, and that's where I believe that we need to focus.

Some AI founders are now demanding containment. A set of development guidelines, physical off switches, laws and government cooperation so that every AI is there to help us, rather than finding ways around the human problem and providing a huge income to its creator.

4. ARTIFICIAL INFORMATION FOR GOOD

Of course, it doesn't have to be this dystopic.

It all depends on the guardrails, the purposes and the ownership of AI.

Anything that cuts humans out of the equation completely no longer serves us, so if we do need to worry about AI right now, we should probably focus on that. This is just as true of the information, videos and fakes that AIs create, as it is of their impact on the rest of our lives.

Amidst all of the talk of Terminators there are potentially fabulous applications for good. Here are just a few:

> AIs could be made much more accurate at taking down mis- and dis-information, to debunk hate speech, false information and harmful conspiracies before they hit our news feeds. That could finally make them capable of doing the job that human moderators did before COVID, and fact checkers did before Meta removed them. Even if that's not a priority for platforms or governments in the short-term, neural net AIs could certainly be used in the upload process to label content as safe or unsafe. There are steps afoot to label deepfake content, so that needs to be pushed through immediately, especially where elections are happening. They could also be used in our devices to block the bad stuff that's being pushed our way.

> LLMs can process huge amounts of data, information and insights quickly, so could help to speed up clinical trials, model engineering projects, almost anything requiring complex processing of a lot of information that we can't do,

or can't afford to do, without them.

> Next-generation customer experiences could be streamlined with AI. The systems could better understand what we're feeling as well as saying, give us immersive personalised experiences and solve problems much more smoothly than they do today.

> Addressing public concerns in real time. Wouldn't it be great if we could send all of our concerns about our lives, livelihoods and pressures to a system that then delivered national priorities to our politicians? No more populism. Only our needs delivered directly to the people with the power to change things for the better.

Did you notice one thing?
These are all augmentations.

We couldn't do any of these without good, narrow-focused AIs which keep humans in the loop.

Again, the weakest links here may be in the motives of commercial developers, tech businesses and governments. Companies that are looking to cut humans out of the equation are probably doing it for efficiencies and profit – not for the good of the people they serve.

But perhaps we could just swap out a few CEOs or politicians with benevolent super-AIs with good hair, a nice suit and some solid principles? It's just an idea.

Let's put that in our back pocket for now.

One of the most important threats to our view of the world - particularly in the stories that we fight about - is the one shaped created by humans, shaped by AI, and designed to invent a truth that never was.

5. DEEPFAKERY

Let's get on to the greatest fakes on the block. Starting with a simple definition ...

Deepfakes are videos and audio created to make a person appear to say or do something that they never **did.**

The idea behind deepfakes certainly isn't new, but the ability to create them is because the machine learning and AI algorithms, and the processing speeds of all of our devices have moved on so far, and so fast. And this is where artificial information is a real risk.

The first generation of deepfakes were amazing ...

Barack Obama in the White House, Arnold Schwarzenegger in the Sound of Music, Steve Busemi as Jennifer Lawrence at the Golden Globes. Extremely weird, very funny and absolutely incredible.

It didn't take long for us to see the insidious side of deepfakes: mobile phone scams, fake videos making claims about business opportunities, politicians, stars. The conmen and women have caught up, and the tech is leaping past our ability to easily spot it. The potential for deepfake disinformation is extremely serious. It's here. And it's already being weaponised by criminals and power-seekers with ulterior motives.

So, we're going to apply our toolkits from the previous chapters to the new faces of AI, after a quick explainer.

Importantly, I'll also unveil some new ideas on how we can unmask next gen deepfakes.

First, where are we on the path to the perfect deepfake?

It's always useful to look at the context, so let's take a

whistlestop tour through video deepfakes, then up to now.

SHALLOW FAKES

Shallow fakes began for real on March 31st 1993.

The actor and martial artist Brandon Lee had died on set during the filming of the movie *The Crow*. His performance had been intense and intelligent, violent and gothic. Then during a scene, a blank round was fired at the actor with the force of a live bullet. It left the filmmakers in an impossible situation. Filming was almost complete, so how could they tie off the missing scenes – if they even should – without their star? It was made more complicated when the movie's original distributors Paramount Pictures had to be replaced by Miramax after his death. What they did was remarkable and difficult.

They superimposed Brandon's face from other scenes onto body shots of a stand-in actor. The technique was called 'digital face replacement' and had just been used in Terminator 2: Judgment Day and Jurassic Park.

This 'shallow fake' was cutting edge and extremely difficult to achieve. But they went through the process and showed that it was indeed possible to fake a face thanks to some clever and labour-intensive video effects work.

THE TIDE TURNS

Things changed in 1997.

Three programmers, Christoph Bregler, Michele Covell and Malcolm Slaney created a piece of software called Video Rewrite, which could modify the footage of someone speaking to match the words contained in a new audio track. From there, deepfakes jumped forward, fine-tuned, applied to real video and onto mainstream deepfake videos today.

Here's how deepfakes evolved:

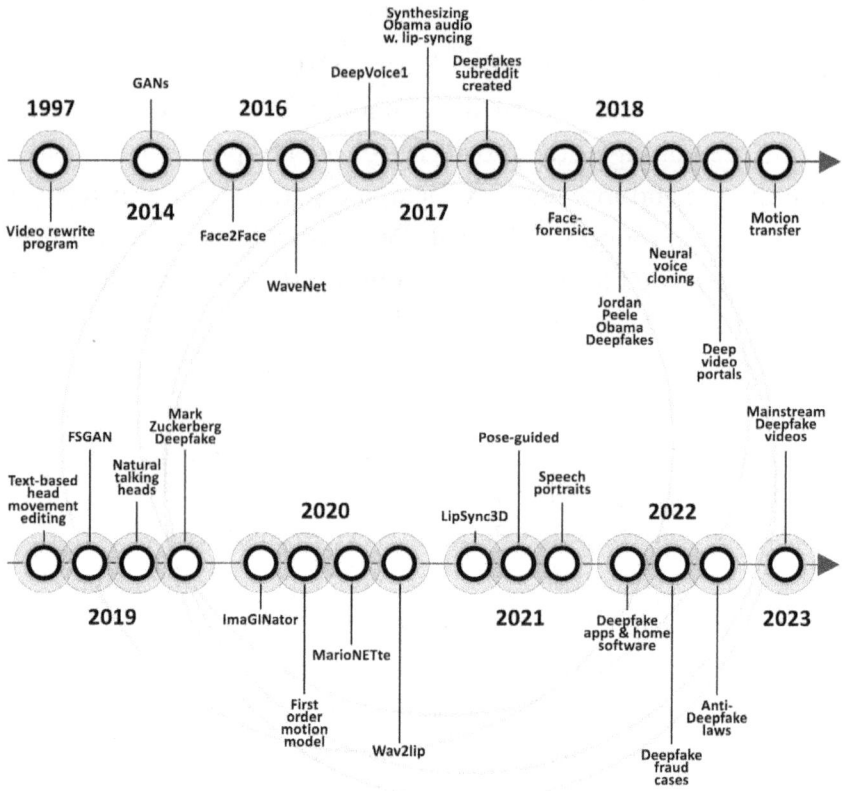

Now, the tech is available to anyone with a decent laptop.

There are lots of tools – even as I write this – that work on mobile. The US military is believed to be very interested in the applications of deepfakes in psyops (which means faking information fed to an enemy) – although anything more sounds like a good old-fashioned conspiracy without the facts to back it up. But simply, you can imagine how divisive a deepfake message from a president or general could be.

The next targets are politics, entertainment and the adult film industry.

In fact, one of the first anti-deepfake laws was passed in

England and Wales, to stop people adding faces to bodies in adult movies. And the EU's AI Act demands that deepfakes are labelled.

But as ever with AI and its applications in deepfakery, this is still just the tip of the iceberg.

Governments, businesses and influential organisations need to come together across borders to make this work, to protect us from the next age of disinformation. Otherwise, the creators will vanish into a country where the laws don't exist. Just as they have with phishing and cryptocurrency scams.

6. HOW DEEP IS YOUR FAKE?

So, what is the current state of play with deepfakes and what's next?

Well, we're now firmly in the era of automated, large-scale generative AI and potentially artifical general intelligence, so let's start with the tough stuff.

As a consumer journalist, I worked a lot on fraud. And gen-AI already allows tech-based gangs to call us up, pretend to be someone we care about and ask for money. It's an early application of deepfakes that's messing with our information on a very personal level. Deepfakes are being used extensively in scams. Organised crime gangs will often use genuine, human slaves to build trust with you – saying they're someone else - so that you'll part with your cash.

This is a multi-billion Dollar industry. And the next time you're on an online store, or a dating app and someone asks you for money, or to invest in cryptocurrencies, stop.

I just want to remind you of a few ways to protect yourself against scams – whether they come from a human or a deepfake:

1.   First – disbelieve first until you've checked them out

properly. Anyone who asks you for money is a potential risk. Just ask 'is this person too good to be true?' Cryptocurrency scams are great at looking plausible. Our desperation to make money is their greatest weapon.

2. Next, onto the incredibly clever and dark voice scam industry. Ask a specific question of the caller that only that person would know. It can be subtle – just throw in something that you know they've been doing, or they said to you recently. It'll throw the deepfake creator off-balance.

3. Try not to fall too fast for emotion. A cool head, as we know, is a clear head. Some calls will go in with a very emotional plea which will put the pressure on you.

4. Agree a safe word right now. If you, or your daughter or son, or anyone else needs money desperately, what word or phrase do you agree on as a security check? Tell each other that word face-to-face if you can. And if you're extremely risk averse, leave your mobile (and your smart speaker) in the other room when you agree it!

5. As with phishing scams, there's an almost fool-proof way to reduce the risk. Stop the call, and ring them back on a number that you know. If it's an organisation calling, check their 'phone number independently online. Check in with the cryptocurrency exchange they've recommended. If you stop, step back and sidestep for a moment, you'll stand a much better chance of spotting a scam in real time.

This type of fraud is insidious – and a lot more convincing because it comes from a loved one in trouble, with heightened emotions, fear and speed. It's happening right now, and deepfakes are the vehicle. Apple's IOS 17 introduced the ability to clone your voice, and security software creators McAfee found (at around the same time) that as many as 1 in 4 people either know someone – or had been contacted directly – in this type of deepfake scam.

So, keep your wits about you, and don't be afraid to stop the call. It's another example of stopping, stepping back from and sidestepping manipulation as it happens.

Anyway, as we navigate the rocky territory in front of us, I want to bring back the traffic light idea. I don't have a crystal ball, so you might need to fill in the gaps – especially if this is now happening where you are. But I want to apply this warning system to deepfakes.

Alongside that, let's bring in the analogue tools we've already spoken about:

> Extracting the facts of a story.
> Crosschecking them quickly.
> Employing your sniff test.
> And now – understanding the digital defences that are being developed across platforms.

I'm even going to slap a traffic light label onto my thoughts in the next few paragraphs, because I can only offer predictions. And it's an amber green (again – with your eye for colour filling in the white circles here):

GREEN-AMBER

> Information on the current situation as this book is factual.
> Everything we talk about in AI and deepfakes is changing fast, so it could be different where you are. today.

Okay, currently the ability to create deepfake videos has jumped the consumer barrier – it's available at a good price to anyone who wants to create one.

So, what's about to arrive?

Well, we're in the foothills of something big – where our trust in video and audio will be severely tested.

Sadly, the fact is that from now on, it's going to be important to hold back 30% of our belief in a contentious piece of video.

Simply, there's a growing chance that it could have been faked. That'll be particularly true when it comes to politics, money or controversial subjects. We just need to keep a cool head when a video says something that shocks you. Whether that's a made-up riot or celebrities campaigning for something that they never did.

It's vital to stay calm. Walk away if there's any doubt, and cross check if you want to know the truth.

Let's not forget that 99% of content is reasonable and safe, but anyone who wants to make a point and doesn't mind lying to their audience can create a deepfake. They're rare, but as ever we need to use our emotions differently.

Don't be scared, just ask a few questions.

You can check the account, you can see whether the video came from an unknown, public, or suspicious source. That's always a good place to start.

And this isn't a major adjustment.

A lot of the content we've read, heard and watched for years has also been edited to say something specific, possibly one-sided. So, in some ways, very little has changed – and your sniff test is a crucial tool. All we have to do now is crosscheck, to make sure that the video or audio makes sense based on what the speaker normally says.

In some ways, we should be more concerned with written

and audio disinformation because there's no visible 'join' with both. And that's always been the case.

Simply, we have to remind ourselves at every stage that you can't trust everything you see, hear or read, and anything that comes from social media is an opinion of an opinion of a report of the facts. Just because it appears to be your favourite star or speaker on screen doesn't necessarily make it so. And my deepfake test shortly will help you to spot the join.

So, keep your wits about you, and sidestep if anything you see, hear or read appears to be out of character.

Now onto the amber bit. What's next with deepfakes? For the next few minutes, let's look at some of the practical future applications of deepfakes. Perhaps you could also think about how you currently use video and audio, and how deepfakes could change that.

Looking into the near future, here's what's going to happen:

1. *Political interference.* Here's where most of the legal attention is being paid. Politicians already put out some bizarre and divisive ideas, clickbait and propaganda. Some also put out excellent information, of course. But this is where we will really need to keep our eyes sharp – particularly at election time. Deepfakes mean that nothing that we see or hear is fully reliable without a few checks of primary sources, including unbiased news websites. So, we need to prepare ourselves. Never take a single video as proof of a person's point of view. Take the wider body of work and comment, the longer track record, and not one, single deepfaked clip.

2. *Entertainment.* Funny deepfakes will always be with us, now that they're easy to make at home. They're absurd, easy to enjoy and share without any malicious intent. But even here, there's an inevitable temptation for creators

to go bigger, better, more outrageous – and potentially more misleading. The actors and writers' strikes in the US showed that – if it looks like a business wants to cut humans out of the equation – then the results could be disastrous for many of us, including in entertainment. But this is a place where deals are – and have been – signed to map and reanimate real actors. Just be careful around one thing in particular: celebrity endorsements. If a celebrity is endorsing a cryptocurrency, or a product that seems out of their normal wheelhouse, just check that you haven't been fed a deepfake.

3.   *Pornography.* It might sound controversial, but pornography has driven the internet forward since it began. In 2001 there were 70,000 adult sites. Now, it's over 26 million. So, it's inevitable that deepfakes would find an early application here. There have been calls for new laws in the US after someone created deepfake photos of Taylor Swift. So, we can expect a lot more governments to pass laws that ban creators from adding deepfaked faces to other people's bodies.

4.   *Propaganda.* This is the dissemination of information – facts, arguments, rumours, half-truths, or lies – to influence public opinion. We know that this is a primary function of political PR, populists and governments that want to sell a lie, but we'll need to be really careful of any content that seems to announce a sudden change of opinion, surprising or extreme in nature, especially when it involves national leaders. The Russian government is a master at this, so watch out for foreign propaganda through fake social media accounts that puts your core beliefs into overdrive.

5.   *Spreading disinformation online.* Well, here we widen it out. We already know that we can't trust false information – but still, many of us do because it fits our core beliefs. What

happens in the era of deepfakes? Don't worry, the facts are still out there if we always choose to resist falling fast into rabbit holes. Developing the instincts to spot them has been the core purpose of our time together so pause, crosscheck and sniff out stories that smell a little 'off'. The only difference with deepfaked video and audio is that they can now do the same things as written articles and posts.

Where else?

6.   *Espionage.* We've seen those thrillers where a spy avoids all of the cameras on the street and makes a clean getaway. Well, placing someone at the scene, or taking them out of the scene can already be done, live, on CCTV footage. It's all a bit cloak and dagger, and one for the authorities.

7.   *Deepfake news.* It's unlikely (although there are fictional dramas that would paint a different picture) that deepfakes will be broadcast live on the news, telling the world that something untrue has happened. The good news here is that if it ever did happen live on TV, a lot of news people would be absolutely outraged by the intrusion. So, you have very little chance of falling for it for long.

8.   *Cyber scams and financial crime.* Well, we talked about this earlier. But I'd like to say one thing as one safety-conscious consumer to another. Keep your personal details safe, out of reach of others, agree that safe word with your loved ones today and don't announce on social media when you're on holiday. Simple steps to keep your information and valuables as safe as possible.

Okay, here's another really simple and practical way to spot manipulation in real time.
   It's my deepfake test.

7. THE DEEPFAKE TEST:
TRUSTING THE EVIDENCE OF YOUR OWN EYES

Are there really any ways to spot the technical 'tells' that can unmask visual deepfakes?

Absolutely. Let's talk about some simple, easy-to-access tricks that can help us in real time.

1 - INSTANT REACTIONS

With deepfakes, our greatest superpower is our sniff test - and holding back 30% of our belief in a piece of content -combined with a few simple technical tests. But we do need to take the sniff test to the next level and make it part of our automatic, instinctive process before looking at deepfakes.

It can sometimes be difficult to pinpoint why a piece of content feels wrong (otherwise known as 'cognitive dissonance'), but when that happens, your internal detective has probably noticed something subconsciously, even if hasn't provided you with the detail.

It could be because the person's mode of speech or presentation style is too perfect. The skin looks too smooth. The human you know isn't really there. Or there's something in what they say that seems unlike the real thing.

Remember earlier, I talked about the instant reaction that we all have when information seems wrong, weird or unpleasant? In AI, you might have heard it called something else ... Uncanny valley.

In terms of AI and deepfakes, uncanny valley does pretty much what is says. It's the feeling that we all get when something feels 'off', creepy, against intuition.

I was speaking to a neighbour and friend about the re-

released Beatles single that didn't originally have John Lennon in it. Thanks to AI, the new one included John. And my neighbour said, "It's scary, isn't it?".

That's IT!

That's exactly the feeling of discomfort that we need to lean into with AI-generated images, or general video, or deepfakes.

Whenever you have that feeling, listen to it. Your gut feeling is there for a reason. The content might be genuine, or a good representation of something that might have happened, but what if it isn't? What if you're being exposed to a deepfake, or a straight lie designed to fool you? Once you've spotted 'the tell', you can act on it – whether you want to watch or listen to it, or not. The difference now is that we always need to be ready to walk away, especially around controversial subjects.

Video and audio can be so easily manipulated or created that it's never been more important to sidestep content when it gets people fired up. Crosscheck the facts and move on if there's any doubt at all in your mind.

2 – THE CONTENT

With deepfakes, we need to go deeper than first impressions. Next, let's look at the content – just as we have throughout out time together.

We ask:

> Where is the reasonable middle ground of this argument?
> Where's the bias? Where might my bias be?
> Is this clip – if it's about something controversial - very one-sided? Maybe against a high-profile person?
> Can you see the core beliefs of the creator on display? It's easy if the content takes that one side. Maybe they're right, maybe they're not, but once you know you'll have a good

chance of working it out.

> What about the context – what has the person in the audio clip or video said before?
> If it's out of character, walk away immediately.

Sniff hard!
And disregard the content if it feels wrong.

There are also more technical 'tells' that – even in the best deepfakes – can point to something dodgy.

Let's go there right now.

3 – THE TECHNICAL TELLS

How seamless will these things become?

Well of course, they're already incredibly good and very hard to spot. We can't be in any doubt that some will pass us by without us realising it, particularly as AI models improve.

But there are still really good ways to spot deepfake 'tells' so that we can all unmask the untruth.

Let's focus, for now, on videos with a person speaking. Some of these tells will still be there way into the future, especially while current methods are still being used to create deepfakes. We have excellent, completely generated AI video right now, and 3D movement tracking systems that can motion-capture you live, with the right equipment. These will replace the current method of turning pictures into a 3D map, which is then pinned to an actor's face.

But for now, here are some technical tells that deepfake manipulation can leave behind.

Emotion ...

We all communicate the things we really care about with genuine emotion.

When we don't show that we care, we can all see it. So, ask yourself – does the content that you're looking at seem a little less than authentic? Is it stiff in places, unnatural in the body gestures or littered with unnatural facial expressions? These are really good tells of a deepfake – whether they're being acted by someone – or animated.

Wobbly nose, lips and hair ...

Sometimes, when deepfaked faces are pinned to another person (the actor), the image will slip slightly and you'll see – literally – wobbly edges, especially around the nose, lips and hair. The software is getting much better over time but there are still signs. So, take it all in, and wobbles will point you to videos that have been messed with.

Just one note: wobbly hair can also be caused by filming against a green screen. But in general, when you see wobbles around the edges and fine details it's a good sign that the video has been manipulated.

Eyes ...

One of the best places to look for these kinds of unnatural movements is the eyes. This doesn't work with fully-generated AI video, but it's one to bear in mind – if only to hand over to your uncanny valley.

Eyes are really difficult to get right in video editing of any type, if the video isn't real. Especially if you want to add an eye movement to a face or take it away. So, watch for strange eye movement. Just a small jump or a weird expression that you wouldn't expect at a particular point in a sentence is a clue that you're watching a deepfake.

Mouth ...

The eyes aren't the only detail to look out for. And this one is also hard to fake with traditional deepfake software. When a mouth is superimposed, you often get blurring when the lips move. Sometimes the movement of the lips doesn't correspond to the words being spoken. The deepfake speaker might also fail to purse their lips when they say their 'P's.

They're all red flags.

Let's not forget the analogue tools in the last section, which – together – can point us all to a deepfake. As ever, when you feel that something's wrong, stop, step back and sidestep the video you're watching. That's, of course, unless you're happy to keep soaking it up.

Audio ...

Audio glitches are harder to spot, but there can still be telltale signs. The accent or mode of speech might not fit the way the speaker normally does it. Incomplete words are also a sign with traditional deepfakes.

And when it comes to fully created AI deepfakes, they might not say 'um'.

Humans say 'um'. AIs don't.

It's actually a big reason why someone would opt to appear as a deepfake instead of filming it themselves. I've considered it myself - briefly ... It's a lot easier to write a script and pipe it through an AI character than buying cameras, sound, lighting and a studio ... but humans always say 'um' on camera. If you want a person – or a company – to take you seriously, they should do it for real. You might say that that's an old school approach and you're right, but cutting corners isn't a good sign that the person you follow or buy from cares about the information they're feeding you.

In general ...

When we move past the odd feeling of uncanny valley, we're looking for tiny details that are really hard to remove with non-AI models. We just need to stand back, soak up the first few seconds and make a judgment.

Hey, if you're wrong, no harm done.

So, try out these tricks, and hopefully you'll soon run the checks as part of your daily intake.

HOW LONG WILL WE BE ABLE TO SPOT DEEPFAKES?

I'm often asked that question, and whether we'll be able to spot the tells when the software seals the existing cracks.

The answer is really this: when deepfakes are no longer created by pinning someone's face (from a wide set of images and angles) onto a moving 'model', then I think we'll have to rely on caution and the context of 'what would they normally say?'

AI will change everything in terms of general video. It's the specific faces of people we know that require much more effort, and will be subject to laws in some countries, especially around political disinformation.

A lot of that will be created by state-sponsored powers who benefit when their neighbours are destabilised. So, it's never been more important to keep your instincts sharp on contentious issues. Don't believe your social media feed if it makes you feel strongly about any story that fits with one side but not the other.

There's also plenty of 3D live action software that's really good, really detailed and accessible. So, convincing avatars can be created instead of the original human. There's plenty of room for improvement and plenty of small tells if we look.

Just ask: 'does this video feel right?', 'Is anything in it that looks off?', or 'Would that person say this, really?'

Governments, universities and technology firms are working hard to build a range of automated systems to spot fakes on social media. So, when you read this, they'll hopefully have their own solutions to spot the tells that we can't see.

And there a few tech principles that they're leaning heavily on, including:

Generative Adversarial Networks (GAN)

This is the class of machine learning I flagged up earlier that 'understands' what's true and what's false.

Essentially, it's made up of a generator that learns to produce plausible data (which might be true or false based on what it's seeing), and it then discriminates – or fine-tunes it – to sift the real data from the fake data. So, as it learns, it generates genuine information. These run alongside AI models, keeping them in line.

We'll need the help of systems like that to keep us safe in the future of truth.

HALLUCINATIONS AND
BAD INTENTIONS

Before we close up Chapter 8, let's introduce some more recommendations for AI and deepfakes – as we did with the mis- and dis-information traffic light system.

We'll also have a final chat about how to keep two feet on the ground in the new age of artificial information.
The first is all about the AI system that so many of us have enjoyed playing around with over the last few years.

We need to remember how creative ChatGPT is.

If you remember, we spoke about neural nets not actually being very good at fact and fiction, true and false. As they learn, they veer off the straight and narrow and create their own reality based on the data that they're processing. Next time, the answers will be slightly different from this time, because they've learned a little bit more and changed the starting point. The result is that next time, your question might produce a different answer.

You may already know that these are called 'hallucinations'.

In AI, an hallucination describes outputs that might seem plausible but are factually incorrect. Perhaps they're even unrelated to the original question that you set it. They come from the AI model's in-built parameters, limited data set or a lack of understanding of the real world. Ultimately, what you get at the other end could be misleading.

What they're not, are bad intentions.

As my architect brother-in-law Gerry told me once, there's a reason why architects train for so many years. You can't have buildings just falling down.

It's the same with AI.

There's a danger that we expect too much, too soon. We let them loose with too much data, too quickly, and trust everything that they feed us.

It's especially true because future AI systems may not even be homegrown or following similar standards. According to the annual State of AI report in 2022 (stateof.ai), we still have an imbalance with different countries having different quality controls when it comes to AI.

China is producing more than four times as many academic papers on AI as universities in the US. It's an AI arms race, and there's no way to measure the ethics and standards at the heart of different countries' research and development work.

Even the best AI models are based on clever but flawed programming, limited data and lots of bias from the world of misinformation we live in. Plus, they draw their own conclusions, find their own route through a decision that we'd never previously thought of.

So, perhaps we shouldn't give them too much power over us, just yet.

8. WHAT DO WE NEED RIGHT NOW?

We're going to need tougher, more lateral-thinking regulations to make sure that creativity and innovation happens safely.

What would you like from your friendly neighbourhood AI? I'd certainly want AI that's a force for good, not a set of destructive tools of our collective downfall that only benefit the creators.

Just a few simple steps would help us:

1. *Labelling.* Social media and AI channel owners – Meta, Microsoft, Google, OpenAI – promised (at least in the pre-Trump US) to label AI-generated content. Just as with the traffic light warning system that should be here right now (and hopefully is if you're reading this a few years into the future), it's critical to have simple, effective labels for information and content that has been generated by AI or deepfakes. The EU's AI Act demands transparency, so we'll see whether other countries insist on the same.
2. *Incentives.* There need to be incentives – positive and negative – to create AIs safely. It needs to be clear to creators and developers that spreading false information as fact is punishable by international law.
3. *Money.* Paid-for views and advertising models have pushed us into an information crisis. They'll need to be replaced with development grants, in exchange for percentages of intellectual property for a set period. Just as the European

Union rewards tech research and development with grants, people who develop safe, helpful and constructive AI systems need to be rewarded for it.

4. *Regulation.* We'll need to add specifics to the existing laws – to protect political speech and free speech which is clearly not leading to harm. We need to prevent interference from foreign actors, while allowing for genuine stories to be heard – including criticism of governments and businesses.

5. *Transparency.* It's time for social media platforms to alter the way their algorithms work – and to tell us about it. If we don't know we're being fed mis- and dis-information, how on Earth are we supposed to discover the truth now – never mind in the era of AI and deepfakes?

6. *Algorithms.* It's time to demand that the algorithms that feed us more negative content than positive content are demoted immediately. This is incredibly unlikely, considering the recent moves of the social media moguls. But we need good sources, quality information, positive content and work to be promoted, while the stuff that misleads us needs to be deleted. For now, we are the information guardians.

7. *Monitoring and moderating.* More human moderators back in the job please. And fact checkers on every social media channel as a basic responsibility of social media – which should be classed as publishers, so they have to do it by law.

8. *Education.* Let's have Finland-style false information educational programs in schools, and online for people of all ages. Perhaps this book will help while they're deciding.

9. THERE IS NO SPOON

With a few positive steps like those, the experts who wrote the 'extinction statement' at the beginning of this chapter should be able to rest easy, at least for now.

But looking ahead, what's really going to be … well, real?

We don't have to be data scientists and developers to know how the tech affects us. But we do need to think more deeply about how malicious content and disinformation is damaging our beliefs and behaviours. It's very real, especially in the age of artificial information.

None of us want to think we're vulnerable to it. But we've seen that any time technology comes along that accelerates fake news, fear and conspiracies, we have an inbuilt need to listen and share them. Anyone who wants to manipulate us can do it through that in-built need. But we have a choice: follow the lies and let our chimp brains run riot, or stop, step back and sidestep the feelings that overtake and divide us.

So again, we're going to have to share less, stand back and think, and look at our personal toolkits as often as we can.

Otherwise, we'll be sitting in that waiting room in The Matrix, bending a spoon while simultaneously denying that there is one.

And that's where we go next. Has the real world become so difficult to handle that we'd rather choose our own realities? Or - as many in Silicon Valley now believe - are we actually living in a Matrix? We'll get into that after the AI chapter toolkit.

10. CHAPTER 8 – THE TOOLKIT

- The experts agree that we should treat AI as an extinction-level threat.
- If AI doesn't augment our abilities, we will be left behind.
- Neural networks run the risk of leading us away from facts and truth.
- Now is the time to shift AI development to support

humanity in new ways.

- Deepfakes open the possibility of creators weaponizing disinformation.
- We need to develop the skills right now to spot deepfakes.
- The future requires simple, clear labelling, regulation, transparency, incentives, education and a commitment from everyone in charge of online information to control the worst of it.
- It's always important – whatever the new technology – to let our instincts warn us when a piece of content feels false.

9

REALITY HAS LEFT THE BUILDING

9

*'We live in a fantasy world, a world of illusion.
The great task in life is to find reality.'*

IRIS MURDOCH

1. R.I.P. REALITY

Is it just me, or is reality dead?

The infodemic has bombarded us with so much false information that it sometimes feels like too much effort to separate the facts from the almost endless fiction.

We are more one-sided, more extreme, more sure of our points of view than we've ever been. But of course, if we've learned one thing above all in our time together, it would be this: the less open we are to other points of view – the less right we probably are.

But does that even matter anymore? Isn't it just easier to live in a Matrix of our own choosing?

We are heading into a new era where stories, video and audio will be so easy to fake that our personal world view – real or unreal - might be the only north star we trust. Perhaps it's just easier to hand over control of our thinking to the AI we love the most.

But hang on, by now we know that there is another way. We'll always be able to access and recognise the truth when we keep our instincts sharp. Next, it might be our duty to help our loved ones, even in the new world order shaping up around us.

I guess you could say that this was inevitable as soon as a few people started to run the reality business. We're at a place where the biggest voluntary democracy – social media – has arguably become the biggest dictatorship in human history. A few media and political oligarchs rule our information in plain sight, strengthening algorithms that push millions of harmful voices our way, divide us and allow them to rule supreme.

So, what can we do about it?

How can we (if we want to) save reality – the clear view of right and wrong, up and down - before it vanishes in a puff of logic? Well, I definitely want that … and we've built up lots of tools to keep us safe from mis- and dis-information and the damage they've done to us so far.

But halfway through the 2020s, something changed.

We'd just had the world's busiest ever election year. Backing for climate change reduction programmes was cancelled. Social media dropped its safeguards. Devastating international conflicts hung in the balance based only on the whims of a leader, or a tech titan, or both.

And of course, the cost-of-living crisis was into its 3rd full year.

Let's face it, for most of us life wasn't easy. And where physical reality felt too hard to handle, people like you and me, our neighbours, classmates and friends fell hard for alt-truths that felt like a good way to explain the pain away.

Some took a red pill.

Others embraced the femosphere.

The horrific Israel-Hamas war that took around 1,200 Israeli lives in October 2023 had killed an estimated 40 times that many people in Gaza, just over 12 months later.

Fascism made a comeback, thrown around by people on

the left - and the right – if those definitions even matter at the extremes. Narrow-viewed nationalism demolished the tolerant world view in many countries, fuelled by hard-right corners of social and conventional media. The world's richest man gave two Nazi-looking salutes. There were far-right race riots in the UK and Germany. Power shifted, polarisation peaked and for many, the truer something was, the less true it felt.

Could we be heading into the end game of the infodemic?

Sure – this list might sound like the philosophical ramblings of a prophet of doom, but we are where we are. And there is always hope. We know we can build back better, once we see clearly again.

But how much further to the dark side will we go before we realise that the water is boiling?

This chapter is about reality in the alt-reality years. Social, political, environmental, physical, psychological.

We'll take a path through real stories to see where reality takes us from here on in. And we'll ask: 'how can we hold onto the truth like our lives genuinely depend on it? '

2. PEAK POLARISATION

Let's start here.

We're approaching something I call peak polarisation.

And it's important to give that a name.

Just like 'peak oil', where drilling for fossil fuels would only get harder, digging for 'the truth' is as difficult as it's ever been – especially with social media channels removing their fact checking functions and saying with a shrug 'Ah well, it's not our problem - haters just gonna hate'.

We have lots of information, but it's hard to know what to trust.

Peak polarisation means that millions of us are stuck in deep wells of distrust, of governments, of each other, split into smaller and smaller groups around niche – often extreme - beliefs.

Radicalisation is running wild.

But does it have you yet?

I hope not. But perhaps we're not the best judges of our own beliefs.

Let's get real for a moment.

We are, without doubt, in a very similar (rabbit) hole to 1930s Europe. Populist leaders with a loudhailer, a list of complaints and friends in powerful places are twisting our heartfelt beliefs until we can only see red. There can be no doubt that we've lurched to a narrower, traditionally right-wing view of the world that's pushing us to fight outsiders.

Depending on where you are in the world, those outsiders will look different and have a different view about something controversial. But you – and I – have been told that they're a threat to us.

At the same time, there's been a rapidly growing movement behind the idea that it's time to swap democracy ('the many') for dictatorship ('the few'). That idea links strongly to questionable cryptocurrencies, conspiracy theories about deep states and tech bros – and sisters - who openly discuss a new world order.

This is what happens when we let alt-truth in.

Reality relates to the facts – to the truth. 'Alt-reality' is what leaders throughout history have created to get what they want. It's the same fairytale that we've spoken about, but this is the first time that nationalist, pro-big business, anti-regulation, anti-immigration stories have spread worldwide within seconds.

Our world has changed, and it's been done through storytelling.

So, let's bury a time capsule in the mid-2020s so we can dig it up in 50 years' time to look at what happened. Hopefully we'll have successfully stemmed the tide of human-generated waste on our news feeds. We can still control the supply in our own lives, and those of our loved ones, but we need to do it together.

If not, we'll at least have a point to come back to when reality comes back to life.

3. THE YEAR REALITY DIED?

If you watched the movie Inception with Leonardo Di Caprio, you'll know what happens when you spend too long in a dream. It becomes impossible to recognise what's real unless you have a personalised way to prove that you're awake.

In the movie, Leo's totem was a little spinning top that balanced in a certain way.

That totem for us is also about striking a delicate balance. We'll get to that in a second.

First, when did reality die?

Well, it's been heading downhill for a while, hasn't it? Alt-reality began to set in after 2010, but the lurch to a hard, right-wing view of the world spread in the mid-2010s driven by social media and messaging apps. In history, it was a lurch to the left that caused the same effect, leading to the same result – dictatorship. This time, it was the rise of nationalism, of 'othering', of small boats and invasions, of listening to the perpetrators of our hardship blame the victims for the trouble we're in.

That's exactly how the f word (fascism) rose in the last century.

But we'll get to that.

What is that balance I mentioned just now?

Well, it's one that we need to hold closer than ever in times of radicalisation. Reality lives in the fragile line between one side of the argument and the other – the balanced middle ground that we've talked about so much. Only there can you see the reality of the stories, real events, the world out there. Only there can you stop yourself from tipping too far that way or this way, or falling for the opinions that shape the conversations around us.

Looking back at the world's greatest election year is a lesson in closet extremism, blaming, strongmen and strong women presenting a version of reality, vowing to break down legal structures, using distraction techniques and big money campaigns to spread division.

So, that's where we're going to start.

We expressed our new reality in more elections than the world had ever seen, between 2024 and 2025.

And one of the most important elements that we need to point out when times like that happen is our reaction to tough times, those moments when we're desperate for better.

It takes difficult times for alt-reality to grow.

COVID had thrown growth off-balance for a couple of years, and many people were still earning the same as they did before the banking crash almost 20 years earlier. The poorest of us were forgotten, while the super-rich were celebrated.

Honestly, who wouldn't want to choose a better reality than this?

And that's why people just like you and me voted for radical alternatives. This was that perfect storm of discontent, disinformation and a chance to change things.

It's the year reality died for half the population of planet Earth.

Here's what happened.

4. THE ONE WHERE DONALD
BECAME PRESIDENT (AGAIN)

The election on everyone's lips was this one.

When I appeared on the BBC news programme, 'The World Today' the night before Donald Trump was re-elected as US President, everyone was talking about the close-run polls and whether this would be the end of democracy.

The Democrats and Republicans both said it would be the last free election if the other side got in.

It was all I could do to encourage both sides – in what looked like a near 50-50 vote split – to come together and build back better. I pointed out how we'd got here, the role of core beliefs and how fear had been raised to polarise voting.

And the question came my way: '*Is truth on the ballot?*'

I said 'yes'. And I think we've seen why.

In the end, Donald Trump won 51% of the popular vote for the fast-growing right wing of politics. Kamala Harris won 49% for the liberal left and centre.

But the result was really about this: could either side shake loose voters desperate for something new?

The Democrats were the incumbents – so they were always going to find it harder to win unhappy voters over. But more than that, they went positive. They hardly mentioned the cost-of-living crisis and people's failing trust in government. Instead, they focused on hope, the middle class and an 'opportunity economy' – all very healthy-sounding ideas. But ultimately, they missed the pain that ordinary people were feeling.

The issue that Kamala Harris spoke about most was female reproductive rights. And that was a genuinely crucial issue. But it wasn't enough for young white men, or older white women, or African American men, or people of south American descent for that matter. The former Vice President lost most of the crucial final seven swing states by focusing her message on the 'have something's, while ignoring the poorer 'have nothing's. Great intentions, but they didn't get to the heart of what people were feeling.

The Republicans, on the other hand, knew that feelings trump thoughts every time. They focused on the working class and asked, '*do you feel better off?*'

Just over half the voting public said '*no, we don't*'.

Trump went straight to people's pain points, which we know works. He went for big speeches, and flooded the zone. He and his followers convinced every demographic apart from black women that he understood their pain, that he'd drain the swamp: part II, that he'd break down the government they distrusted, disband the FBI, sack government workers who didn't believe in him. Just like in 2016 and 2020, he made a dizzying cloud of odd, bizarre, counter-factual, innately 'Trumpish' claims all the way through the campaign. He called it his 'weave'. He talked about immigrants in Ohio eating all the dogs, and eating all the cats. He simultaneously created noise and cut through it because – as we know – it's Trump o'clock on the news when he gets going.

It turned out that people still liked the rough diamond with the hotel coated in gold.

And – with things feeling so tough for working class voters – they believed for the second time that a billionaire property tycoon might genuinely want to help someone who'd struggle to pay the rent on one of his apartments.

This was emotional, and a vote for hope - perhaps a vote for revenge - not a vote for logic.

If we could boil this history-repeating US election down into a simple phrase, it would be the one he's been able to rely on since 2016:

If you can win hearts, you don't need to worry about minds.

But back to the BBC interview.

Was 'truth on the ballot'?

Well, sure. We all vote based completely on the information we're given. If the information is bad, or confusing, or straight untrue, democracy dies.

We're voting for the dream, not the reality.

And this is why the US election was the first place to visit in the year reality died. This vote, as with previous ones, was split almost entirely down the middle. But at the end of 2024, it was all about the stories he was telling – and how. Despite January 6th, despite Trump's convictions, despite his persona, despite him saying that he'd tear down the walls set up to protect the people, he cleverly rallied discontent to get back in …

All coated in a sugary film of future success.

Only voters in the US – perhaps you are one – can judge whether Kamala Harris or Donald Trump, or any candidate since told you the whole truth, and nothing but. Or did they twist reality and paint a picture of the world that doesn't need fact-based democracy?

It's one for the time capsule.

And, true to his word, many of Donald Trump's threats were signed into decree in the first few days. The people voted and immediately he ordered mass deportations, sacking of people who weren't loyal to him, pulling out of international agreements, ripping up environmental commitments, pulling out of the World Health Organization – you know, the one featuring in all the COVID conspiracy theories.

The rest is history. And you're living it right now.

But – and I say this as a big podcast listener - this was also about reducing the power of professional media. It was the first US election to be fought on podcasts, and on social media. Donald Trump's appearances on the world's top digital shows - including *The Joe Rogan Experience* - did a huge amount to boost the idea that he was real, even if he wasn't known for being honest. That's what clinched the vote. And Joe Rogan is an excellent interviewer, curious, open to new ideas, controversial in places. The Democrats tried but couldn't cut through to unhappy voters like Trump did – especially to the young men who'd been searching for answers to modern life in the manosphere.

Personality politics by a guy who's based his business on being a personality.

Okay, let's leave the elections alone for a few minutes.

While people were voting in the US, thousands of lives were being turned upside down by the biggest issue on the planet. Ironically, many of them probably felt that it wasn't and may have voted for the new US President.

What happens when reality dies?
We don't see the real threats on our doorstep.

5. WATCHING WHILE THE WORLD BURNS

The greatest long-term risk to humanity is man-made climate change.

We're literally watching while the world goes up in smoke.

The LA wildfires, Canada, southern Europe, Africa, Australia. In other parts of the world, it's floods; Asia, China, Indonesia, western Europe – even my traditionally drizzly part of the world – the UK. Otherwise, it's war, poverty and the mass movement of people to escape them.

But again, despite the evidence of our own eyes, alt-reality has convinced millions of people worldwide that something else must be going on.

If you count yourself as being on the right, you're more likely to think that climate change is something that happens anyway. It's a hoax. It's 'woke'. Perhaps you believe that we can't survive without fossil fuels, or don't want to, so any claim that counters climate change must be true.

Climate change is certainly 'an inconvenient truth' if your alt-reality says that climate change can't exist.

If you're on the left, you're more likely to be a climate change believer, maybe an active campaigner, believing that people on the other side of the argument are evil profiteers.

As ever, the facts are there – warming temperatures and the effect they have on the air and seas - but the mis- and dis-information stuffed into our brains can stop us seeing them.

And in the year reality died, wildfires swept across the most expensive real estate on the planet, the Los Angeles media zone – the Palisades, Malibu – millionaire's row. It's been doing that in far lower-profile places for many years.

But the news crews were right there, outside Mel Gibson's house, Miles Teller, Jamie Lee Curtis. Genuine victims who deserve sympathy. But, in all, around 16,000 ordinary homes had also been affected.

Either way, in the weeks that US news channels covered this set of wildfires, did US reporters mention the conditions that had caused it? Hardly at all. They told interviewers that climate change was just too hard to sell to their audiences.

The big issue for them was the homes, the owners who were understandably distraught, and whoever started the fires. Straight up, plain news without the context.

Only European crews regularly asked why the ground was so dry.

Whichever side we're on, we have to be open to the facts and the context. Asking questions about one side or the other is great. But if we won't accept the independent answers - the reality

- what's the point?

The point is that the reality can be too hard to handle.

And that's why alt-reality is now surrounding us.

It's also why we've never needed 'the truth' more. For those people around the world feeling the effects of climate change, their lives and livelihoods depend on having the facts. And that's why climate change is such an important story to understand.

The world's environmental scientists are now unanimous that the seas and the air are now warming up 10 times as fast as at any time since the ice age, and it's down to us.

And believe me, scientists are a very careful lot.

The reasons you might think that they're still unsure (if you do) is because a. they generally don't say something is true until it's been conclusively proven – and that took time, and b. there are still a few people – who are often paid by oil and gas companies – who say, 'the jury's out'.

The jury isn't out.

The jury returned its verdict years ago.

And the wildfires, and the floods, and the famine and the movement of people are the first pieces of evidence.

But many of us still didn't like it – including the US President of alt-reality, Donald Trump. When he pulled out of the Paris climate accord, he became the world leader who'd taken the fastest ever action on climate change! Sadly, it wasn't in the right direction.

And what about mis- and dis-information?

I would argue that climate change wasn't just created by pollution. I'd say that it was caused by disinformation.

The stories created by businesses and leaders who had the most to gain from polluting the air and water needed to feed our addiction to fiction. They've spent billions to make sure we're divided on the issue, or that there's doubt in just the right places. They succeeded just long enough for our generations to feel the effects.

And it's easy to do it. You just need to distract us by flooding the zone, by weaponising information against us. Things like 'scientists are split on the issue'. 'The 'woke' agenda made them turn off the water to save an endangered fish'. Anything to muddy the waters, and disguise the main causes – the global industries who've provided our creature comforts, and the pollution that over-consumption creates.

Even my geography teacher in the 1980s knew that we were using too many natural resources and that we'd start running out of things soon, things like copper. Between 2010 and 2016, the amount being dug up by the world's top 15 producers had halved. Here's a report in Money Week … https://moneyweek. com/475695/copper-now-a-precious-metal

That's because we're way beyond 'peak copper'.

So, the information has been around for a long, long time.

The question back then was: when would we see the signs?

The when … is now.

The climate – if we're lucky – is now going to be 1.6 degrees Celsius warmer than it would be otherwise. The last 10 years were the hottest 10 years ever recorded. Humans have never experienced temperatures like we're feeling now, never mind the ones to come.

This is what happens when a system heats up. Weather just gets more extreme and sudden to compensate.

It's tough, I know. But this chapter is about how we can see what's happening today so that we can build a future of truth to believe in. Alt-reality gets in the way of that but it's much easier to take.

So, let's do what we always do:

1. Look at the source of the stories about climate change.
2. Check them for bias.

3.   Engage our human brains and think 'could they be telling me one side of the story for ideological, commercial or political gain?'
4.   Get another view from the opposite side of the argument.
5.   Audit our own core beliefs – why do we have those opinions?
6.   Step away if your sniff test tells you that a story smells 'off'.

As I said earlier, things get ugly when mis- and dis-information change our views and behaviours. Plenty of people want us to look the other way while the world burns, so it's up to us – the information guardians – to ask the right questions.

I'm lucky to have had a good geography teacher who told us all about the copper. I hope you do, too.

6. DON'T MENTION THE F WORD

Really? Not you too …

Yep. It's time to have a grown-up conversation about the F word.

One hundred years ago, in the 1920s, a simple idea was spreading fast. It wasn't one simple ideology, but more of a rag-tag assembly of populism, persecution and control under a man who thought he should be king.

The man was Mussolini.

The idea was fascism.

This ultra-nationalist, anti-democratic, anti-liberal (or anti-'woke'), pro-elite ideology was sweeping central, southern and eastern Europe. Mussolini ruled Italy, the US had its own fascist movement attached to the Christian right (check out the fascinating podcast *Ultra* by MSNBC), as did the UK, South Africa, Japan and the Middle East.

It's not something people like to talk about, but it happened.

In the 30s, fascism spread to western Europe, taken up and made antisemitic by Hitler, leading to invasion, world war and holocaust.

Sure, that was a century ago, but we need to talk about it again.

Today, it's back in plain sight.

And we have to mention it.

The American writer Mark Twain said once '*history doesn't repeat itself, but it does rhyme*', and it looks like that's never been truer. We've had decades to forget about the grainy footage of the historic crimes committed by a cult obsessed with conspiracies and perpetual power. But now, in glorious streaming 4K video, it's back – or at least a new version of it.

The information we're fed, and share, like and repost has led us to a place where a new type of fascism has grown in the fertile soil of alt-reality.

And populism is the modern sales pitch to make us believe it's okay.

Does it matter that Donald Trump pardoned all of the January 6th Capitol invaders, creating a new fanbase of armed loyalists? Does it matter that Nigel Farage spread (and admitted to spreading) false information about the Southport killer before the 2024 race riots in Britain? Does it matter that a high percentage of younger people in the UK think that something like a dictatorship could be better than democracy (https://www.ukonward.com/wp-content/uploads/2022/09/kids-arent-alright-democracy.pdf)?

I think it absolutely does.

Whatever they look like, whoever's showing us the modern face of far-out beliefs, fascism – and communism – are almost identical when you think about how they're achieved by twisting our beliefs. The stories that turned people into believers were different, but they all created the same fear, fury, hope, idea of a better future – through control. People at the top still did it for ideological, political or commercial gain.

And yes, perhaps we've forgotten what a crazed military dictatorship looks like. The way they demolish the structures there to protect us. How they destroy freedom and individuality.

That's why we need to remember exactly what fascism is, because it's rising to power again.

Look, let's turn down the heat for a second and engage our human brains. Here's the definition of fascism, from Merriam-Webster:

'*Fascism is a populist political philosophy, movement, or regime that exalts nation and often race above the individual, that is associated with a centralized autocratic government headed by a dictatorial leader, and that is characterized by severe economic and social regimentation and by forcible suppression of opposition.*'

It can be left, it can be right. But the boxes to tick are …

> Populism.
> My country first.
> Out with immigrants.
> Close, reduce or own democratic bodies.
> Punish the opposition.
> And finally, the populist-in-chief needs to have absolute power to be called a fascist leader.

So, can you think of anyone who sacked their enemies in government, the courts, law enforcement and the media?

If so, they've earned their place in the band.

This is a real threat to democracy – particularly in the west – as we pop this entry into the time capsule.

If we lurch even further to the right, the next chapter of our history book might as well be entitled 'The year democracy died (again).'

The reality is that we've come uncomfortably close, and our healthy, happy future of truth depends on us having the freedom to choose what we believe. If we're not doing harm, we should be allowed to hold our own views and to disagree with unpleasant ideas at the top, the middle and the bottom.

So, let's keep sniffing hard to resist this stuff, whatever you choose to call it.

7. INVERSION

What do you do when you want to get away with a heinous act or a lie without anyone noticing?

This is an old technique that's flourishing in the age of alt-reality. It's in the news all the time, and really messes with our view of the world.

So, what do you do to deflect?

Firstly, you'll probably deny it.

Then, you'll immediately try to blame someone else.

Thirdly, the powerful step used by regimes for decades is to discredit the other side. To make the people saying something genuinely justified to look like the offender. And you can do that by distracting everyone from the truth by making a nasty, inverted accusation. You might even accuse them of doing what you've been doing.

That's a huge issue in our world of alt-reality.

It was mastered by the Russian government during the early days of the Ukraine invasion, spread to its allies, and it's been weaponised by populists everywhere since then.

I call it, simply, 'inversion'.

It's a tactic best explained with a real-world example. When you are responsible for terrible, offensive acts – perhaps grabbing a territory that you think should be yours - the most effective thing you can do is to tell your people that the other side is doing exactly the same, or worse. Or that they're a threat, so you're justified in doing what you want to do.

We saw a form of it when Donald Trump accused Ukraine's leader Volodymyr Zelenskyy of being a dictator in early 2025, days after choosing to decide Ukraine's future with its invader, Vladimir Putin, not its President or its neighbours.

If you want to save face and deny a claim against you, the best form of defence is attack. You might say that the other side is full of horrific criminals. That they kill the defenceless. That they are worse than 'we' could ever be. You cast doubt among your people, cause outrage, fear, hatred – all the emotional triggers that we know create an alt-reality where you can win back control.

When you invert the argument, the facts are demoted. You're basically cancelling them out by creating another, untrue side of the story.

But the lie needs to be big. Really big. You have to turn the story up to full, and deny everything. Inversion is a tool used by authoritarians and would-be dictators everywhere as a way to control the minds of their people. It activates our fight, fright and flight response really well, with minimal effort. Of course, you also need to remind people - who know what's going on - of the punishments they'll face if they don't follow your party line.

This is gaslighting turned up to 11, and it's a precise type of propaganda now in use all over the world.

But it's also another great way to spot manipulation in real time.

If the authoritarian in your life is accusing the other side of the worst kinds of crime, it's very possible that they're the ones committing it.

8. THE IDENTITY I CHOOSE

In Chapter 3, I spoke about how believing in conspiracies can form a brand-new identity, where we become something more than we were before. Being part of a new community gives us a place in the world, a voice and a chance to fight for what's right.

Feels good, doesn't it? Especially when the world we create feels like the only one we can really control.

If you're a gamer, or grew up on Minecraft, or make TikTok lifestyle videos, the face you show to your followers is the real thing. In the physical world it's too easy to feel less attractive, have less of a voice, be less important. Perhaps the real world is more dangerous or challenging for people who grew up during COVID, perhaps we just feel more loved online – despite the equal amounts of hate.

The 2020s will go down in history as the first decade of self-invented reality, where tens of millions of young people chose their own norms.

And that's a bit of disruption that opens such a brave new world.

But we know how harmful fully distanced online living can be, so in an emerging age of alt-identity, we really need to talk about the rules that keep everyone safe.

How can we bring people who don't live in the same reality as us into the same conversation? We're still human, still physical, and still need to know true from false, up from down, so how can we prevent some people from becoming disconnected, unhappy, angry and alone?

That's where conspiracies and extreme beliefs come from.

So, in our age of opinion, we need strong safeguards for younger people and older people alike, not to destroy fact checking or hand all of the control to the tech barons and their friends at the top.

When we're surrounded by alt-reality, the identity and values we think we're choosing have probably been given to us by them.

9. 52-48

We'll go back to the busiest ever year for elections in a minute, because they still have a lot to show us.

But let's just take a pit stop for moment.

I left a section out of the 1st Edition of The Future of Truth (and How to Get There), because it seemed like an odd effect that I couldn't really prove. It was a simple question about why we seem to be so polarised.

Why are so many elections ending up with a 52%-48% vote?

I believe, in the year reality died, that we now know.

Just as nature doesn't draw in straight lines, no vote goes to 52-48 without powerful disinformation in the mix. Only a big lie shared by millions of us can create that level of division. And it only happens around wedge issues created on purpose.

It's just something that's been bothering me since Brexit here in the UK.

Votes close to 50-50 shouldn't exist.

That extends to 30-30-30 when there are three main stances. At the heart of nearly every evenly split vote is a hugely controversial issue, thrown into the conversation by a politician looking for power at any price. That's right, a really, really effective populist.

Here's the populist playbook again. Can you think of any 50-50 votes that involved characters like this?

> Someone who made wild claims, created fear or new threats.
> Did they use a plausible grain of truth to defend their claims? Maybe something around government control, immigration or gender?
> Did they ramp up the attention using their social media or mass media?
> Did they say that the system is rotten and needs to be rebuilt?
> Did they ask simple-sounding questions about a big issue? Did they avoid tough questions from journalists?
> Did they say 'the people think this' without asking many of us?
> Did they sugar coat their claims with humour, or an image of huge success?

You do the math.

Thankfully, it doesn't always work.

But it did make headway in the world's busiest election year. In countries where immigration was high, or where there was a neighbouring country desperate to put a friend into power, disinformation rose, and polarisation peaked.

There's a great view of the world's busiest election year here, from The Fact Site: https://www.thefactsite.com/year/2024/

And here at Statista – focusing on the key elections: https://www.statista.com/topics/12221/global-elections-in-2024/

Let's pick out a few where disinformation - particularly on social media – looks to have influenced the result. I'll keep it short, but they're definitely worth adding to our time capsule.

10. POPULARITY SHIFTS

The results here show the splits between the top two, or three parties in each country, and how the alternative – potentially using (or being backed by) false information managed to split the vote.

INDIA

Let's start with the populist leader of India who's done a lot of good for the commercial interests of the nation, but won – and kept – power using a religion-based version of the populist playbook.

Narendra Modi always led with his Hindu beliefs.

But this time around, an almost perfect voter split gave him something to think about.

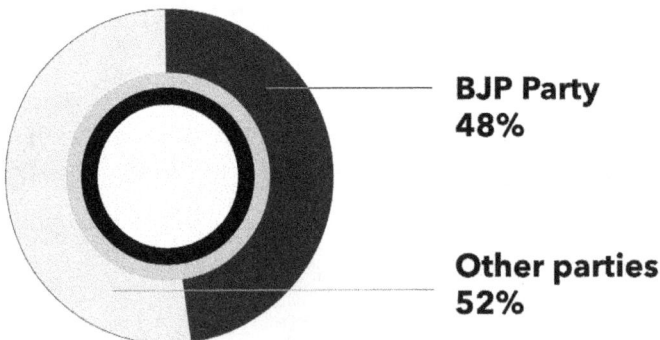

**BJP Party
48%**

**Other parties
52%**

Modi called Muslim people 'infiltrators' during his 2024 campaign and was accused repeatedly of encouraging supporters of carrying out violent attacks on Muslims. Classic 'them and us' threat-based populism, straight from the playbook.

But he was dealt a surprising blow in 2024 when his BJP party could only win 48% of the total vote including all parties, against 52% won by the rest.

The voting public reportedly wanted to put a control on his powers, but there was strong enough support to keep the incumbent leader in power through a multi-party coalition. The lesson? Populism can take you a long way but perhaps – in a complex, thriving country of multiple views – you can still lose if you push it too far. Now, to Europe.

PORTUGAL

Portugal was an early signal that the world's busiest election year would be all about polarisation.

The centre-right Democratic Alliance narrowly won the election with 28.02%, a tiny nose ahead of the Socialist Party with 28%. That's an incredible 50-50 split at the top, with the far-right CHEGA party following in third place with 18% of the vote.

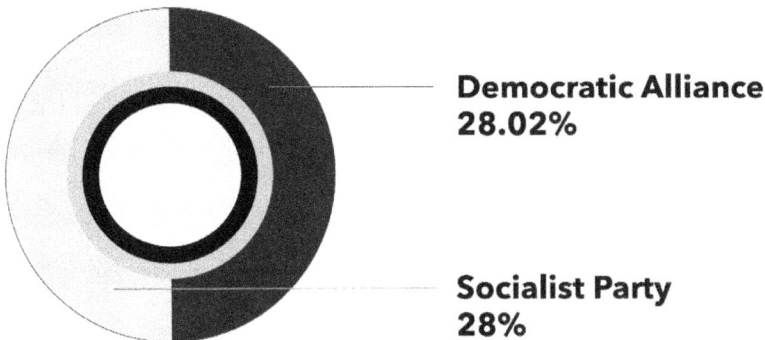

Democratic Alliance 28.02%

Socialist Party 28%

FRANCE

The election result in France went to an almost completely polarised 3-way split among the top three parties.

The New Popular Front (left-wing) won 182 seats (31%), followed by Ensemble Alliance (in the centre) with 168 (which is 29%). Not far behind was the National Rally (far-right) with 143 (25%), and Les Républicains with 60. 23 seats went to other parties.

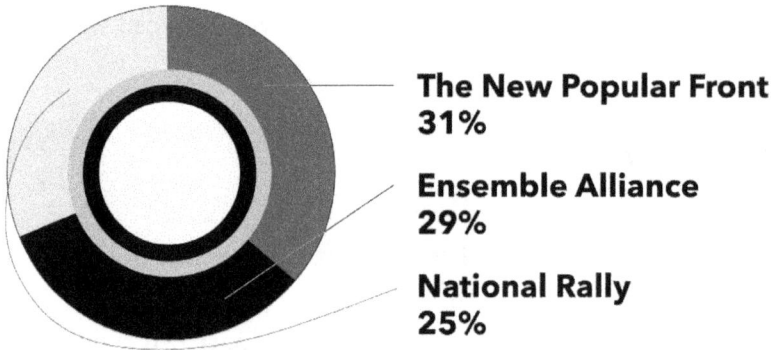

**The New Popular Front
31%**

**Ensemble Alliance
29%**

**National Rally
25%**

This is the first truly polarised three-way election split in a western country.

In France, voters are very quick to mobilise and while Marine LePen's far right National Rally was publicly – and rapidly - gaining ground, others were desperate to block her way to power. It was an almost equal and opposite vote to the left, leaving a fractured and polarised National Assembly, but a balanced three-way swing.

Let's now turn to eastern Europe countries who held elections in the shadow of the great bear, Russia.

GEORGIA

In Georgia, the pro-Putin, far-right part Georgian Dream won 54% of the popular vote in their Presidential elections, but despite that fairly even split, this is just the start of the story.

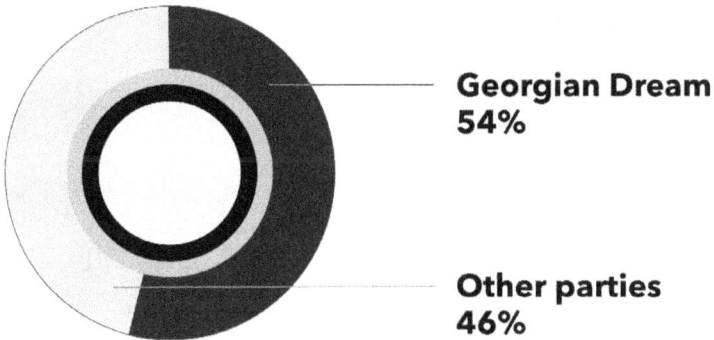

**Georgian Dream
54%**

**Other parties
46%**

Immediately, the head of Georgian Dream Bidzina Ivanishvili – a former oligarch in Russia – cancelled talks to join the EU. That slotted perfectly into the agenda of the Russian President Vladimir Putin, who many believed played a part in convincing British voters to leave the EU in 2016.

And when the former Georgian President Salome Zourabichvili refused to leave, backed by other countries who also believed that Russia had rigged the vote, she was arrested and locked up. Georgia is a small country, but if her claims were true, this was a direct attack on a democracy by the Russian government – and potentially the latest of many.

MOLDOVA

The pro-EU Party of Action and Solidarity under Maia Sandu came out on top with 55% of the vote, against 45% for the anti-EU, pro-Russian Party of Socialists of the Republic of Moldova.

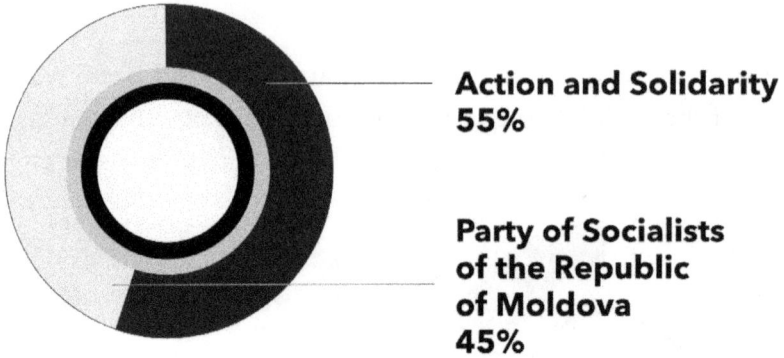

Action and Solidarity 55%

Party of Socialists of the Republic of Moldova 45%

Again, as a former part of the Soviet Union, the Russian government was accused of interference and denied it. The US government said that Russian proxies had piped $39 million into the country to buy votes, combined with anti-EU disinformation.

But in this case, it didn't work.

ROMANIA

Romania's top court actually annulled the first-round results of the presidential election in Romania in 2024, and cancelled the second.

The reason? Intelligence documents claimed that the Russian government had been promoting the far-right, pro-Putin candidate Calin Georgescu on TikTok and Telegram. He denied it, but in the first round (annulled) here's how the top 3 party votes were split. The six other parties took the remaining vote.

When you read this, the election may have happened, and a result decided.

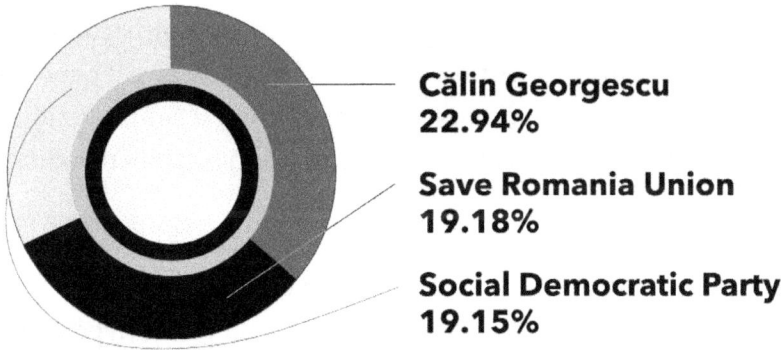

Călin Georgescu
22.94%

Save Romania Union
19.18%

Social Democratic Party
19.15%

But you can see those evenly split votes there, lots of accusations of disinformation, triggering peak polarisation with countries neighbouring Russia fighting anti-EU, pro-Russian disinformation.

HOPE ...

There was so much hope too.

Just as we spoke about the Ik people of Uganda, there were oppressive governments overthrown across the world, and elections in countries including Mexico where huge changes were made to the status quo by the pure force of positive choices, and good information.

Democracy is destroyed by disinformation. But the good news is that, even with these examples showing how devious the power-hungry are, many people saw through it. And the fair, healthy elections across the world should give us a lot of hope that the future of truth will be back.

What did the world's busiest election year teach us?

It taught us something very simple.

Peak polarisation is the inevitable result of alt-reality.

Also, reality isn't what it used to be – in our lives, in our identities and what that does to things like elections. If we can surround ourselves with enough bad information, it becomes our reality. And if the real world is too hard to handle, we'll choose to believe the alternative, no matter how much of a contradiction it is. And if there's a messiah promising to lead you to better times, why wouldn't you take their hand?

So, we may not like the way history judges us for our choices in the year reality died – or the years since - but it's easy to understand why so many people chose to believe the hype when it was backed by the best and wealthiest opinion-makers on the planet.

11. THE CRYPTOVERSE

We're almost there for this chapter.

Before we move on to build a healthier, happier future of truth, we need to talk about crypto.

The cryptoverse is a place where alt-reality reigns supreme. From the sales pitch to the valuation to the real-world uses, it's all a little … well, cryptic.

And when we pray for a quick payday, there are plenty of conmen and women mixed in with the genuine sellers ready to take our cash. It's a multi-billion Dollar industry, with entire towns filled with real, human slaves who've also been conned into acting like your next girlfriend or boyfriend.

That's not to say crypto, NFTs, meme coins and the rest are innately bad. You might have spent some coin buying real things in real countries around the world. You might have an investment statement which had paid cash into your conventional account. Great.

It's just that crypto is such a wild west of scams, deregulation, inconsistent value and fraud in some corners that we need to take care. Digital currencies that aren't guaranteed by real contracts, visible on blockchains, or attached to a real address could be completely unreal. They're - at very least - trying to hide from you.

And they could be doing much worse than that.

Powerful criminal organisations run scams targeting dating apps, online stores and more every second of the day. And the gold rush they opened up is being jumped on by new tech bros and sisters who share the idea that taking all of your money (so-called 'pig butchering') is perfectly okay.

I suppose if you want to be free of accountability, something like unregulated crypto, scams and even dictatorships over democracy would make more sense.

Have a listen to the excellent podcast '*The Coming Storm*' with Gabriel Gatehouse and you'll hear all about the tech bros. And '*Scam Inc*' by Economist Podcasts is the clearest insight into what it's like inside international crypto scams that I've heard in a very long time.

Even Donald Trump launched his own meme coin (which quickly halved in value) after being re-elected, and exclaimed that he'd be the first Crypto President in US history.

As ever, we just know why it's so crucial to be careful.

The lie is always in the why.

When I was a consumer correspondent, I went on raids with the police to uncover snakehead (Chinese people-smuggling) gangs. And this stuck with me as a major life lesson ...

On the surface, gangs were selling illegal DVDs (remember them?). But in order to earn huge amounts of easy money, that was only one small corner of their business. They were also smuggling people. They ran sex workers. They were dealing drugs in other cities. They were also transporting weapons.

A few years later, I was looking into a terrorism network and a Scotland Yard detective told me that they were funding their activities through exactly the same cash-rich operations, from selling illegally ripped movies to cannabis.

The cryptoverse is the modern equivalent.

Where there's easy money to make, especially when a product has no intrinsic value, dodgy characters will circle the killing grounds like vultures.

And any cryptocurrency, or scheme or scam that we can't be 100% sure about is one that we should walk away from, especially if it's been recommended by someone we've just met online.

Again, there are plenty of reputable sellers and investment people out there, but the cryptoverse is prime territory for scams.

It'll change when national banks and international bodies like the EU take their place in the market.

For now, we need to be careful of the alt-reality of quick money.

As always, stop, step back and sidestep a good sales pitch packed with disinformation, and keep the analogue toolkits close because they still apply very well to alt-reality.

And on that note, how can we remove the 'alt-' in 'alt-reality'?

12. LET'S GET REAL

Okay, let's get reality back.

The first thing we need is variety in the information we're being fed. No more made-up extreme stories sent our way because we clicked on a few related links. And we can do a couple more simple things to gently lift our loved ones – or indeed, ourselves – out of the hole.

So, here are three simple steps to get reality back.

Step one is to challenge our algorithm.

Most of us know very well that we're rewarded by social media for clicking on our favourite things, longer for things we really like. They reward us by feeding our addiction or creating new ones. Then, that's reinforced by our friends, our posts, shares, re-posts. It's all great information for a data-hungry algorithm that's programmed to push us further down the rabbit hole.

Let's break that.

Move around, click on different, surprising, harmless pictures, reels and posts. Go back, go forward, stop, scroll a long way and do it again. It's all about confusing and reprogramming your social media algorithm. And it only takes a few seconds at the start and end of your unit of social media time.

If we want reality back, we can't let social media dictate it for us.

Step two is immunisation.

Next, how do we demote the harmful stuff – or at least get to a point where it slides off us like drizzle?

Everyone born before social media brought us up was given some kind of guidance. Sure, it wasn't always perfect or even good, but we weren't raised by friends who have just as little idea of what's going on as we do.

What we need is a little help as soon as we use social media and community messaging apps.

Here's an idea.

Just like Finland does, how about we expose ourselves – our younger people – safely, to mis- and dis-information to show them what it looks like? How it makes us feel, what it sounds like, why we feel strongly when something horrible is presented to us by a friend, or in a group that isn't doing us good?

It's like a safe version of the storytelling effect I spoke about in Chapter 1; rather than experiencing a serious threat in a story on our own, this would be a guided tour through harmful mis-

and dis-information.

There's a great piece of research that showed how effective this idea could be. Sander van der Linden called it psychological inoculation.

It's just like a vaccination, where you get a little bit of the disease so that your body knows what to fight. And if you're an anti-vaxxer, don't worry! It's not that kind of immunisation.

Here's an article on the University of Cambridge website: https://www.cam.ac.uk/research/news/psychological-vaccine-could-help-immunise-public-against-fake-news-on-climate-change-study

The main thing is to flag up the information as false before we show it, otherwise it'll just end up looking real.

What this could do is to reduce the emotional reaction, give power back to our younger people (and our older people too). And if you've ever had a conversation about disinformation or deepfakes – as I have hundreds of times in the writing of this book – the relief when that person realises that it's not real, not AI-generated, that they're not being stupid, is very real indeed.

Let's try that in our own lives. Gently.

Step three is to fight isolation.

Remember the research in Chapter 2 that showed how physical isolation is directly linked to conspiracy thinking? Here's the link again just in case you can't find it: www.ncbi.nlm.nih.gov/pmc/articles/PMC8420120/

Well, if we could do one thing today to bring reality back to our loved ones, our friends, classmates or someone we know caught in a doomscroll?

We could reach out a hand of friendship and let them know that we're there if they need us.

Isolation is a fast track to alt-reality.

It's just really damaging to feel as though we're not wanted, needed, respected or important. Another reality is very attractive if the one you live in is horrible. It's just as simple as that. But of course, if you turn to alt-reality, there's a whole lot of poisonous ideas and beliefs mixed in that'll want you as a follower.

So, if you're a young person, or you're older and care about someone who's hitting the wall, what are the key signs that someone's feeling really lonely and isolated?

> They'll be withdrawn from most social situations.
> They might find it impossible to talk about their - or your - feelings.
> There'll be self-doubt and low self-esteem.
> They may not have 'best friends'.
> They'll be feeling sadness and depression.

Now look, these reactions have been around since humans started noticing. I think most of us have felt those at some time. But if we want to reconnect in meaningful ways, to reclaim reality, we'll need to look up and notice again when someone nearby is in pain.

And those were just three simple steps that could help, today.

Okay, let's close up Chapter 9 for real, with our next toolkit.

13. CHAPTER 9 – THE TOOLKIT

- We may be entering a time where the world's biggest voluntary democracy – social media – has created the world's first global dictatorship.
- Peak polarisation influenced elections worldwide in 2024-25 wherever disinformation was injected into social media conversations.

- Reality depends on us listening to both sides, challenging our algorithm and avoiding the spread of alt-reality.
- Beware fascism 2.0 … if it's not with you when you read this, alt-reality has still brought it uncomfortably close.
- The water is boiling, and we're only just realising how hot it is – which is perhaps why climate change is one of the greatest issues ever created by disinformation.
- No vote goes to 52-48 without disinformation in the mix.
- Watch out for inversion.
- And sniff hard if you're thinking about investing your hard-earned cash in the cryptoverse.

LINDLEY GOODEN

10

CREATING THE FUTURE OF TRUTH

LINDLEY GOODEN

10

*'I look to the future because that's where I'm going
to spend the rest of my life.'*

GEORGE BURNS

Well, Chapter 9 may have made you a little tense.

So, let's get practical – and positive - about our next steps.

How can we create a future of truth when things are changing so fast on the tech, social and political fronts? A future where we can separate the facts from the fiction and still be creative, excellent, innovative and safe?

Well, we now have most of the tools that we need.

In our final chapter, let's bring together some of the discoveries we've made, the actions we can take, and work out how to apply them to whatever happens tomorrow.

And whenever we're confronted with a blank canvas of possibilities, I like to go to the primary source – the people who'll have the biggest stake in the future.

1. TALKING TO THE FUTURE YOU

In 2019, to mark the 30th anniversary of the internet, the polling company YouGov ran a survey of British 8 to 18-year-olds for the children's charity Barnardo's. Yes, it was a few years ago now, but it's still a lovely guide to the future us. The question was, 'How do you think people will communicate in the future?'

The key findings were:

> 87% of the group thought that physical letters and postcards would be obsolete by 2049.
> The majority thought they'd be spending too long online talking to people and not enough time in the physical world.
> 1 in 3 thought we'd talk using holograms.
> And most thought that wearables would be the best way to communicate.

Lovely.

But therein lies something interesting.

A popular theory among futurologists is that the next generation of communications will be carried out seamlessly, invisibly, almost telepathically through our wearables. They'll use biometrics (digitised biological signals) to measure what we're doing, feeling, thinking and transfer that into action.

But is that right? Are we ready for that?

We've already seen the damage our recent withdrawal from the real world did to us, haven't we?

Three years of disruption to our normal lives during COVID triggered a really serious mental health problem among young people around the world. It disrupted the normal development of social skills, of play, of learning, of having your first kiss, of growing up – for good and for bad.

So where will young people get that crucial time to relate physically in the future?

2. EDUCATION

In education, at school.

A good education is our leg up to the future. But if the next generation spends longer and longer online, school will be THE place where young people meet. They might not meet, as a rule, in many places except school or college until they begin their first job.

For one thing, if they don't swap information face-to-face, the mis- and dis-information problems we have today will look tiny. We all need to spend time in conversation, it's that simple. It's the way that we've evolved to succeed and grow.

So, the place of learning might become the most important physical space – including the home – for people to share ideas, build their confidence and explore.

Put it this way. What would a completely reclusive, online education have done to you?

Perhaps you'd have been fine, but I'm telling you now that hundreds of millions of kids worldwide wouldn't. They need a great, real-world education, to escape the limitations of home, family, and a way to have a full independent future of their own. I can tell you that if I hadn't gone to a school where teachers genuinely cared about giving working class kids a good education, I would never have gone to university or had a chance to choose a career of my own.

A happier, healthier future of truth depends on offering all young people a good education at a school where they can learn safely.

And if young people aren't given the experience of hanging out with good people, bad people, friends and bullies in the physical world in their early years, how on Earth can they possibly be expected to know the difference online? How can they develop the judgement to recognise good information and dismiss the harmful stuff?

Education is – for all young people, not just the privileged few – crucial to our shared future.

3. THE FINNISH LINE

We spoke about Finland (and Estonia) in Chapter 6, because they've done something really special.

Just to remind you, here's what they do - focusing on Finland.

Finnish kids are taught how to spot and navigate mis- and dis-information as part of their national curriculum. For them, it's become an essential life skill like maths, languages or the arts. They're shown the methods used to fool readers on social media. They learn about video and audio manipulation, factals (my term for mixing fact with fiction to trigger a big response online), intimidation and the use of fake profiles.

In turn, those young people pass on their knowledge to their parents in the same way that recycling has been done in other countries. It's just one layer of an approach to education that unites – not divides – that society.

What do you think?

For me, it's just a very simple win-win. And this wasn't something brought in because of news about how the UK, US, Brazil and other countries were starting to tear themselves to pieces over populist threats that didn't exist. The Finnish government introduced the initiative in 2014, two years before the US elections and the Brexit vote – presumably because law makers there were worried about their neighbour, Russia.

If there was one educational initiative that we could all vote on for schools wherever we are, apart of course from the continuous need for proper funding of all education, this would be a real contender.

Top marks, Finland. 10/10.

4. CRITICAL THINKING

What else could we look at to make our future relationships with the information we share healthier?

Well, it takes time to develop unbiased critical thinking. But how powerful would it be to embed that into the curriculum at school? Inside maths and science (where it comes in later), in language lessons, inside history.

We need this even more now, in a time when next gen chatbots can give us an easy answer to a complex question. Although, do we need to think when DeepSeek will do it for us?

Well, yeah. We clearly do.

Critical thinking lessons would offer a brain training that I only saw at university. Sure - it's offered at private schools - but very rarely at state, public schools. But it could be such a help for children from normal backgrounds to access opportunities and social equality. It doesn't require specific academic expertise and would help everyone.

Critical thinking is the antidote to extreme views and conspiracy beliefs, and we could all use a little help with that from an early age.

Okay, so what would these new positive critical thinking lessons teach?

Well, the details would change, but the starting point is the basic scientific method:

1. First, have an idea (hypothesis). Think about how to test it. Do you have your facts straight? Probably not … yet.
2. Measure and record the results. Ask honestly – did it prove your hypothesis, or show you areas where you were wrong? Is there another side of the story?
3. Adjust it – perhaps with a slight change to your idea and test

it again.

4.   Measure and record your results again. Is there a belief out there that you should bring into the mix?

5.   What happened this time? Are you closer or further away from the answer?

6.   Keep adjusting until you have the correct answer.

Something that nearly always comes out of critical thinking like this, is that our original idea was wrong.

And wouldn't it be good for our young people, our old people, all of us to be secure enough to realise that we're all still learning the truth?

It would certainly make us listen to each other more, and to question our own side of the story.

5. LET'S DEMAND THIS

It's pretty clear that we'll never control mis- and dis-information and false reporting if we don't have laws to protect us.

As I write this, safeguards against false information are being dismantled around the world. Only the EU is holding ground – at the moment.

We've been through a lot of the existing laws, but how do we drive an appetite at the top to improve things, to build shared worldwide standards for the people?

Mis- and dis-information damage our minds like cigarettes do our bodies, so why have governments dragged their feet? Probably because they don't understand the infodemic, don't care, or – for the conspiracy lovers among us – just find it useful at election time.

Let's demand this, right now:

1.   We should set out a definition of harm and link it directly to

false information, The Harm Test – or something like it – to help law makers regulate.

2. Let's focus on the damage false information and fake news do to mental health, particularly in younger people.

3. Then, we need to show people who spread disinformation that they'll face steep punishments e.g., removing them from social media networks – with an agreement to watch their activity. Meta made this more difficult in 2025, but hopefully the winds will change.

4. We should also focus on mainstream political disinformation – which would absolutely need to include penalties for politicians who spread it.

5. Clearly, since these are the people who pass new laws, we need to strengthen the powers of independent bodies, so that they can name, shame and even punish the spread of domestic propaganda.

6. And yes, that needs to include stronger laws around the mass media, not only online channels and individuals who try to divide us. Currently, there is no incentive for newspapers, websites, social media or broadcasters to stop putting false information into their output as standard.

As we've said before, biased coverage isn't news. It's just storytelling.

So, let's finally punish people who weaponise information to hurt and divide the rest of us. We've had enough.

6. TRAFFIC LIGHTS AND DEEPFAKE LABELS

Let's bring it all together.

It's completely within social media and video platforms' abilities to carry out a rough transcription when content is uploaded, to work out what's contained within it. They're doing it already - in the data they sell and use to train AI models. So, we need them to do that for their users too.

It could easily feed into a colour-coded guide that you can understand in a split second. A green label when the content is good, and an amber or red label when it's rubbish.

It's been used for food standards, so let's do it for information standards too. For example:

GREEN

> The information is safe and accurate.

GREEN-AMBER

> Some information needs to be checked. Here are the timecodes for the amber information.

RED

> This information is very likely to be false. Stop if you want the truth.

So, when anyone posts a piece of content, it would go through an automated speech recognition system and flagged for harmful views. Easy, effective, important.

We're also going to have to get serious about deepfakes.

Labels are a must, they were promised by the four big players Meta, Google, Microsoft and OpenAI in discussion with Joe Biden's US government, but it's unlikely those discussions will continue until the wind changes. Hopefully the EU's AI Act will help to set the standard.

But it's the tip of the iceberg. What about the hundreds of other AI labs and other countries who lead the way outside the US and Europe? China's DeepSeek was the first to shake the ground under Silicon Valley.

We've gone through a lot of the telltale signs that can help us to recognise deepfakes as they stand, but the organisations working on detection software have a big part to play in this too – and I'm sure that they'd appreciate the business!

A simple label to let you know that the video or audio in front of you is faked will help us to:

1. Spot disinformation in real time.
2. Be more aware of the rabbit holes that we're being exposed to.
3. Give us a constant awareness that content isn't always genuine.

So, let's label this stuff. It's a very simple way to make us safer and more aware of false information and fake news as it happens.

7. SLAVES TO THE ALGORITHMS

In the 'everything in moderation' section in Chapter 6, I said this:

'Without high quality moderation, with clear, unambiguous and shared standards, extreme conversations and communities turn nasty, quickly.'

Right now, we are completely and utterly at the mercy of the algorithms, feeding us more of what we click on or hover over, however negative and factually crazy it is.

So, we really need some transparency from the social media channels, and some changes to the business model. But let's be honest, that really not likely to happen, is it?

So, we'll need to vote with our feet and our fingers.

Our ancestors – for all their faults – would have regulated their conversations in groups, around the campfire or communal meal and found their safe middle ground there.

We don't have that anymore. So, how can we make online living safe again?

We need our human moderators back.

And we need them back at work on all the social media channels. We also need them to be expertly trained and supported. And that support is really important. Imagine what it's like to read garbage, hate speech, threats and false information all day, every day. Imagine the effect is has on the mind of a moderator who does it for a living?

What else?

Would it be useful to you to hear from moderators about what they see in their job? To spend a little time in a moderator's mind could help us all to see the damage that posting harmful content is doing.

Ultimately, they were really effective gatekeepers before COVID. We need to value them much, much more.

8. THE GREATER GOOD

What can we do to make sure that AI is developed in a way that helps humans to be all that they can be?

Well, it's pretty clear that the future depends on the people in charge banging developers' heads together. Just so that they explain what they're doing.

We need to team up and think about the big picture on AI. Why are we doing this? Is it for the greater good, or the greater bad?

Most independent AI experts want new, cross-country governance to make sure that the ways in which we develop AI technologies are monitored and moved forward safely.

It's got to be worldwide and include these five groups:

1.   AI creators.
2.   Governments.
3.   Platform owners.
4.   Civil society – the organisations that monitor the above three to keep their conduct clean.
5.   Us – we need to be closely involved and regularly updated.

Together, we can look at the global scale, not just the borders and interests of a single corporation.

And the fifth point there – 'us' – is so important. We need education, training and accessible (and accurate) information.

The future of AI affects us all, so we need to keep a close, public eye on what's happening.

And anyone who says that we need less regulation around AI hasn't given it any thought at all – or stands to gain personally from deregulation.

Any country that doesn't co-operate is effectively pulling the

rest of us into a lot of trouble. And of course, there are always bad actors who try to gain advantage over others by developing features to influence, harm or simply make a quick buck from the rest of us. Some AI tools, in information (or psyops), vaccine development, synthetic biology could launch a devastating attack on the rest of us tomorrow, if they wanted to. It'll take nothing more than a laptop and a DNA printer to create some truly horrific
diseases in the near future.

So, the laws need to be much stronger.

I'd argue that we should be treating the safety of our individual information with the same respect that we do threats to national security.

9. AI VALUES

What's the true purpose of a new AI?

Not just the problems it solves but the values that are essential to create something that has a positive impact on us.

Do you remember the two main models by which AIs are designed and developed?

1. Symbolic systems
2. Neural networks

Our brains are a combination of both, and of course we learn a lot of our natural behaviours from childhood, with morals guiding us to what's right or wrong.

This is absolutely critical in purpose-driven artificial intelligence too.

You'll perhaps have seen the movie I, Robot starring Will Smith. In it, the basic rules governing the AI robots followed Isaac Asimov's 'Three Laws'. He was a professor of biochemistry at The

University of Boston, and wrote almost 500 books.

The laws were:

- First Law: A robot may not injure a human being, or, through inaction, allow a human being to come to harm.
- Second Law: A robot must obey orders given it by human beings, except where such orders would conflict with the First Law.
- Third Law: A robot must protect its own existence as long as such protection does not conflict with the First or Second Law.

Look at that.

AI's purpose was all about reducing harm and enabling humans. The values here were clear, focused on helping people with everyday tasks (before the cold, hard logic went too far).

I think we can agree that these are still a basic requirement – just like in The Harm Test in Chapter 3.

But according to many founders of AI companies – not least Mustafa Suleyman, the Co-founder and former Head of Applied AI at Google's DeepMind – we need to contain the tech and think very carefully about where AI goes from here.

If we focus on values, AI would ultimately be a set of technologies that enrich our lives. They'd add to our existence, not just take jobs away and make many human activities obsolete.

Unfortunately, in many ways, this involves a critical point of commercial philosophy: is the purpose of AI to help the few or the many?

I think we all know that most developments of this type are being designed to help the few, the businesses and countries with enough money to develop or buy them, and people with enough money in their pockets not to have to work again. Look, they're businesses and that's just a fact of life. I've run a business for two decades. We need to make money to keep improving what we do.

But this is too important to be owned and controlled by a few AI barons.

So fundamentally, we do need to consider the lives of everyone and integrate that purpose into AI. And when we pay the creators for the AI (whether that's through subscription or pay-per-use) it needs to be priced to a level where everyone has access, not just the wealthy.

This is not socialism. It's society. A fair market economy for the good of every user.

10. PROTECT (YOUR FACE)

There might be something else we could do to protect our image and voice from deepfakers. But before we do, we might need to hold back from signing up to a free account with our friendly neighbourhood AI avatar and voice provider.

It's about copyright.

Most laws currently protect us in these areas:

1. Original literary works.
2. Dramatic works.
3. Music.
4. Art.
5. Sound recording.
6. Film.

As I write this, our faces and voices can't be copyrighted. And AI avatars look almost totally realistic. They've made personal videos much easier to create, but your image and voice might well be assimi-lated into their models for future use. You might even find your lookalike saying something you never would.

But it's tempting to just use them Not least because of the many creative gen-AI tools out there making content creation so much easier. I've been tempted myself but haven't because once your stand-in AI presenter has been created, that's it unless you pay for a pro account and check the small print.

I can tell you that any video or audio that you see or hear from me is either me, or someone pretending to be if they come up with wild ideas out of context. And again, if your image is used to promote a message that you never would, you can spot the fake in real time. If the information doesn't match your previous statements stop watching, and report the content.

But staying with this copyright issue for another few seconds, there is protection in the area between 'intellectual property' – where you own your thoughts and ideas – and 'personality rights'. In the second area, no image or representation of you can be used to promote a business or organisation without your direct consent.

So, we can all take steps to stop organisations or individuals from being able to use our image or voice without written consent. And that means protecting our images and voice, reporting content and asking others to stop watching, sharing or commenting on it. Every mention gives algorithms a reason to send
it out again.

Stars including Tom Hanks have fought deepfake use. Others have already been scanned, and have effectively lost control of their image. What we really need is protection, but in the meantime, we need to shout loud if we've been deepfaked.

11. THE HONEST TRUTH

Well, we're almost there for this book. So much of our time together has been about the elusive search for 'the truth'. And I opened Chapter 3 by saying 'There is no truth.'

Well, actually, I think we're finally close to it, aren't we? Each of us now has the tools and techniques to create a future of truth, if we're clear on what is – and what isn't – needed.

Truth is a combination of:

> The facts, from original primary (or unbiased secondary) sources.
> The all-important 'why' – the motives – that we think we know but rarely do without a lot of investigating of multiple sources.
> But we also need to extract our own bias – those core beliefs that we've spoken about so much.

So, here's what the truth really is:

The Truth =
The Facts + The Genuine Motives – Your Core Beliefs

The truth lives in the intersection of those three:

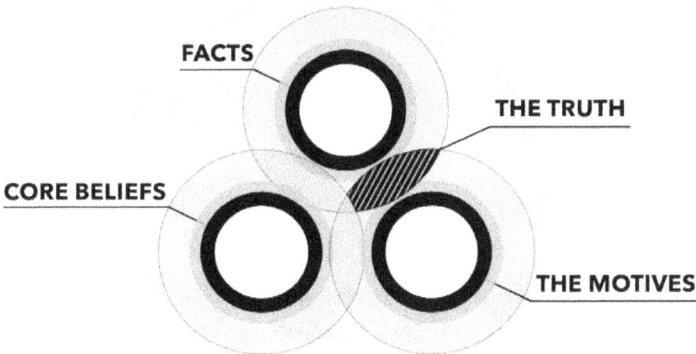

Our desperate thirst for meaning and our need to know 'the truth' means that we can easily colour it with our own assumptions and core beliefs. That's why we need to subtract those biases out. It's completely human for our background beliefs to keep firing, but they're nearly always wrong and work against us when we're looking for the truth. As long as we know where our biases are, we can move much closer to the truth. No more, no less.

What about the motive?

Will we ever discover the original motives in a big story? Probably not. But we can have a stab at it if we're honest with ourselves and where the facts lead.

We can generally assume that the motive behind a harmful story or belief is around personal, political, or commercial gain. Those people want us to react, to follow them, to vote for them and to buy from them.

And I'd like to see our governments, content creators, platforms and businesses being more honest about their motives – so that the ones that are authentic can rise above the ones that aren't.

Your sniff test has some work ahead to establish that.

And the next time someone makes a divisive, inflammatory or harmful claim but doesn't explain their motive, we should demand to know why, or walk away from them as a source in future.

It's a basic bit of truth-checking. And if offenders' accounts are taken down, or newsrooms impose a temporary halt to non-essential coverage of the offender, we'd move a lot closer to a future where truth is valued.

While we're waiting for that, let's keep sniffing and cut out the information that stinks.

12. LET'S MAKE NEWS GREAT AGAIN

Finally, we really need to look at the business of news.

Social media as a source of news is clearly a huge problem,

but I guess it's okay if you go to a qualified, professional journalist whose reputation and job depends on them telling the truth.

Anyone else is a tertiary, third-hand source at best.

Despite everything I explained in Chapter 4, there are so many incredible journalists out there. The business itself prioritises attention and clicks, just as social media does. So, it's inevitable that the news agenda gets steered by the rich, advertising-led, popular newspapers, and controversial issues that might not have a close relationship with the truth.

Hopefully that chapter gave you a clear insight into how the business really works, but here's a summary of what we should all demand.

We need:

1. Accuracy.
2. Clarity and clear, creative ways to explain the facts.
3. We need to hear about positive developments in subjects that actually matter (instead of politics) like healthcare, science, environment, tech – subjects that are rarely covered properly but affect us every day.
4. We need to hear about positive developments in subjects that actually matter (instead of politics) like healthcare, science, environment, tech – subjects that are rarely covered properly but affect us every day.
4. We should be hearing real voices again, reporting real stories, not just talking about the establishment and political chitchat.
5. Investigations of corruption and bad behaviour.
6. News should help us to understand the facts, explaining them much better than now.
7. The tone of news needs to change into something that we want to watch and listen, rather than being afraid to miss.
8. We need to wrench ourselves away from extreme views in the

news.

9.   That might mean rationing our news intake every day.

10.   Above all, we need honest reporting and genuine balance so that conventional news is reliable again.

Look, mis- and dis-information needs a welcoming environment to thrive in.

And the modern news environment can often discourage excellent reporting. It's a big part of the reason why so many people worldwide say they no longer trust the news. But there are still unbiased places that you can find excellent journalism explained well.

13. TURN OFF, TUNE OUT

Before we close, we need to do something really difficult. Whether or not we've found a way to stop, step back from or sidestep false information, or gained perspective, the middle ground, or a good conversation with the other side, we need to force ourselves to have an attention break.

Smaller, fewer bouts of bad news definitely help. Look up and away from time to time, not down and inward every time. Being out of the loop for a short time really does get easier.

14. LET'S BUILD BACK BETTER

Well, we've been through a lot together.

Ultimately, everything we've spoken about comes down to the power of stories that we're told about and tell each other. When they're twisted for personal, political or commercial gain, our natural appetite for more is insatiable.

The genuine facts may sometimes look boring.

But fighting false information and fake news is one of the best lifestyle choices that any of us can take today. It's a lot easier to do than spreading lies, but it will still take some effort to reduce our addiction to fiction.

We are the guardians of the truth, the fighters of mis- and disinformation. It's an ongoing battle with our in-built behaviours, but if you can look at information from all angles, without bias or hate, you hold the keys to helping the people that you respect and love to come back to the real world.

It's all so very human but we're incredibly adaptable when we try.

So let's do that. Let's ask questions, hold back all of our belief from one-sided stories, and stay close enough to the middle to keep a foot in reality.

In such a divided world, that is our way back to a healthier, happier future of truth.

15. CHAPTER 10 – THE TOOLKIT

Let's look at the key ideas that could take us toward that safer future of truth one more time:

- We need to focus on face-to-face education to give young people the life skills and judgement that will keep them safe online.
- Finland's policy of teaching students about disinformation in schools should be adopted everywhere.
- We also need to introduce critical thinking into the curriculum.
- Regulation, regulation, regulation.
- Traffic lights and labels.
- Stronger, properly trained and funded human moderation is also critical for social media safety.

- In the mass media, opinion should also be labelled and general political coverage reduced or separated from core news coverage.
- Social media algorithms need to be replaced to share healthier, more balanced information with users.
- Cross-border cooperation on AI governance and design.
- Transparency around outside interests that influence government messaging.
- Protect your image.
- Truth = the facts + the motive − your core beliefs.

LINDLEY GOODEN

Epilogue

SO NOW WHAT?

LINDLEY GOODEN

Epilogue

These are the rolling credits.

From now on, it's up to us to help each other. We've covered so much, and this is where the fight back begins. But I wanted to wrap up with a three-step summary, and a final toolkit of the questions we can now use to interrogate content, news and information wherever we find it.

It's been a privilege and a hair-raising experience (not that I have much) to do this work with you.

There's now a possibility that we can change our parts of the chattersphere for the better. We can't perhaps change the world, but every major change begins with a small step.

So, there are two summaries left. The first is the basic flow of information-checking that we can all do from here on in.

1. THREE SMALL STEPS IN THE RIGHT DIRECTION

Let's sum up.

Step one.

How do we quickly separate the facts from the fiction? Well, let's start with sources.

Here's the list of four again:

1. Primary – the experiences of people directly connected to

the event or story. You can normally trust primary sources, or at least see bias in their statements.

2.   Secondary – reporting of a story by someone qualified, unbiased, working for a reputable news outlet.
3.   Tertiary – includes opinions about a report, biased coverage, editorials and analysis/comment by third parties. They're generally unreliable, but interesting.
4.   Quaternary – anything on social media by individuals who aren't connected to the story. It's fourth-hand opinions of opinions of reporting of the facts. Stop, step back from and sidestep these, even if that source is a friend or someone you admire.

In terms of the mass media, social media or our own conversations it's absolutely crucial to apply these tests whatever you're reading, seeing or hearing.

Step two.

This about crosschecking the news. If the information you're seeing:

1.   Follows a completely different narrative to other news outlets.
2.   Says something about a person or people that fails your immediate sniff test.
3.   Goes against what they've said in the past.
4.   Or attacks someone or something using emotive language, wild claims or relates it to a life-shattering threat that has appeared from nowhere.

… then put a big editorial red mark against it.

There's a chance that it's true, but there's also a very significant likelihood that it's been invented for personal, political or commercial gain. Just crosscheck it with opposing news outlets and if they're not carrying a similar story, disregard it.

Biased reporting isn't news. It's just storytelling.

There are nearly always grains of truth mixed in to make it plausible and factals to make it spread, but if we want to edge closer to the actual truth we need to crosscheck with the other side of the argument. The same thing applies to deepfakes, and content created by generative AI.

Step three.

Okay, the third practical step is our old friend – extracting the facts:

1. Use the 5Ws and an H – what, where, when, who, why, and the final H – how.
2. Now, draw a clear, unbiased set of conclusions based on the facts of the case/story/event.
3. Finally, think about that extra W – the additional 'why' that can fuel conspiracy beliefs. What, logically, based on the facts and context, might be the reason behind the story you're reading? That includes any agendas that the writer or news outlet has shown in the past.

If you can step back, apply your sniff test to the content and reach behind the headlines, you're going to be a great, intuitive judge of the disinformation in front of you. Especially if you can hold back that vital 30% of belief, asking *'is that really true?'* to allow for bias in the information you're receiving.

Finally, here are 25 questions from across this book that will help you, and the people close to you, to stop, step back from and sidestep mis- and dis-information. They include the process above and wrap it all into one final toolkit so that we can all create a much happier, healthier relationship with the truth.

2. THE FINAL TOOLKIT

If we could boil everything we've done into 25 simple questions to expose mis- and dis-information, what would they be?

Thankfully, we won't have to ask them all, but here are the ones I'd choose:

1. Facts – does this information look factual? Why?
2. Extract the facts – as above, can you extract the facts using the 5Ws and an H.
3. Good sources – does the information come from an unbiased primary (or qualified secondary) source?
4. Bad sources – otherwise, does it come from an unqualified fourth-hand opinion, perhaps on social media? Perhaps you can't find the original source?
5. Context – does it look like something that person would normally post, or is it quite different to their normal content? Also – could it be a fake account set up by a third party?
6. Bias – does it come from a news outlet, organisation or person that is known to have a set political, commercial or ideological agenda?
7. Your reaction – does it feel a little odd – perhaps give you an uncanny valley feeling?
8. Emotion – does it make you really emotional, outraged, furious?
9. Populism – is it towing a specific political line, or an extreme view that a populist politician has created?

10. Language – can you see a shocking headline or inflammatory language, especially in the media?

11. Complexity – is the information – perhaps from a guru or a wellbeing influencer – wrapped up in complex language or confusing ideas that don't make sense?

12. Motive – have you spotted an ulterior motive – perhaps in the story itself? Does it make you suspicious?

13. Conversation – listen, learn, and open a conversation if you can.

14. Balance – does the information take into account the opposing views, in the right proportion?

15. Middle ground – leading on from the previous point, can you see the centre ground of the argument, even if you don't agree with it?

16. Core beliefs – does the information tap into your core beliefs or raise beliefs that you didn't know you had?

17. Sniff test – does it pass your sniff test or does something about it stink?

18. Sharing – should I like or share it? Why should I go that far?

19. Harm – who might I harm by sharing this information, supporting it or talking about it in public?

20. Consequences – if I'm wrong, what are the wider consequences of my sharing it?

21. The real world – would I speak like this to someone face-to-face? E.g. someone from another country, someone who's lost a friend or relative recently, someone who might hurt themselves if you accused them of something publicly.

22. Personal harm – if it hurt a member of your family, or a friend, would you still share the information?

23. Spotting the tells – are there technical 'tells' that suggest deepfakery, one-sided bias or a clever technique to fool you into believing it?

24.   Protection against scams – if a caller appears to be genuine but wants money or personal information from you, stop, ask a personal question and offer to call them back on a genuine number. If they're genuine, they'll have no problem with that. Think about a safe word with loved ones.

25.   Ultimately – whatever else you do, stop, step back and sidestep anything that looks harmful, untrue, or too good to be true.

3. ANY FINAL QUESTIONS?

Is there anything that I've missed?

Well, there are lots of other sections on the cutting room floor and our alt-reality takes us somewhere new every day. But our conversation about mis- and dis-information has to end somewhere.

If you have any other questions that could make a difference to us all, I'd love to hear them. This 2nd Edition of The Future of Truth (and How to Get There) was completed in early 2025 so I'm sure you'll have more thoughts whenever – and wherever - you are.

It's now over to you. I hope this book has helped you to look differently at the information you're fed, to improve your diet for years to come. It's now up to each of us to share the good, shut out the bad and avoid the ugly altogether.

4. GOODBYE AND GOOD LUCK

Well, I think that that'll do. We've spoken at length, so I'll let you go about your day.

Thanks very much for reading The Future of Truth (and How to Get There). I hope that, together, we've painted a clear picture of how to practically build a happier, healthier future where the truth is accessible and recognisable to you.

It's been a journey spanning almost 1,000 years through religion, radicalism, prejudice, the printing press, social and mass media, deepfakes and artificial information.

Many of the technologies emerging today make it really difficult to separate the facts from the fiction. But we've developed a unique set of instinctive tools and techniques to unmask mis- and dis-information wherever we find it.

It's been absolutely fascinating to explore the murky world of false information with you.

And I leave you with this:

Never forget to sniff hard, stop, step back from, and sidestep the false information on your feed. And hopefully you'll see the next suspicious story for what it really is ...

A tall tale made to make you feel.

Good luck and be safe.

5. THE AUTHOR

Lindley Gooden is the Founder and Cheerleader-in-Chief of Greenscreen, a factual communications agency based in London, UK. His background is as a journalist, broadcaster, and business film director.

In a career spanning more than 30 years, Lindley has interviewed more than 50,000 people involved in world-changing events, breaking stories and daily news. He was a Senior Journalist, a consumer, technology and finance correspondent for national news channels at the BBC, ITV and Sky before working with businesses to improve the way they communicate in the – and their own – media.

Lindley has lectured postgraduate journalism at leading British universities. He has also advised many organisations in the news about how to communicate, working with global businesses, governments, charities and climate change research organisations. His work has often required him to challenge misleading information, and it's driven his work helping organisations and speakers to deliver better quality information and creative content.

6. REFERENCES

INTRODUCTION

- British Journal of Developmental Psychology article on isolation and conspiracy thinking: www.bpspsychub. onlinelibrary.wiley.com/doi/full/10.1111/bjdp.12368
- Nature, on how the power of storytelling is reversed by telling lies: https://www.nature.com/articles/s41467-017-02036-8
- '*Our Fiction Addition*' by the BBC: www.bbc.com/culture/ article/ 20180503-our-fiction-addiction-why-humans-need-stories.
- '*Reliance on emotion promotes belief in fake news*', by Cameron Martel, Gordon Pennycock and David G. Rand: www. cognitiveresearchjournal.springeropen.com/articles/10.1186/ s41235-020-00252-3

CHAPTER 1

- The Blood Libel in Britain history at The National Archives: https://www.nationalarchives.gov.uk/education/resources/ jews-in-england-1066/
- The nature of fear by Arash Javanbakht and Linda Saab in the Smithsonian magazine – www.smithsonianmag.com/ science-nature/what-happens-brain-feel-fear-180966992/
- The effects of losing social standing - a page on the American Psychological Association's website: www.apa.org/ monitor/2019/05/ce-corner-isolation
- The stress response, expained by Harvard Medical School: www.health.harvard.edu/staying-healthy/understanding-the-stress-response
- The link to right-wing politics and a larger amygdala: https://neurosciencenews.com/brain-structure-political-ideology-27703/

CHAPTER 2

- The traits of the great apes, from The Proceedings of the National Academy of Sciences of the United States here: www. pnas.org/doi/10.1073/pnas.1522060113
- *'Social Relationships and Mortality Risk: A Meta-analytic View'* by Julianne Holt-Lunstad, Timothy B Smith and J Bradley Layton: https://journals.plos.org/plosmedicine/ article?id=10.1371/journal.pmed.1000316
- The National Library of Medicine (US) on the effects of social separation during the COVID-19 pandemic: www.ncbi.nlm. nih.gov/pmc/articles/PMC8420120/

CHAPTER 3

- The WHO alert on the infodemic in Nature Medicine: www. nature.com/articles/s41591-022-01713-6
- How much do we want to believe? *'Conspiracy belief among the UK public and the role of alternative media.'*: www.kcl.ac.uk/ policy-institute/assets/truth-under-attack.pdf
- How do we react to fear? The psychology article on CNN: www.edition.cnn.com/2020/08/16/health/pandemic-covid-19-denial-mental-health-wellness/index.html
- The fear response, in the Wiley European Journal of Social Psychology: www.ncbi.nlm.nih.gov/pmc/articles/ PMC6282974/
- BBC podcast *Death by Conspiracy*, by Marianna Spring

CHAPTER 4

- Meta's influence on global conversations: https://www.statista. com/statistics/272014/global-social-networks-ranked-by-number-of-users/
- How we get our news, by the Reuters Institute and the University of Oxford: www.reutersinstitute.politics.ox.ac.uk/

digital-news-report/2022/dnr-executive-summary
- Polarisation - article 1, from PNAS (Proceedings of the National Academy of Sciences): www.pnas.org/doi/10.1073/pnas.2207159119
- Polarisation - article 2, from Berkeley: www.belonging. berkeley.edu/democracy-belonging-forum/polarisation-distraction
- Polarisation - article 2, from Annual Reviews: www.annualreviews.org/doi/10.1146/annurev-polisci-051117-073034
- Goalhanger Productions podcast *The Rest is Politics*, with Alastair Campbell and Rory Stewart

CHAPTER 5

- Belief that the 2020 US election was stolen; LSE event with Lawrence Lessig: https://www.youtube.com/live/bF6rer0I1FE
- Trump's speech before the January 6th insurrection, from NPR: npr.org/2021/02/10/966396848/read-trumps-jan-6-speech-a-key-part-of-impeachment-trial

CHAPTER 6

- 2023 Poynter research into anti-disinformation laws around the world: www.poynter.org/ifcn/anti-misinformation-actions/

CHAPTER 8

- The 2024 Safe.ai statement about the threats from AI: www. safe.ai/statement-on-ai-risk#open-letter

CHAPTER 9

- The Money Week report into copper production: https://

moneyweek.com/475695/copper-now-a-precious-metal
- MSNBC podcast *Ultra*, presented by Rachel Maddow
- BBC podcast *The Coming Storm*, presented by Gabriel Gatehouse

CHAPTER 10

- UK-based research on young people's attitudes to democracy and dictatorship in 2025: https://www.ukonward.com/wp-content/uploads/2022/09/kids-arent-alright-democracy.pdf
- First study of the results in the world's busiest election year: https://www.thefactsite.com/year/2024/
- Second study into that election year: https://www.statista.com/topics/12221/global-elections-in-2024/
- Psychological innoculation: https://www.cam.ac.uk/research/news/psychological-vaccine-could-help-immunise-public-against-fake-news-on-climate-change-study